The Arms of Kiangnan: Modernization in the Chinese Ordnance Industry, 1860-1895

A Westview Replica Edition

This book is a Westview Replica Edition. The concept of Replica Editions is a response to the crisis in academic and informational publishing. Library budgets for books have been severely curtailed; economic pressures on the university presses and the few private publishing companies primarily interested in scholarly manuscripts have severely limited the capacity of the industry to properly serve the academic and research communities. Many manuscripts dealing with important subjects, often representing the highest level of scholarship, are today not economically viable publishing projects. Or, if they are accepted for publication, they are often subject to lead times ranging from one to three years. Scholars are understandably frustrated when they realize that their first-class research cannot be published within a reasonable time frame, if at all.

Westview Replica Editions seem to us one feasible and practical solution to the crisis. The concept is simple. We accept a manuscript in camera-ready form and move it immediately into the production process. The responsibility for textual and copy editing lies with the author or sponsoring organization. If necessary we will advise the author on proper preparation of footnotes and bibliography. The manuscript is acceptable as typed for a thesis or dissertation or prepared in any other clearly organized and readable way, though we prefer it typed according to our specifications. The end result is a book produced by lithography and bound in hard covers. Edition sizes range from 300 to 600 copies. We will include among Westview Replica Editions only works of outstanding scholarly quality or of great informational value and we will exercise our usual editorial standards and quality control.

The Arms of Kiangnan: Modernization in the Chinese Ordnance Industry, 1860-1895

Thomas L. Kennedy

In the late 19th century Chinese leaders made efforts to transform the defense industry in China along lines suggested by European and U.S. counterparts; this was the first such instance of a large-scale concerted effort to change a critically important area of government operations. The Confucian leadership confronted the traditional Chinese economy and educational system, attempting to overcome communications and cultural barriers and to introduce Western industrial technology, through foreign advisers, to China. Despite tradition and the semicolonial influence of foreign governments, the major industries were modernized with remarkable speed and success and with some benefit to the Chinese society and economy.

Thomas L. Kennedy is professor and chairman of the Committee on Graduate Studies, Department of History, Washington State University. He received his Ph.D. from Columbia University and has served as Chinese language and intelligence officer in the U.S. Marine Corps.

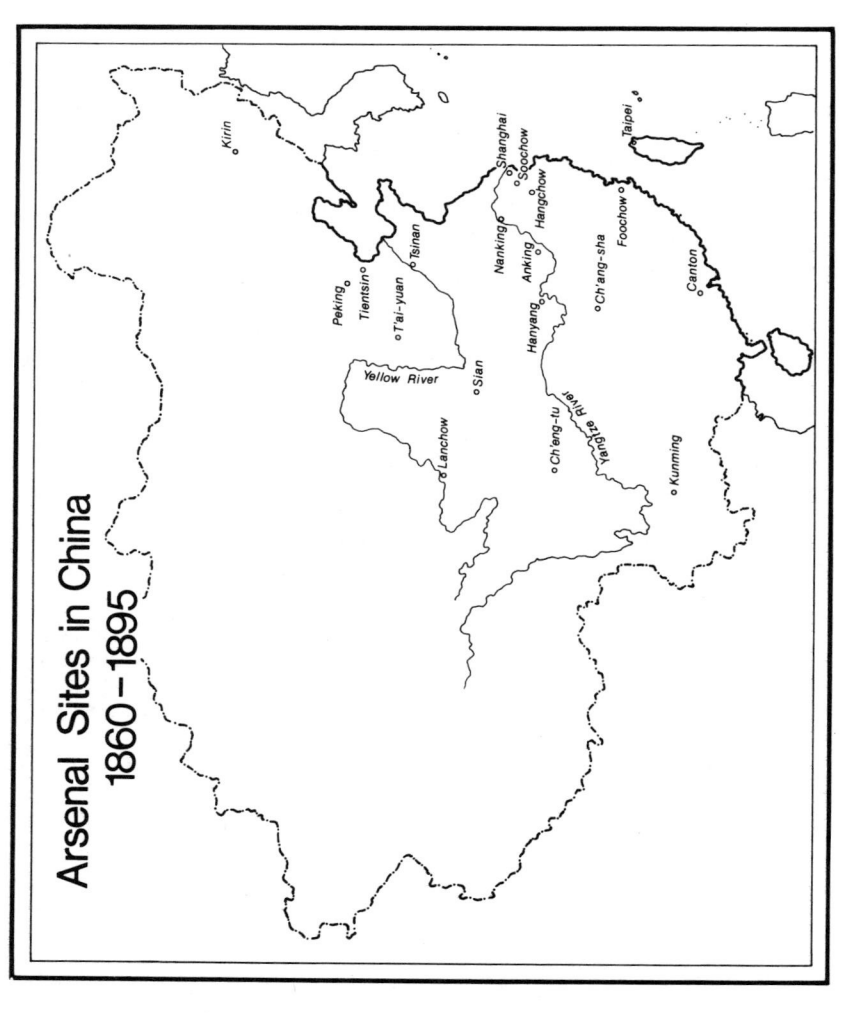

The Arms of Kiangnan: Modernization in the Chinese Ordnance Industry, 1860-1895

Thomas L. Kennedy

Westview Press / Boulder, Colorado

A Westview Replica Edition

This book is included in the Studies of the East Asian Institute, Columbia University

All rights reserved. No part of this publication may be reproduced or transmitted in any form or by any means, electronic or mechanical, including photocopy, recording, or any information storage and retrieval system, without permission in writing from the publisher.

Copyright © 1978 by Westview Press, Inc.

Published in 1978 in the United States of America by
    Westview Press, Inc.
    5500 Central Avenue
    Boulder, Colorado 80301
    Frederick A. Praeger, Publisher

Library of Congress Catalog Card Number: 78-60679
ISBN: 0-89158-258-4

Printed and bound in the United States of America

For Micki

Studies of the East Asian Institute
of Columbia University

The East Asian Institute of Columbia University was established in 1949 to prepare graudate students for careers dealing with East Asia and to aid research and publication on East Asia during the modern period. The Studies of the East Asian Institute were inaugurated in 1962 to bring to a wider public the results of significant new research on modern and contemporary East Asia.

Contents

ILLUSTRATIONS	xiii
TABLE OF EQUIVALENTS	xiv
ACKNOWLEDGEMENTS	xv

I. THE ORDNANCE INDUSTRY OF TRADITIONAL CHINA — 1

    The Production of Weapons — 2

    The Early Development of Firearms — 7

    The Introduction of Western Ordnance — 10

    Conclusions — 15

II. THE REFORM MOVEMENT OF THE MID-NINETEENTH CENTURY AND THE ROLE OF THE ORDNANCE INDUSTRY — 18

III. THE ARSENALS OF LI HUNG-CHANG: THE ESTABLISHMENT PHASE, 1860-1868 — 34

    The Anking Arsenal — 35

    The Yung Wing Mission — 37

    The Shanghai-Soochow Arsenals — 38

    The Kiangnan Arsenal — 45

    The Nanking Arsenal — 49

	The Tientsin Arsenal	50
	Initial Operations of the Kiangnan Arsenal	53
	The Nien Rebellion and the Tientsin Arsenal	55
	Conclusions	57
IV.	THE ARSENALS OF LI HUNG-CHANG ENTER PRODUCTION, 1868-1875	58
	The Kiangnan Arsenal	58
	The Nanking Arsenal	66
	The Tientsin Arsenal	70
	Conclusions	76
V.	THE EVOLUTION OF A NATIONAL POLICY FOR THE ORDNANCE INDUSTRY, 1872-1875	78
	The Decision to Terminate Shipbuilding At Kiangnan	79
	The New Maritime Defense Policy of 1875	87
	Conclusions	98
VI.	PRODUCTION UNDER THE NEW MARITIME DEFENSE POLICY, 1875-1885	99
	The Kiangnan Arsenal	99
	The Nanking Arsenal and Powder Plant	112
	The Tientsin Arsenal	115
	Conclusions	119
VII.	THE MODERNIZATION OF ORDNANCE AND AMMUNITION PRODUCTION, 1885-1895	121

The Kiangnan Arsenal	123
The Nanking Arsenal and Powder Plant	139
The Tientsin Arsenal	142
Conclusions	146

VIII. CONCLUSIONS — 149

APPENDIX I — 161

- Table 1. Specifications and Cost of Vessels Built at the Kiangnan Arsenal, 1867-1885 — 161
- Table 2. Income of the Kiangnan Arsenal, 1867-1895 — 163
- Table 3. Machinery, Arms, and Ammunition Producted at the Kiangan Arsenal, 1867-1895 — 164
- Table 4. Distribution of Arms and Ammunition from the Kiangnan Arsenal, 1867-1895 — 165
- Table 5. Expenditure of Funds by the Kiangnan Arsenal, 1867-1895 — 170
- Table 6. Income and Expenditure of the Tientsin Arsenal, 1876-1892 — 172
- Table 7. Income and Expenditure of the Nanking Arsenal, 1879-1894 — 173
- Table 8. Income and Expenditure of the Nanking Powder Plant, 1884-1891 — 174

APPENDIX II. ARSENALS ESTABLISHED IN CHINA, 1860-1895 — 175

NOTES — 179

GLOSSARY — 209

BIBLIOGRAPHY	223
INDEX	236
STUDIES OF THE EAST ASIAN INSTITUTE	244

Illustrations

ARSENAL SITES IN CHINA, 1860-1865   Frontispiece

AN EARLY SPECIMEN OF HEAVY BUILT-UP
    ORDNANCE, CHINESE GUN CREW AND
    FOREIGN TECHNICIAN   132

THE TIENTSIN WEST ARSENAL AFTER THE FOREIGN
    BOMBARDMENT IN THE SUMMER OF 1900   148

Table of Equivalents

Tael = 1 Chinese ounce or 1.2 English ounces of silver; approximately ₤.33 or $1.6 depending on fluctuations in exchange rate and local Chinese standards.

Li = 1/3 mile; ½ kilometer

Ch'ih = 1 Chinese foot; 14.1 inches.

Acknowledgements

I am deeply pleased to add my name to the long list of authors who acknowledge the central role which Professor C. Martin Wilbur has played in the development of their scholarly endeavors. This study which began as a doctoral dissertation at Columbia University in the 1960s has profited at every stage from Professor Wilbur's criticism, encouragement, support, and the example of his scholarship. Over the years I have received detailed comments and suggestions on preliminary drafts from Professor Kwang-ching Liu of the University of California, Davis, and Samuel C. Chu of Ohio State University. Professors Yi-chu Wang of Queens College, CUNY, and Erh-min Wang of the Chinese University of Hong Kong provided invaluable assistance and direction at particularly difficult stages in my research. To Professor Yi-chu Wang I owe a special debt of gratitude. The patient support and encouragement of Professor Raymond Muse, Chairman, Department of History, Washington State University, greatly facilitated the final phases of research and writing.

I would like to acknowledge the financial support of the Social Science Research Council, Joint Committee on Contemporary China and the Committee on Exchanges with Asian Institutions, the Graduate School of Washington State University and the East Asian Research Center of Harvard University. The Institute of Modern History of the Academia Sinica and the East Asian Institute and Department of East Asian Languages and Cultures of Columbia University have made their research and personnel resources readily available to me when needed.

The photograph of a specimen of heavy built-up ordnance was provided by the Museum of the American China Trade, Milton, Massachusetts, through the courtesy of Mr. Frank Carpenter.

Finally, I wish to thank my wife, Micki, for untold

hours of editorial assistance and stylistic criticism. To Micki and to my children, Elizabeth, Joseph, and Maida, I owe the greatest thanks for patience, encouragement, understanding, and love without which this book would not have been written.

Thomas L. Kennedy
Pullman, Washington
January 1978

I. The Ordnance Industry of Traditional China

On October 16, 1964 the primeval calm of China's remote Central Asian vastness was shattered by the explosion of a twenty megaton atomic bomb. China had become the fifth world power to enter the nuclear club. The Chinese bomb, a response to the partial nuclear test ban treaty which Britain, the United States, and the Soviet Union had signed the previous year, also marked a centennial. China's entry into the nuclear age followed by almost one hundred years its entry into the machine age; the Kiangnan Arsenal, the first Chinese machine industry, had opened in Shanghai in the spring of 1865. Foreshadowing by a century the motivation for the development of atomic power, Kiangnan had introduced steam-powered machinery to produce the military hardware which it was hoped would secure the Empire from threats of the leading world powers. Thus began a century in which the armament industry became the cutting edge of industrial modernization as well as the focal point for the introduction of new technology, new types of education, and new organizations aimed at strengthening China against those enemies, foreign and domestic, real and imagined, which its leaders perceived; a century which ended with nuclear dust settling over the Middle Kingdom.

The years from 1860 to 1895 witnessed the first stage in the establishment of China's modern ordnance industry. Steam-powered machinery was employed in government arsenals to produce iron and steel ordnance and ammunition in what was otherwise a preindustrial social and economic setting. It was not long before the arsenals became the foci of controversy; not only were the kinds and amounts of production debated, the extent to which the existing economic, social, and educational systems should be adjusted to accommodate these new institutions was also discussed. These matters pass far beyond the scope of ordnance technology and production and touch upon broader issues such as the adaptability of the institutional structure of the empire, the motivation of individual leaders, and the openness to socio-economic change at various levels of Chinese society. In short, the problems associated with China's new arsenals were essentially the problems of initiating and implementing change in traditional Chinese civilization.

To catch the signficance of the change involved in the establishment of modern ordnance production, the new plants must be measured against the production norms of the traditional civilization and viewed in the context of China's initial interaction with the West in the nineteenth century. The manufacture of firearms was an ancient and well-established technique of Chinese civilization. In fact, the evolution of the technique had tended to parallel and reflect the development of the civilization throughout the centuries. This development in the nineteenth century was subject to new forces, a devastating series of rebellions, complicated by the aggressive probes of Western imperialist powers and the stimulating influx of Western technology and learning. This combination of historical circumstances, domestic rebellion, foreign aggression, and the availability of new technology provides the background in which China's ancient firearms industry became the first sector of the traditional civilization to undergo radical alteration. For the first time, a significant group of China's leaders attempted to engineer a change in a major thread of the political-economic fabric of the Empire along lines suggested by the technology of an alien civilization. This thread, the government ordnance industry, had a history as old as that of the Empire itself.

THE PRODUCTION OF WEAPONS

The invention of paper, the magnetic compass, printing, and gunpowder were the four great technological achievements of early Chinese civilization.[1] In the case of gunpowder, its momentous consequences have been felt in every inhabited corner of our planet. In China, it has had a pervasive influence not only on warfare, but on social and religious life as well. Fireworks, for example, have become a ubiquitous sign of the gaiety which Chinese people express through their celebrations. Gunpowder and the firearms that eventually were devised to exploit it were regulated by the enduring institutions which guided China's civilization during the imperial age. Thus it was that in the third century B.C. there were evolving administrative institutions that would shape the subsequent discovery and use of firearms right through the critical years when modernization was attempted in the Ch'ing dynasty.

In the third century B.C., while the material culture of East Asia was well along in the transition from bronze to iron, a major advance in political centralization also took place. The administration of Chinese civilization was, for the first time, brought under the control of a single ruling authority, the Ch'in dynasty (221-206 B.C.). It was only after centuries of political strife, during which larger states expanded at the expense of smaller ones followed by a period of internecine struggle among the larger states, that Ch'in emerged victorious over an empire of Chinese culture extending over the North China plain and the northern fringes of the Yangtze Valley. The teachings of the Legalist school of philosophy, an iron-fisted control of society and a monopoly of wealth and military power in the hands of the rulers, had provided the theoretical basis upon which Ch'in rose to power. On the same basis, the First Emperor of Ch'in moved to consolidate his rule over his new Empire.2

This epoch-making centralization of Ch'in also owed a great deal to the concurrent development of iron technology. The economic growth upon which the new political power was founded resulted partially from employment of the new iron-tipped plow. Other tools and utensils were also made chiefly of iron while weapons were made of both iron and bronze. The early policies of the Ch'in dynasty leave no doubt about the importance which they attached to weapons as a factor in their rise to power. One of the First Emperor's earliest and most conspicuous moves was the confiscation of all weapons held by the conquered peoples. These were transported to the Ch'in capital at Hsien-yang, near the present day city of Sian, where they were melted down and cast into twelve enormous statues of men. This appears to be the first concrete instance of what became a persistently recurring policy in later dynasties: the prohibition of the production or ownership of weapons by private individuals outside of the government.3

During the Ch'in dynasty and its lengthy successor the Han (206 B.C.-A.D. 220), official concern with the development of iron technology and its military applications appears to have been great. Official rosters included works officials (kung-kuan) and iron officials (t'ieh-kuan). The former were, in some instances, concerned with the production of weapons, and the latter were involved with all sorts of iron production both military and civilian. The iron officials were more numerous, possibly reflecting the spread of iron technology during these years.[4] However, government control was not unchallenged. Once the Han had replaced the Ch'in, Legalist economic controls, which the Ch'in had carried to the extreme, virtually wrecking the economy, were relaxed. Laissez-faire policies aimed at promoting economic recuperation characterized the first century of Han rule. Under these conditions, private commercial development flourished--so much so that by 178 B.C. the Emperor Wen Ti complained of food shortages caused by cultivators abandoning their lands for the pursuit of commerce. Though such complaints probably stemmed from concern over potential diminution of agricultural tax revenue, nevertheless it was a fact that commerce was expanding and with it there was a growth of private capitalism and the emergence of a class of wealthy merchants. Among these, at least three are known to have grown wealthy through iron mining.

During the Former Han dynasty (206 B.C.-A.D. 8), this emergent merchant class, socially ascendant and economically powerful, gained in influence at the expense of imperial officials. They disrupted the officially advocated Confucian social structure, which relegated them to the lowest level of society. Furthermore, the costly expansionist policies of Emperor Han Wu Ti (r. 141-87 B.C.) bankrupted the imperial government and the agricultural economy upon which it was founded. But by opening up new trade routes through Central Asia, expansion of the Empire actually promoted an increase of wealth among the merchants. In domestic trade also, iron merchants probably profited from the demand created by Han Wu Ti's military requirements. Fortunes must certainly have been accessible to those who could supply the Emperor's troops with the superior iron weapons that were just coming into general use. This merchant class, which tended to dominate the production of iron and iron weapons, soon emerged as the sole prosperous group in the midst of the general poverty created by Han Wu Ti's empire building. But when the Emperor turned to the merchants for contributions to the state treasury, his appeals fell on deaf ears.

In the face of this fiscal dilemma, imperial advisers worked out a system to mobilize merchant wealth for the service of the state. In essence this consisted of four points: the issuance of new currency to replace that held by the merchants; the introduction of new business taxes; government purchase and sale of commodities; and a government monopoly on the two key items of trade, salt and iron. The iron monopoly was actually established by a wealthy iron merchant who formulated concrete plans through which the entire industry was taken over by the state. From that time on private individuals were forbidden to engage in iron mining or in the manufacture of iron tools or implements. Violations were to be punished by fettering of the left leg. Though the establishment of the iron monopoly had the effect of excluding small merchants from the iron trade, the big merchants simply transferred their services from private enterprise to the government. They accepted appointments as iron officers to superintend mining, processing, and sale of iron in a stipulated province or principality. At least forty-eight of these were appointed. Petty officers were subordinate to the iron officials, and at the lowest level were the laborers, mostly slaves. By the reign of Han Yüan Ti (48-32 B.C.), the monopoly had been extended to include copper; in the mining of these two metals, about 100,000 men were employed annually.

Through the establishment of the monopoly on iron, the government had, in effect, strengthened its control over the production of weapons, for these were the years when iron was coming into its own as a war material. The need for such control was clearly articulated during the famous debates on salt and iron (yen-t'ieh lun). These debates, which took place in 81 B.C. after the monopolies had been functioning for almost four decades, raised a whole series of questions concerning the propriety of state control of the economy in the context of Confucian political theory. General dissatisfaction with the monopoly products as well as with other aspects of the state's manipulation of the economy led the Emperor Chao Ti (86-73 B.C.) to summon the Confucian scholars, who were foremost among the critics, to the capital where they confronted the Legalist officials, the masterminds of the monopolies. The clash of ideologies--Confucian disdain for official participation in economic affairs versus Legalist insistence on state economic controls--ranges far beyond the scope of this study. However, among the arguments of the Legalists for continuation of the salt and iron monopolies is an early and unmistakably clear statement of the rationale for government control of arms production. The operation of these industries by private entrepreneurs, argued the Legalists, led to the accumulation of enormous power in the hands of certain families, power which could challenge and threaten that of the central government. Numerous historical examples were cited to support this point, but the concurrent development of iron weaponry gave real cogency to their arguments. The possibility of equipping antigovernment rebels with superior weapons and denying the use of these to the Emperor's forces was intolerable to the imperial government. Iron weapons were regarded as important to the maintenance of the Empire and were not to be placed in the hands of the masses.

The Confucian attack on the monopolies was unconvincing and only partially successful for a variety of reasons, one of which must have been the failure to offer an alternative program to remedy the financial weakness of the imperial government. Nor were they successful in rebutting the Legalist position on production of iron weapons. The monopolies survived for more than one hundred years, and the Legalists' fears about letting the production of iron slip out of government control proved to be very well founded, for trouble broke out even within the purview of government control. Imperial iron workers revolted in 22 B.C., invading nine different provinces and principalities, and again in 14 B.C. when the revolt spread into nineteen provinces and principalities. The wisdom of a policy of strict government control over the production of arms was indelibly fixed in the minds of China's rulers, and this policy has been adhered to by Chinese governments, insofar as possible, right up to the present century.[5]

During the Ming dynasty (1368-1644), for example, the production of weapons was controlled by a government monopoly and all private production was prohibited. In the early Ming, even government production was restricted to the metropolitan cities of Peking and Nanking where it could be kept under close scrutiny by imperial officials. An arsenal established by a frontier general in 1441 was closed by imperial order, and an edict of 1496 explicitly limited production to the capital where it could be closely controlled. It was only in the final decades of the dynasty, when the Manchu threat dominated every aspect of government policy, that the provinces were permitted to produce guns for presentation to the imperial government. Furthermore, the Ming were careful to keep firearms from falling into the hands of the Manchus; it was partially through their superior fire power that they were able to beat back Manchu attacks during the first several decades of the seventeenth century. The eventual acquisition of firearms by the Manchus was one of the decisive factors in their final overthrow of the Ming.[6]

During the Ch'ing dynasty (1644-1912), government control of the arms industry was rigidly maintained. The Manchus, a minority of a few million ruling a Chinese population of several hundred million, were particularly fearful of dissidence and kept a close guard over potential sources of power such as firearms. They had learned the wisdom of close government control of firearms the hard way. Consequently, the high regard which the rulers of the Ch'ing dynasty attached to arms as an instrument for maintaining state power is not at all surprising and it is reflected in the statutes of the dynasty. There it is explicitly stated that weapons production would be entirely controlled by the Board of Works of the Imperial Government. Elaborate procedures were set forth to control current inventories of arms held by the armed forces and to regulate resupply. Private dealing was strictly prohibited. Casting of heavy artillery was to be supervised by an official appointed by the Emperor or by the board; smaller caliber arms could be cast as needed.[7]

THE EARLY DEVELOPMENT OF FIREARMS

Government monopoly of arms production was one of the basic assumptions underlying the maintenance of ruling power in imperial China; as such, it also provided the administrative and institutional framework within which the traditional firearms industry developed. The technological antecedent of firearms, of course, was gunpowder, one of the important discoveries of ancient Chinese civilization. Although the earliest written record of the formula for gunpowder appears in a volume on military affairs dating from about A.D. 1040, it is certain that the skill necessary to combine sulphur, saltpeter and charcoal into the exact mixture described in this work was perfected only after many years of experimentation. Hence the discovery of the explosive mixture in a crude form presumably preceded this date by a considerable period. It is even possible that the earliest production took place, quite by accident, around the end of the third or the beginning of the fourth century A.D. when, in the course of alchemical experimentation, saltpeter and sulphur were mixed in the amounts necessary to produce gunpowder and exposed to temperatures sufficiently high to produce explosion. In one instance it was reported that the substance produced "blew up suddenly burning the hands, the face, and the house."[8]

In any case, it was not until the tenth or eleventh century that there were indications of military applications of gunpowder. Even then, it was the incendiary rather than the explosive properties that first attracted the attention of ordnance officers. The new mixture was used on fire arrows, some of which may have employed the rocket principle between 970 and 1040, and in crude flame throwers between 919 and 1000. Employment in mines and smoke screens dates from the early eleventh century and about this time, incendiary objects containing gunpowder began to replace the stone projectiles that Chinese armies hurled from their catapults. Gunpowder was produced in large quantities to meet this requirement. But it was not until 1103 that fireworks containing gunpowder were used at the capital and the explosive properties of the mixture were first officially noted. A composition of lime and sulphur, resembling Greek fire, was employed in smoke grenades (which exploded on contact with water) at the battle of Tsai Shih Rock in 1161 by forces of the Ju-chen Chin dynasty, which ruled North China from 1126 to 1234.[9] These cannot be considered true firearms, however, since they were designed solely to blind and confuse, rather than to wound or kill.[10]

True explosive grenades were first employed in the early thirteenth century, possibly as early as 1206, and certainly by 1232, when they were used in connection with a catapult, again by the Chin forces, this time against the invading Mongols at the battle of Pien-ching. Meanwhile, the prototype of the gun was slowly evolving. A tubular weapon constructed of durable and reusable paper, which projected burning powder for more than ten paces, was also used by the Chin forces at Pien-ching. By 1259 a bamboo barrel had been fashioned. During the next several decades bamboo was replaced by metal, and in 1274 the Mongols used an iron barreled gun which shot out iron balls in their unsuccessful attempt to invade

Japan.[11]

Between the discovery of gunpowder in China and the development of a firearm employing the explosive force of the powder to propel a projectile through a predictable trajectory, a minimum of three to four centuries had elapsed. These centuries, from the tenth to the thirteenth, were a time of thoroughgoing social change. A general recrudescence of Confucian learning followed from the adoption of the Confucian classics as the basis for the civil service examinations during the T'ang dynasty (618-906) and the educated Confucian official class increased sharply in number and in prominence.[12] The movement of this group, well-known for its disdain of the military arts and for its preoccupation with humanistic rather than scientific learning, into the leadership of society presumably slowed the development of firearms technology. This was the case even though the eighth to the thirteenth century was a time of steadily intensifying military pressures from non-Chinese peoples on the northern borders. The very survival of the Empire seemed to hinge on the ability of the Chinese of the Sung dynasty (960-1278) to develop military strength sufficient to resist the Ju-chen and the Mongols, and still they were unable to do so. These trends--the growing pacifism of Chinese civilization coupled with a growing aggressiveness on the part of their non-Chinese neighbors, as noted above--resulted in the fall of northern China to the Ju-chen Chin dynasty in 1126, and in complete occupation by the Mongol Yüan dynasty in 1279.

The Mongol armies were probably the first in China to employ firearms, that is explosive grenades and guns, as organic weapons. It also seems likely that it was through the Mongol Empire, spanning as it did the entire land mass of Asia, that gunpowder was introduced to Europe. Whatever its origin, it is clear that gunpowder became known in Europe during the thirteenth and fourteenth centuries and was followed promptly by the development of firearms. Meanwhile, production technique in China seems to have developed slowly under Mongol rule. The earliest dated specimens of Chinese iron cannon are from the years 1356 and 1357, weighing 666 and 466 pounds respectively. These and models of several decades later, which may be observed in Western museums, substantiate literary evidence that cannon were produced in large numbers by Chu Yüan-chang, founder of the Ming dynasty (1368-1644), and by another fourteenth century rebel leader and aspirant to the throne, Chang Shih-ch'eng.[13]

The Ming dynasty was a critical period in the development of firearms production in China. Though the variety and design of ordnance gives evidence of significant advance in the indigenous technology, the Ming failed to keep abreast of the progress being made in the West. During the fifteenth, sixteenth, and seventeenth centuries, Western firearms moved well ahead of those produced in China and, when Western ordnance first reached China in the early sixteenth century, the Ming were quick to purchase pieces and to model their own production after that of the West. Meanwhile, several types of small arms had been produced by the Ming: a gingal thirteen feet or more in length with a supporting rod to facilitate aiming and a somewhat shorter small bore weapon of which there are no extant specimens. Both of these used fuses, a marked advance over the flint firing devices previously employed. A variety of heavy ordnance was also produced from both bronze and iron. The most common was a short iron gun of rather large caliber, stubby in appearance like a present day mortar; unlike the mortar, however, these guns fired on a flat trajectory. Longer curved trajectory guns were also produced. These were fired by fuses. They had a better range and were considered more formidable than earlier models. They were employed for coastal and border defense as well as in operations against the Manchurian tribes.[14]

The Manchus of the early Ch'ing dynasty adopted the ordnance employed by the Ming armies which surrendered to them--for the most part, Portuguese guns that the Ming had begun to import or domestically cast pieces based upon these models. As the Ch'ing consolidated their rule over China proper, they continued to employ ordnance inherited from the Ming. Up until the mid-nineteenth century, the only advance in indigenous technology was in the gingal. These weapons, which were employed on a limited scale in the Ch'ing armies, were reduced in length to about five feet; the quality of the barrel was improved, and the specifications were made uniform.[15]

THE INTRODUCTION OF WESTERN ORDNANCE

Western ordnance first appeared in China in 1520 --only six years after the arrival of the Portuguese at Macao. In that year the Ming Scholar-General Wang Yang-ming employed a Portuguese gun, which the Chinese styled the Fo-lan-chi, in subduing a local rising and was sufficiently impressed to record the event with a short poem. Fo-lan-chi guns based on Portuguese models were promptly produced in China beginning in 1522 and their awesome reputation was firmly established during the 1520s and 1530s when the Portuguese used them to turn back Chinese forces in Kwangtung. These pieces varied in weight from twenty to seventy catties and in range from six hundred paces up to six li; they were generally regarded as far superior to earlier ordnance produced by the Ming.[16]

Though they were produced throughout the sixteenth century, it was not until the early seventeenth, when the Ming began to feel acute pressure from the Manchu tribes on the northern border, that the employment of the Fo-lan-chi was sharply expanded. A determined group of officials, which included some early Chinese Christians such as Li Chih-tsao (Leo Li) and Hsu Kuang-ch'i (Paul Hsü), seeking vainly to save the crumbling Ming Empire, not only promoted the production and employment of the Fo-lan-chi gun, they even went so far as to hire Portuguese to supervise and instruct in the casting of the guns in Peking and to assist in their battlefield employment. By 1622 the efforts of Hsü, Li and others over the previous several years began to bear fruit; ordnance training began in Peking under Portuguese gunners, and imperially authorized production commenced the same year under the direction of three Portuguese technicians. During the 1620s, foreign-style artillery appears to have been an important factor in the Ming success in staving off the steadily increasing military pressure from the Manchus. At the battle of Ningyüan in 1626, for example, the Hung-i-ta-p'ao, or barbarian artillery, employed by the Ming was extremely effective. It was at this battle that the Manchu chieftain Nurhachi was reported to have been seriously wounded. He died very soon thereafter.[17]

During this decade, however, the Ming requirement for Portuguese style guns became so great that production could not keep up with the steadily increasing demand. Consequently, in 1629, Portuguese technicians from Macao were again recruited to come to the capital. Bearing ten additional ordnance pieces and accompanied by the missionary interpreter Johannes Rodriquez, this group established their reputation by repulsing a Manchu attack at Cho-chou before they ever reached Peking. After they arrived at the capital, Hsü and Rodriquez attempted to increase the number of Portuguese even further;

however, their plan was blocked by opposition from the Imperial Censorate. Subsequently the Portuguese gunners were assigned to forces defending the P'eng-lai area in Shantung. There they used their artillery but ultimately were unsuccessful in checking the Manchu advance. After the fall of Teng-chou the survivors of the badly decimated Portuguese contingent were sent back to Macao. As a result of this sustained experience with foreign artillery the Chinese came to regard the Fo-lan-chi and the Hung-i-ta-p'ao as integral items in their own arsenal of weapons. Production was vastly expanded, and, after 1621, the government monopoly was relaxed to allow for production by certain provincial governments in addition to the imperial arsenals at Peking and Nanking.[18]

Until about 1630 the Manchu forces had no firearms at all. As noted, this seems to have been one of the important factors that helped the Ming maintain the upper hand during the first several decades of the seventeenth century. During the late 1620s, however, Chinese troops equipped with firearms joined the Manchu forces and about 1630 Manchu bannermen began employing captured firearms themselves. The first record of Manchu production of firearms was a Hung-i-ta-p'ao completed in 1631. In that year also, firearms were an important factor in the Manchu victory at Ta-ling-ho and, subsequently, the savage Manchu artillery barrages on Ming strong points did much to demoralize the imperial armies. Possession of artillery also became an important bargaining factor for Ming generals negotiating surrender terms. By the late 1630s, although both sides were producing ordnance as rapidly as possible, the Manchus had gained experience and surpassed the Ming in the employment of their guns.[19]

After the capture of Peking in 1644, as the Manchus and their Chinese subordinates moved south against the fleeing remnant of the Ming court and their remaining loyal military forces, firearms were used extensively by both sides. Cheng Ch'eng-kung, the leader of the Ming loyalist forces based on Taiwan, employed guns in raids on the mainland in the 1650s. Production by the Manchus was stepped up in 1674, when the Emperor K'ang-hsi, faced with the Rebellion of the Three Feudatories in South China, ordered the Jesuit missionary Ferdinand Verbiest, then serving in the imperial government, to cast cannon for the Ch'ing armies. In the next three years, more than 120 pieces were completed and, by the time the rebellion had been put down in 1681, more than three hundred cannon had been cast, a feat for which Father Verbiest received lavish imperial praise. Subsequently, foreign style artillery was employed by Chinese forces against the Russians at Fort Albazin on the Amur River in 1685, and again in 1686. These victories established China's military superiority in the border area and laid the foundations for the Treaty of Nerchinsk (1689), which stabilized northwest border relations for more than a century.[20]

During this next century and one half, a time of unprecedented domestic peace and prosperity, development of the foreign style artillery, which China had assimilated during the seventeenth century, came to a standstill. Nor was there further introduction of new foreign ordnance; the Ch'ing policy of strictly regulating all intercourse with the West within the ritual framework of the tributary system presumably prevented this. Consequently in the next important test of arms with a foreign foe, the Opium War (1839-1842), the Chinese found their ordnance vastly inferior to that employed by the British. The explosive shell, for example, which contained gunpowder and was ignited by fuse, was unknown in China until used by the British outside of Canton during the war.[21]

Explosive shells and other superior British ordnance items, as well as their steam-powered naval vessels, created a deep impression on Chinese officials in charge of defensive operations during the Opium War. Imperial Commissioner at Canton Lin Tse-hsü called for the adoption of Western-style ordnance and warships as part of China's long-range defense planning. More specific proposals were made by the well-known, reform-minded scholar Wei Yüan who suggested establishment, in the Canton area, of a shipyard and arsenal to produce Western-style vessels and ordnance and the use of French and American technicians to teach production, gunnery, and navigation. Further proposals came from the French ministers in 1843 and 1844. In a move calculated to offset the predominant influence enjoyed by Great Britain, the French invited China to send students to France to study shipbuilding and ordnance production with the assurance that the Chinese would quickly be able to overtake British technology in these areas. Although the imperial backing necessary to implement such far-reaching plans was not forthcoming, defense-conscious gentry and officials, with imperial encouragement, responded to the challenge of British military technology at the local level with concrete and practical achievements. In Canton, Ting Kung-chen, a holder of the Chien-sheng, a degree implying marginal gentry status, was successful in casting iron ordnance and producing gunpowder while Ting Shou-tsun, a second class secretary of the Board of Revenue, developed a process for making mines. Both also wrote treatises on ordnance production as did Kung Chen-lin, a former district magistrate, who developed the first iron mold to replace the sand molds generally used for casting ordnance. In Canton also, Taotai P'an Shih-ch'eng invented an underwater mine and authored a volume on naval mines.[22]

In the 1840s these and other students of Western ordnance technology continued their efforts to improve China's military hardware. By the end of the decade, however, peace and with it a false sense of security engulfed the Empire, numbing the court to the urgency of China's international position. Those who favored changes such as the adoption of Western ordnance were regarded as dangerous innovators. A prototype of the percussion cap developed by Ting Shou-tsun, though far more reliable for igniting propellant charges than the flint and priming powder method then in use, was not adopted during the 1850s and did not become widely used in China until introduced from the West more than a decade later under wholly different conditions.[23] Thus it was that foreign intelligence reports during the Arrow War (1856-1860) showed that Chinese ordnance captured at Canton in 1857, and at the Taku Forts in 1860, was still for the most part vastly inferior to that employed by their British and French adversaries.[24]

During these decades while firearms technology advanced slowly, the Taiping Rebellion broke out in the south central province of Kwangsi in 1850. By 1853, the rebels had moved north and were in control of the rich central Yangtze Valley from which they launched expeditions toward Peking and westward into Anhwei. Both sides used firearms in this rebellion, and production of traditional models, some of which incorporated improvements developed during and subsequent to the Opium War, was greatly stimulated. Eventually, during the last years of the rebellion (1860-1865), the machine production of Western-style ordnance was initiated--a development that will be dealt with in detail in a subsequent chapter.

As early as 1850, however, at the time of the initial Taiping uprising at Chin-t'ien in Kwangsi, the rebels already had firearms in their possession. In the same year, one of the Taiping kings, Shih Ta-k'ai, began casting guns at Kuei-p'ing in Kiangsi. Guns were also cast by the Taipings at Yung-an in Kwangsi during the same year and by 1853 British merchants were supplying foreign small arms and powder to the forces of another Taiping king, Lo Ta-kang, at Chin-kiang in Kiangsu.[25]

Local officials in the provinces affected by the rebellion responded promptly to the challenge presented by the Taiping's use of firearms. The earliest instance of local pacification forces employing foreign style firearms seems to have been in 1853, when Tseng Kuo-fan, imperially appointed to organize militia forces in his home province of Hunan, ordered one thousand Chinese and foreign cannon from Canton. Though the offensive launched with these cannon was unsuccessful, use of firearms in counterinsurgency operations continued. In 1853 Anhwei Governor Chiang Chung-yüan proposed the establishment of an arsenal, but it was Governor Lo Ping-chang of Hunan who first succeeded in completing such an establishment. After failing in an attempt to have Kung Chen-lin, the inventor of the iron casting mold, and his son Kung Chih-t'ang transferred from Chekiang, Lo commissioned Huang Mien, a former aide of Lin Tse-hsü, to cast wrought-iron guns in Hunan. Subsequently the Hunan Gun Bureau became an important ordnance supply point. Tseng Kuo-fan also continued to display an interest in firearms. In reporting his victory over the Taipings at Yo-chou on the Yangtze River in July 1854, he noted the arrival of 180 guns from Canton and requested further supply. During the same year Kung Chih-t'ang, who had successfully cast iron guns, and naval personnel skilled in the production of submarine mines joined Tseng's staff. In the course of the next two years, 1855 and 1856, while campaigning in Kiangsi, Tseng established three small arsenals for the casting of guns and ammunition as well as a shipyard. During the same period, Hupeh Governor Hu Lin-i was purchasing more than seventeen hundred pieces of foreign ordnance through Canton. Subsequently, at Wu-ch'ang in Hupeh, he established a Powder Bureau which, along with the Hunan Gun Bureau, became an important source for the supply of firearms to the forces fighting the Taipings during the 1850s.[26]

CONCLUSIONS

In looking back over the development of firearms

in China, the facts seem to warrant certain generalizations. First, the Confucian formula for rule placed the authority for the production of iron weapons entirely with the imperial government or its designated agents. This government monopoly initiated during the Former Han dynasty was an established institutional feature of the Empire when firearms became an important item in the imperial arsenals from the fourteenth to the nineteenth centuries. Secondly, the discovery of gunpowder in the latter half of the first millennium A.D. coincided roughly with the recrudescence of Confucian learning in the late T'ang (618-906) and the Sung (960-1278) dynasties. Recent studies have suggested that the gradual adoption of this neo-Confucianism as the required learning for the civil service examinations resulted in the transformation of the official class from a group known for its martial orientation and aristocratic traditions to one of humanistic interests and bureaucratic organization. The rise to power of these Confucian bureaucrats possibly influenced the slowness with which the Chinese governments of the eleventh, twelfth, and thirteenth centuries developed the use of gunpowder in firearms. Native Chinese firearms technology was probably further retarded by the Mongol occupation (1278-1368). Third, although there was considerable progress in both gun and small arms production during the early Ming dynasty (1368-1644), when Portuguese guns appeared in China in the second decade of the sixteenth century, the Ming Chinese regarded them as superior and quickly imitated their production. In the early seventeenth century, foreign ordnance was completely assimilated by the Ming and subsequently by the Manchu Ch'ing dynasty (1644-1912) which employed foreign-style ordnance successfully against both foreign and domestic foes. Fourth, the eighteenth century, a time of domestic peace and prosperity was another period of stagnation in the evolution of Chinese firearms technology. Presumably this lag resulted from the continued ascendancy of the educated Confucian official class and the absence of any serious military threats to China proper. At any rate, by the mid-nineteenth century, China's seventeenth century ordnance was no match for that of Great Britain. This was dramatically demonstrated during the Opium War.

Finally, the bitter experience of defeat in the Opium War followed by the domestic challenge of the Taiping Rebellion stimulated advances in firearms technology by individual defense-conscious and technically inclined officials. As a result, a substantial beginning was made in technological innovation, showing not only that China, employing its own resources, was capable of moving toward parity with the West but also that technological progress measured against the domestic standards of the Ming and early Ch'ing dynasties was quite significant. The most important developments were the iron mold, which replaced the sand mold and facilitated the casting of more durable ordnance, and the percussion cap, which made the ignition of propellant charges far more reliable. Nevertheless, in 1860 China was behind the West in important areas of ordnance production. Explosive shells had still not replaced the solid shot produced in Chinese ammunition plants. Nor had rifled barrels and breech-loading mechanisms, both widely used in the West, replaced the smooth bore muzzle-loading ordnance of the Middle Kingdom.

II. The Reform Movement of the Mid-Nineteenth Century and the Role of the Ordnance Industry

The development of the domestic firearms industry through 1860 was influenced both by the general civilian bias of Chinese civilization, which slowed advances in ordnance technology, and by the periodic military pressures on the Empire, which provided a countervailing stimulus. The year 1860, however, was the threshold of a new stage in the growth of some of the fundamental forces influencing Chinese civilization and a critical juncture when military pressures reached unprecedented intensity. One result was a reordering of priorities and values in the minds of certain of China's leaders beginning in that year. Military modernization, particularly the modernization of ordnance production, became a central concern. The next thirty-five years, the period of primary focus in this monograph, were a time of furious activity in the ordnance industry when these leaders struggled to lay the foundations of a military industrial complex to produce the military hardware that was the index of big power status in the late nineteenth century. Their struggle culminated in 1895 when the Chinese armed forces were crushed ignominiously by those of a small Asian neighbor, Japan.

Although the significance of the year 1860 as the point of departure for the reform movement in modern China is widely acknowledged, it has not been adequately stressed that the intellectual foundation for reform had already developed in the domestic tradition before the foreign intrusion and the domestic rebellion culminating in that year underscored the immediate necessity for reforms. From the very outset Confucian political theorists during the Ch'ing dynasty had exhibited an overwhelming concern with reassessment of the assumptions upon which contemporary Chinese civilization was founded. This tendency was initially exemplified by the philosophers of the late seventeenth century who assayed the intellectual foundation upon which the defunct Ming dynasty had rested. In general, they regarded the orthodox Sung School of Neo-Confucianism, which had flourished during the Ming, as excessively concerned with metaphysical speculation while they attacked the Wang Yang-ming School of the late Ming for its overly idealistic view of the world and its subjectively established moral norms. Their criticism of these schools and the weakening influence that they had upon the Ming rule led them to an insistence that government policies be derived directly from the text of the Confucian canon, the true Confucian Way. It was thus, they argued, that morality could be restored to government and order to society. This concern for the canonical validity of socio-moral norms inspired the textual criticism and philological study of the Confucian classics, efforts that were the hallmark of the eighteenth century School of Empirical Research.[1]

The potential for social and political reform inherent in the School of Empirical Research failed to materialize during the eighteenth century, however. Whether it was the fear of retaliation by a Manchu court still wary of political criticism from the Chinese literati or the attractive spell of classical research, which tended to make scholarship, rather than its application, an end in itself, or a combination of these two forces, the scholars of the School of Empirical Research, for some reason, usually shunned the arena of social and political reform. Indeed, the socio-political issues upon which a reform program could have taken hold were disappearing during the eighteenth century as an aura of peace and prosperity enveloped the Empire--a striking contrast to conditions in the early seventeenth century, which had given rise to the spirit of criticism and to calls for reform. Aside from the School of Empirical Research, the orthodox Sung School was the most vital intellectual force of the middle Ch'ing. Scholars of this school, however, tended to focus on the problems of moral cultivation of socio-political leaders to the exclusion of such considerations as the reordering of political or social norms.[2]

It was not until the turn of the nineteenth century, when socio-economic and political problems precipitated by overpopulation and aggravated by growing bureaucratic inefficiency overtook the Empire, that the essential socio-political concerns of Confucianism began to reassert themselves among China's intellectuals. Initially this took the form of criticism of the sterile scholarship of the School of Empirical Research during the previous century by scholars of the orthodox Sung School who began to emphasize practical statesmanship as the corollary of their primary concern, moral self-cultivation of the ruling class. Eventually scholars of the School of Empirical Research also manifested a renewed interest in the moral and social implications of the Confucian Way, which they were engaged in defining with such painstaking scholarship.[3]

Concurrent with this reemphasis on the traditional Confucian problem of the ordering of the state and society was the development of the New Text School of the late Ch'ing dynasty. This school, which had grown out of the tendency of the School of Empirical Research to retreat ever further into the past in search of valid exegetical and annotative analysis of the Confucian canon, was based on the freewheeling interpretation of the Confucian Way derived from the so called New Texts of the Former Han dynasty (206 B.C.-A.D. 8). It advanced an apocalyptic theory of historical evolution derived from the writings of the Former Han in which various states in the development of civilization were accompanied by corresponding changes in the socio-political institutions of the Empire.[4]

Although the institutional reform potential of this school was not realized until the end of the nineteenth century, it contributed to the growing socio-political orientation of nineteenth century Neo-Confucianism, an orientation which was epitomized in the School of Statecraft. This school drew extensively from the Legalist philosophies of the late Warring States Period (403-221 B.C.), which held views of the state almost diametrically opposed to those held by Confucianism. Whereas Confucianism regarded the mission of the state as the moral transformation of the populace through the agency of the ruler's virtue, Legalism regarded the paramount goal as the increase of state wealth and power. Observing the ferocity of the interstate struggle of their day, "the legalist philosophers of the Warring States Period concluded that it was wealth and power--and the relationship of the two was very clearly understood--that could insure survival." "Enrich the state and strengthen the military" became their watchword, and the socio-political measures that they advocated were invariably aimed at building up economic power as a basis for military power, which could be controlled and wielded by the authoritarian head of state. Although Legalist-inspired advocacies cropped up repeatedly in Chinese political theory throughout the imperial period, they were frequently cloaked in Confucian terminology, for the harsh realism of Legalism never held the appeal of the humanitarian teachings of Confucianism.[5]

Thus, Neo-Confucian scholars of the School of Statecraft in the early nineteenth century, echoing the economic and socio-political concerns of the scholars of the late seventeenth century, concerned themselves increasingly with the adjustment of institutions and the improvement of administration for the purpose of bolstering the wealth and power of the faltering imperial regime. Now a seemingly insoluble problem beset that regime, the adjustment of international relations with the newly arrived and unruly barbarians of the West. These interests are nowhere more apparent than in the content and organization of the Huang-ch'ao ching-shih wen-pien (Collected Documents on Statecraft) published in 1826 under the editorship of two Hunanese officials, Ho Ch'ang-ling and Wei Yüan. This collection sets forth guidelines for organization and administration of the state and discusses the general problem of policymaking. It goes on to reflect on the theory and practice of state administration under each of the six boards of the imperial government. Though the Confucian assumptions upon which the traditional political order was founded are unchallenged, the emphasis that it places on the technique of bureaucratic administration reflects a legalist orientation in clear contradistinction to the Confucian emphasis on moral cultivation of the ruling class as the central ingredient of statesmanship. Furthermore, the reform potential inherent in the institutional and administrative concerns of the School of Statecraft was reenforced by some of the notions of historical evolution advanced by the New Text School. The idea of timeliness or accord with the times (ho-shih), found in the New Texts, was widely understood by scholars of the School of Statecraft to mean that Confucianism advocated reliance on the past only when it could be of assistance in the present.[6]

The convergence of these ideas is perhaps best exemplified in the writings of the New Text scholar Wei Yüan, co-editor of the Huang-ch'ao ching-shih wen-pien and one of the earliest advocates of reform for the purpose of strengthening China. Wei Yüan minimized the differences between Legalist Realpolitik and Confucian moral idealism, seeing the congruence rather than the conflict of the Legalist goals of wealth and power and the Confucian ideal of kingly government. Nevertheless, his emphasis seemed to be in the direction of Legalism and the School of Statecraft. "In this world there is wealth and power without the kingly way," he said, "but there is no kingly way without wealth and power."[7] These ideas, which were already prominent in Wei Yüan's writing before China's first disastrous encounter with the West, the Opium War (1839-1842), reached the form of concrete proposals in a document written in 1842 and included in the Hai-kuo t'u-chih (Illustrated Gazetteer of the Maritime Nations), published two years later. Here Wei Yüan, preoccupied with the problem of consolidating state power to resist barbarian incursions, enunciated two general principles for the guidance of Chinese policy: one was the age old Chinese strategy of employing barbarians to control barbarians; the other, a new idea, "Learn the superior techniques of the barbarians in order to control them." The latter principle, he advised, should guide Chinese policy while a state of peace existed between China and the barbarians. The superior techniques of the barbarians, he observed, fell into three categories: warships, firearms, and the maintenance and training of troops.[8]

Pursuing this tack, Wei Yüan made concrete recommendations for the establishment of Western-style military industry. These wide-ranging proposals in some respects represented a dramatic departure from existing institutional arrangements. Had they been adopted, they would have altered the face of Chinese civilization considerably for some time to come. Included were plans for a bureau to translate Western books; a Western-style shipyard and arsenal to be established at Chuenpi and Taikoktow outside the Bogue in Kwangtung; the employment of Western technicians to direct production and teach navigation and gunnery; and revised methods of recruitment and advancement for artisans and military personnel skilled in Western techniques. Wei Yüan's farsighted suggestions had no lasting or important influence on the court. They no doubt had a Legalist ring to many of the officials at the capital where the Sung School of Neo-Confucianism enjoyed imperial patronage. In any case, the imperial backing that was the sine qua non for such a radical reform program was not forthcoming.[9]

During the decade following the Opium War, while the court settled back in the false security of temporary peace, still another strain of reform ideology developed, one that despite certain Legalist aims was essentially Neo-Confucian in its perspective, acknowledging the central position of the imperial institution and the need to effectuate reform through its agency. Its author was Tseng Kuo-fan, who in the 1860s became the cofounder of China's modern ordnance industry. From 1840 to 1852, Tseng, a native of Hunan province and a holder of the highest civil service degree, <u>chin-shih</u> (class of 1838), resided in the capital where he served in the Hanlin Academy, the center of Confucian learning for the Empire, until 1847. In July of that year he was appointed sub-chancellor of the Grand Secretariat with the title vice president of the Board of Rites, the first in a series of bureaucratic appointments in a long and distinguished career of government service.[10] As the result of his Neo-Confucian studies and his exceptionally broad administrative experience during this decade, Tseng gained an understanding of the need for reform in the imperial bureaucracy and developed a strategy for implementing it that would influence his decision, more than a decade later, to revolutionize arms production in China by introducing steam-powered production machinery.

Though Tseng was closely identified with the orthodox Sung School of Neo-Confucianism, the influence of the contemporary School of Statecraft, combined with his intense personal commitment to remedy the administrative, military, and economic woes of the dynasty, led him to recommend solutions that were less doctrinaire and more pragmatic than those advanced by others of the Sung School. For example, he shared with his contemporaries in the School of Statecraft a belief that enrichment of the state was a proper aim of government and that the institutions of antiquity should be discarded if they did not meet the needs of the present. It would, however, be naive to regard Tseng as a reformer in the modern sense of that term since, by and large, he clung to the view that the existing institutional structure of the Ch'ing dynasty was not in need of a general overhaul. Instead, he recommended specific changes as he saw that they were needed. He advocated currency reform based on a realistic acknowledgment of the flight of domestic silver, military streamlining designed to demobilize corrupt and inefficient units, administrative reforms calling for wider consultation by the throne in the decision making process and a greater role for ministers and censors. His position that administrators should be appointed only upon the advice of censors, whom he regarded as the voice of the people at court, clearly reflected a commitment to the Mencian principle that government should be for the people and shows his determination to push administrative reform based on this commitment even to the point where it affected political institutions. This advocacy can only be understood as an attempt to mitigate the intensifying trend toward imperial autocracy, which Tseng saw as the foremost reason for dynastic decline.[11]

Of even greater importance in understanding Tseng's subsequent role as a reformer in the ordnance industry is his approach or strategy of reform. Because of his unquestioning adherence to the Neo-Confucian idea of hierarchical bureaucratic government with the Emperor at the summit of the hierarchy monopolizing all powers of appointment within the bureaucracy, Tseng felt that the key to effective reform lay in influencing imperial appointments. Talented officials would then be at the crucial posts at the moment that they were needed. His preoccupation with this personnel-administrative aspect of reform leaves no doubt that the pragmatism that had led him to recommend limited institutional adjustments had not altered his faith in the fundamental Confucian belief that good men were the most important ingredient of a good government, a belief that later led him to channel the careers of highly talented and reform minded officials into the government-operated ordnance industry.[12]

In 1852 an imperial edict directed Tseng to recruit and train militia in his home province of Hunan for employment against the Taiping Rebellion, which had spread northward into Hunan. His skill as a recruiter and disciplinarian, coupled with careful planning and dogged determination, brought him limited success against local uprisings in Hunan and catapulted Tseng and his Hsiang (Hunan) Army into a position of prominence in the campaign, which began in early 1854, to dislodge the Taipings from their stronghold in the central Yangtze Valley. As noted previously, Tseng took a pragmatic and innovative approach to the problem of ordnance supply, seeking whatever was effective to insure the survival of state power in the struggle with the Taiping menace. He placed his first order for foreign ordnance in 1852, and it appears that from that time through 1860 occasional shipments of foreign and foreign-style ordnance items reached his forces. The Hsiang Army used these arms, often successfully, and Tseng recognized their excellence. It was this recognition, no doubt, together with his realization that state military power could be best consolidated from domestic rather than foreign supply that led to his first groping attempts at ordnance production in the years 1856-1860.[13]

The emphasis that Tseng placed on the proper use of human talent during this period also bore important implications for the establishment of a modern ordnance industry after 1860. As early as 1843, Li Hung-chang, who twenty years hence would be a cofounder of the modern ordnance industry, attracted Tseng's attention. Beginning about that time, a teacher-disciple relationship formed between the two. Although there is no record to indicate that Li immersed himself in the examination of reform ideologies as did Tseng, nevertheless Tseng recognized Li's great talent as early as 1845. Two years later, in 1847, Li reached the pinnacle of scholarly attainment when he won the chin-shih degree himself. He was also named to the Hanlin Academy. It was not until he embarked on a military career in the antiTaiping struggle that Li won real distinction, however. After returning from the capital to his home province of Anhwei in the spring of 1853, he led a force of more than one thousand in victory over the Taipings. His accomplishment was praised by Tseng Kuo-fan who was then commanding forces in Hunan and with whom Li was corresponding. From 1853 through 1856 Li served with distinction as a military commander and as an adviser to the government of Anhwei. In early 1859 he accepted an invitation to join the staff of Tseng Kuo-fan, who was then campaigning against the Taipings in southern Anhwei. During the next three years, as a member of Tseng's personal staff (mu-fu), he gained further recognition. By 1860 Tseng was convinced that Li was ready for an administrative appointment at the provincial level and an important military command.[14]

It was in that year that Tseng Kuo-fan received an imperial appointment that gave him the military muscle and administrative autonomy necessary to mobilize the wealth and resources of the lower Yangtze provinces for an all-out effort against the Taipings. The imperial forces guarding the Taiping capital at Nanking were decisively defeated in May 1860 at the battle of Tan-yang by a Taiping army under the able leadership of Li Hsiu-ch'eng. The imperial headquarters collapsed completely and within two months the Taipings had occupied all the important cities on Lake T'ai, the richest area in the delta. By mid

August 1860 Li Hsiu-ch'eng's forces were nearing Shanghai. At this critical juncture the throne took extraordinary measures. An edict of August 10, 1860 named Tseng governor-general of the Liangkiang provinces (Kiangsu, Anhwei and Kiangsi) and imperial commissioner in charge of all imperial armed forces in these three provinces as well as northern Chekiang, a precedent-breaking eleventh hour move to unify administration, military command and supply functions when the rebellion threatened to engulf the entire Yangtze Delta.[15]

Many local officials in the lower Yangtze Delta favored soliciting foreign assistance to deal with the Taiping menace. The foremost advocate of this course was Ho Kuei-ch'ing, governor-general of the Liangkiang provinces before Tseng's appointment. The idea of asking to borrow foreign troops was not seriously entertained by the court, however, for the simple reason that China's relations with Britain and France were strained almost to the brink of war as the result of the British minister's efforts to force his way into Peking to exchange ratification of the new treaty signed in 1858. Furthermore, Ho, the leading advocate of borrowing foreign troops, was dismissed for unprincipled behavior during the Taiping rout of the Yangtze Delta, and was replaced by Tseng Kuo-fan as acting governor-general in early June 1860. Like it or not, however, the imperial government was about to receive aid from the British and French. The commercial stake that these two powers had in the port of Shanghai was too great for them to ignore the threat that the approaching Taipings posed to the city. A joint declaration released by the foreign consuls in Shanghai on May 26 asserted that the city was an international port where Chinese and foreign interests were inextricably intertwined. If the rebellion were to reach Shanghai, there would be extensive losses to British and French trading interests. Therefore the armed forces of these two countries would be employed to prevent acts of violence and to maintain order. Accordingly, when Li Hsiu-ch'eng's army finally did enter the city on August 19, it was expelled by British and French defense forces.[16]

This move against the Taipings by the British and French at Shanghai came at a time when the military forces of these two powers in North China were threatening to crush the imperial court. The apparent inconsistency in the Anglo-French policy toward the court in Peking and toward the local authorities in Shanghai can be resolved by recalling the origins of the controversy that brought British and French troops to North China in August 1860. The incidents that provided the British and French with a casus belli for the Second Opium or Arrow War (1856-1860) were but thinly veiled pretexts. Their real motivation was to compel China to agree to revised treaties that would be more advantageous to the Western nations than the first set of unequal treaties signed in 1842-1844. The latter had fallen far short of securing the commercial, diplomatic, and evangelical gains that the powers had hoped for in China.[17]

The British and French forces of 18,000 men that stormed the Taku Forts guarding Tientsin on August 21, 1860, a scant two days after the forces of these two powers had turned back the Taipings at Shanghai, pressed on to occupy Peking in October. There they compelled the imperial government, represented by the Emperor's brother, Prince Kung, to ratify new treaties. These provided for the exchange of diplomatic representatives, a revised tariff schedule, reparation and indemnities, extension of extraterritoriality, expanded rights for foreigners to travel and evangelize in the interior, the opening of Tientsin and new ports on the Yangtze to foreign trade, and the cession of Kowloon to Great Britain. The motive of commercial access that had prompted the Anglo-French intervention in Shanghai was clearly an important motivation for the occupation of Peking and the pressure for treaty revision as well.[18]

Although the Anglo-French forces were withdrawn from Peking in early November, the general situation had changed irreversibly. The humiliating occupation of the imperial capital, the new and more favorable treaties that the powers had obtained, the stepped up Taiping activities in the Yangtze Delta, and the personnel changes that these multiple crises had prompted among China's leaders all combined to create a new atmosphere at Peking. The necessity for bold new steps to rescue the waning fortunes of the dynasty was becoming apparent at the highest levels of the imperial government. The young Emperor Hsien-feng, who had fled the capital with his antiforeign advisers as the British and French forces approached, remained in his retreat in Jehol even after the evacuation of the allied forces. De facto control of the government was in the hands of Prince Kung. Though Prince Kung's policy views at the time that he assumed the onerous responsibility of making peace are unknown, it seems that he quickly became convinced of the utter folly of further military resistance to the foreigners. For the time being at least, he felt that the most prudent course was adjustment of China's relations with the West within the framework of the treaties. Having guided the imperial government through the gravest crisis in the history of the dynasty, Prince Kung's voice now carried a new note of authority.[19]

One of the earliest concrete signs of Prince Kung's attitude was a proposal to establish an office exclusively for the management of foreign affairs. This bureau, the Tsung-li ko-kuo shih-wu ya-men, usually referred to as the Tsungli Yamen, was approved, and Prince Kung himself was named head, a position that he held through 1884. Initially he was assisted by two officials of a similar turn of mind, Grand Secretary Kuei-liang and Vice President of the Board of Revenue Wen-hsiang. At about the same time the positions of the superintendents of trade for northern and southern ports were established. These officials, who were subsequently termed northern commissioner (pei-yang ta-ch'en) and southern commissioner (nan-yang ta-ch'en), were charged not only with superintending trade at the newly opened treaty ports but also with the regulation of all official contacts with foreigners. The Tsungli Yamen and the commissioners also extended their cognizance to all domestic matters that bore directly upon foreign affairs such as foreign language schools, shipyards, and ordnance production.[20]

The ascendancy of Prince Kung, the apparent willingness of the dynasty to adjust its relations with the West, and above all the very favorable terms of the new treaties clearly changed the stake that Britain and France (and other powers such as the United States and Russia who by virtue of the most favored nation clauses in their treaties enjoyed the same privileges as Britain and France) had in the maintenance of the existing political order in China. No longer could the powers sit by maintaining official neutrality while their hard won treaty rights slipped away as control of the Yangtze Valley passed from the Ch'ing to the Taipings.[21]

This was the changed international climate in which Tseng Kuo-fan found himself as he took control of the devastated imperial forces in the lower Yangtze Valley in the fall of 1860. Offers for foreign assistance were not long in coming. In November Nicholas Ignatiev, the Russian consul general who had mediated between the Anglo-French forces and the Chinese at Peking in the fall of 1860 and in return gained a treaty in which the transUssuri provinces of Manchuria were ceded to Russia, offered to dispatch a Russian force to assist imperial troops along the Yangtze. The court referred this offer to Tseng Kuo-fan, Hsüeh Huan, the governor of Kiangsu, and Wang Yu-ling, governor of Chekiang, for comment. Though the latter two strongly supported the idea and Hsüeh even felt that the Russians should be rewarded, Tseng Kuo-fan prudently opposed it. The import of the recent Russian treaty must have made it clear to a strategist of Tseng's experience that, with friends like the devious Ignatiev, China had no need for enemies. Tseng favored only limited borrowing of Western military techniques to be employed in pacifying the rebellion and was opposed to large-scale foreign intervention. The views submitted by Tseng, Hsüeh, and Wang were weighed by Prince Kung, who in January 1861 decided to follow Tseng's suggestion to emphasize the production of Western style warships and weapons in Shanghai and to decline direct military assistance. This decision marks the point of departure for the establishment of the modern ordnance industry in China.[22]

The multiple crises of 1860 not only focused official attention on China's urgent need for military modernization, they intensified the concern for related reforms among Chinese intellectuals. The reform ideas, which had been germinating during the past several decades as a result of the influence of the School of Statecraft, were expanded and formulated in a coherent program designed to bolster state power by the far-sighted Confucian scholar Feng Kuei-fen. Feng, who had won the chin-shih degree with highest honors in 1840 and was subsequently named to the Hanlin Academy, was serving as director of an academy in his native Soochow when that city fell to the Taipings in June 1860. After taking refuge in Shanghai, he is reported to have won the recognition of Tseng Kuo-fan for his advice on a strategy to recapture Soochow. Subsequently Feng served Tseng as a personal adviser, and in 1864-1865 he joined the staff of Li Hung-chang (who by then held the post of governor of Kiangsu) as an adviser on reconstruction and provincial affairs. During these years, 1860-1865, Tseng and Li formulated their plans to introduce steam powered machinery to mass produce Western style military ordnance and ammunition. The influence of Feng's ideas was acknowledged by both.[23]

Feng's proposals on reform are contained in the collection of essays, Chiao-pin-lu k'ang-i (Protests from the Study of Chiao-pin), which, with only a few exceptions, were written during 1860 and 1861 in Shanghai.[24] Perhaps the most important aspects of

Feng's proposals are the balance and range that they reflect when considered in toto and the thoroughgoing practicality evidenced in individual proposals. The reforms that he proposed were not confined to any single area of Chinese life, nor can they be characterized as surface adjustments that would leave the basic timbre of Chinese institutions unchanged. For example, Feng recommended extensive changes in the existing political order. Though he derived his political principles of reducing superfluous government personnel, eliminating meaningless bureaucratic procedures, and consolidating ties between ruler and the ruled from his studies of Chinese antiquity, his recommendations for putting these into practice were sometimes quite revolutionary. This can be seen in the system that he outlined for the selection of government personnel so as to strengthen ties between the ruler and the ruled; it incorporated the ideals of a democratic government and went far beyond earlier proposals in attempting to mitigate the autocratic power of the ruler. He advocated procedures under which officials, gentry, and elders would select personnel to be advanced to higher office. At the local level, that is below the district, he recommended that officials be popularly elected to specified terms with stipulated salaries. In a separate but related area, his advocacies for the revival of the clan welfare system of antiquity incorporated the goals of modern welfare policies in advanced Western states and amounted to a proposal for complete reform of China's social system.[25]

But Feng's foremost concern was the foreign threat to China; he clearly regarded it as more dangerous than the problem of rebellion. Rebels, he observed, could be exterminated, but foreign powers were too numerous and diverse to eliminate completely. If one type of foreign problem was solved another would arise from an entirely unexpected direction. Therefore he felt that what was needed was a reasonable strategy to deal with foreigners, not foolhardy attempts to eliminate them. From what he had learned of Western nations, he judged that an appeal to reason in countering their demands would not fall on deaf ears, for the foreigners always attempted to rely on reason as their ultimate authority. For an understanding based on reason, communications were the first essential. Accordingly, Feng advocated the establishment of foreign language schools in Shanghai and Canton, an advocacy that resulted in Li Hung-chang establishing such a school in Shanghai in 1863. Subsequently one was also started in Canton.[26]

With respect to policies for the immediate present, he felt that Wei Yüan's strategy of using barbarians to control barbarians failed to comprehend the complexity of contemporary foreign relations. China was patently incapable of manipulating or sowing dissension among foreign powers. Feng's views, however, were in accord with Wei Yüan's strategy of learning the superior techniques of the barbarians in order to control them. The traditions of broad scholarship, espoused by the School of Empirical Research and the School of Statecraft, led Feng, as it had Wei Yüan, to investigate foreign civilizations and to draw comparisons. When he found areas in which foreign civilizations excelled, the statecraft ideals of objectivity and practicality sometimes led him to recommend that China study and adopt such features. But not always. There were also cases in which he felt that China's shortcomings could be remedied without extensive learning from the West. This was so, for example, in matters such as employing human and natural resources and in consolidating ties between the ruler and the ruled. In each of these areas he saw that the West was ahead of China but he felt that enlightened imperial leadership was the key to reform (even though his proposals for strengthening ties between the ruler and the ruled were informed by the Western notion of democracy).[27]

It is clear that Feng's perception of China's shortcomings went far beyond that of Wei Yüan who saw inferiority only in the area of ordnance and ships. But it was precisely in this area that Feng was in close agreement with Wei Yüan; he also urged that China should study and adopt superior Western ordnance and ships. This was the key to China making itself strong (tzu-ch'iang). These were the barbarian's techniques of which Wei Yüan had spoken and which would enable China to control the barbarians. He recommended the establishment of a shipyard and arsenal in each treaty port and the employment of foreign technicians to instruct Chinese personnel in ordnance production and shipbuilding. Furthermore, he proposed that incentives should be provided and avenues for upward socio-political mobility should be opened for Chinese personnel who distinguished themselves in such pursuits. Those who mastered the art of production as well as the Westerners should be awarded the chü-jen degree, the second highest in the civil service examination system, and be recommended for the metropolitan exams; while those whose achievements in production excelled the foreigner's should be awarded the chin-shih and be recommended for the palace examinations, the pinnacle of individual status. At least half of China's intellectuals should be diverted from pursuit of literary degrees in the civil service system to the study of foreign techniques. Moreover, Feng's interest in learning from the West did not stop with ordnance production and shipbuilding, although it has sometimes been asserted that it did. He advocated intensive study of fundamental sciences such as mathematics, mechanics, optics, chemistry, and even foreign geography. When the translation of books in these fields had progressed far enough, he wanted students who showed a mastery of them and who could make valuable contributions based on this knowledge to be awarded the chü-jen degree upon recommendation by the northern and southern commissioners.[28]

There is no doubt that Feng's primary interest in studying the West was self-strengthening--self-strengthening that would enable China to expel the foreigners. And he took serious issue with those Chinese whose disdain for the foreign powers kept them from studying foreign techniques. In Feng's view, these people wanted to expel the foreigners from China but were unwilling to take steps necessary to achieve that end, primarily because of the disruptive effect which they feared foreign techniques would have upon Chinese civilization. Feng reasoned that the use of certain techniques derived from Western civilizations need not be disruptive nor necessarily entail a substitution of Western state and social organization for Chinese. Although this viewpoint of Feng's, together with his emphasis on military industrialization, has been understood as the origin of the superficial approach to reform (sometimes called t'i-yung) in which only such functional aspects of the state as the military establishment would be modernized while all fundamental elements of the civilization such as the educational system would remain untouched, the total impact of Feng's works leaves quite a different impression. It is clear that he favored reforms in the educational system, the distribution of political power, and other matters that pertained to the most fundamental aspects of Chinese civilization when reason and practicality dictated that such changes would promote the self-strengthening that he felt was imperative for survival. Sometimes such reforms were inspired by foreign models, as in ordnance production and scientific education. Sometimes they were influenced by Western ideas, as in his plan for distributing political power, and sometimes they were based on traditional models, as in his proposal to solicit public opinion for guidance of the government, which was based upon the early Chou dynasty practice of collecting poems from the people to sample their mood.[29]

The objectivity and practicality of the Neo-Confucian School of Statecraft as exemplified in the reform proposals of Feng Kuei-fen provided an eclectic, flexible, and pragmatic intellectual basis for self-strengthening in many areas of Chinese civilization while placing an immediate high priority emphasis on military modernization, particularly ordnance production. Feng's proposals supplied the intellectual framework within which Tseng Kuo-fan and Li Hung-chang, China's earliest self-strengtheners and cofounders of the modern ordnance industry, would conceive their reform programs.

III. The Arsenals of Li Hung-Chang: The Establishment Phase, 1860-1868

By the beginning of the 1860s, the notion that Chinese civilization would have to undergo fundamental changes to meet the foreign threats and domestic challenges which the dynasty faced was gaining acceptance by a small number of influential Chinese leaders. Saddled with the responsibility of pacification and stimulated by increasingly frequent contacts with foreign military technology, these officials became absorbed in schemes for military modernization though, as will be shown, they did not lose sight of the broader vision of change that had inspired the writings of Feng Kuei-fen. Foremost among their efforts at military modernization was the production of ordnance, which, in the view of leaders such as Li Hung-chang, held the key to pacification. Indeed, it was Li who dominated the three major arsenals established during this decade, the first large-scale modern machine industries in China, and the pacesetters of the industry until 1895. Li's concept of strategic industry shaped the production missions and operation of these plants throughout most of the decade, until it was challenged by Tseng Kuo-fan beginning in 1867.

Although the Taiping forces under Li Hsiu-ch'eng had been repulsed at Shanghai in August 1860 by foreign intervention, they remained active in Kiangsu and Chekiang during 1861, occupying one city after another. Finally in December of that year Hangchow, the capital of Chekiang, fell to the disciplined and highly effective army under Li Hsiu-ch'eng's command. As Taiping military pressure mounted in the lower Yangtze Valley, responsible Chinese officials echoing the logic of Feng Kuei-fen's reform proposals began to call for military modernization based on Western models to meet the Taiping menace. In the changed international climate resulting from the signing of the new treaties of 1860, the Western powers were more than willing to assist with their arms and arms technology.

Early in 1861, while supporting before the throne Tseng Kuo-fan's advice to decline Western military aid and concentrate on domestic production of Western-style arms and warships, Prince Kung of the Tsungli Yamen reported that France had already expressed its willingness to sell arms to China and to provide technicians to instruct in arms production. This idea was also referred to Tseng Kuo-fan along with other proposals to sell steamships to China, which had been advanced by Robert Hart, the British inspector general of the Imperial Maritime Customs Service. Tseng's reply was written in mid-1861, shortly after a relief force had reached his headquarters at Ch'i-men in southern Anhwei where he had been bottled up by the Taipings. It reflected a deepening determination to take immediate steps toward military-industrial self-strengthening. The purchase of foreign guns and ships, he observed, was China's most urgent need at the moment. He felt that they would be of great immediate use in checking the advance of the rebels and stressed that, in time, possession of these arms and skill in their use would equalize China's power relationship with Western nations. Moreover, he advocated that Chinese scholars and artisans become adept with foreign ships and guns and learn how to make them themselves. Optimistically, he forecast that within several years, the steamer would become a common phenomenon on the Chinese scene.[1] This advocacy led directly to the beginning of machine production of Western-style arms in China.

THE ANKING ARSENAL

Although the suggestion to employ French technicians in ordnance production did not materialize, it was not long before Tseng Kuo-fan was in a position to attempt production himself. After the recapture of Anking, a Yangtze port in southwestern Anhwei, by Tseng's brother Tseng Kuo-ch'üan in early September 1861, Tseng moved his headquarters to that city. In December he ordered the establishment of a powder plant, an ammunition plant, and an arsenal (nei chün-hsieh-so), which was to produce foreign-style ordnance. This arsenal was staffed by some of the most distinguished Chinese engineers and scientists of the day, reflecting the great importance that Tseng placed upon having the right man in the right job. Included were Hsü Shou, a renowned engineer whose son went on to play an important role in the development of China's strategic industry; Hua Heng-fang, an accomplished mathematician; Kung Chih-t'ang, son of Kung Chen-lin, one of the pioneers of strategic industrial development at the time of the first Opium War who had perfected the iron mold for casting ordnance and conducted experiments aimed at construction of a steam engine; and Wu Chia-lien, another engineer. In 1863 Li Shan-lan, the distinguished mathematician and translator of Euclid's Elements, books seven to fifteen, also joined this group.[2]

Meanwhile, in 1862 a team headed by Hua Heng-fang completed work on a steam engine, and in 1863 a small steamer, the Huang-ku, about fifty-nine ch'ih in length was completed and tested under the direction of Tseng's aide, Ts'ai Kuo-hsiang. The arsenal at Anking also turned out ordnance items including explosive shells, air bursting shells, and large guns up to thirteen hundred catties in weight. Tseng summarized his attitude toward the production at Anking in the summer of 1862: "The way to self-strengthening," he wrote, "is urgently to put governmental affairs in order, to seek out men of talent, and to take the learning of ordnance production and shipbuilding as our initial task."[3] Although far more cautious than the bold steps proposed by Feng Kuei-fen in the critical matter of the emphasis on military industry, Tseng's views bore the clear imprint of Feng Kuei-fen's ideas.

Initially, Tseng was quite enthusiastic about the ability of his engineers at Anking to master Western techniques of production, but as time wore on, he took a more realistic view. In January 1863 he anticipated expanding production to include foreign-style percussion caps. He felt uncertain, however, as to whether or not his artisans could be successful at this. In 1868 he memorialized that the staff at Anking had been entirely Chinese and, though they had built one steamer, it was slow and they had not grasped the techniques involved very well.[4] It seems that the experience at the Anking Arsenal convinced him that the successful production of Western-style arms and ships would require foreign technical assistance and the use of foreign-style machinery.

THE YUNG WING MISSION

In this connection Tseng, on the advice of several of his engineers, summoned Yung Wing, a Yale-educated Chinese businessman, to his headquarters during September 1863. When asked by Tseng what type of machinery would be best for China to acquire, Yung Wing replied that he felt that machine production should not be confined to the narrow military limits that Tseng had in mind.

> I would say that a machine shop in the present state of China should be of a general and fundamental character and not one for specific purposes...a machine shop that would be able to create or reproduce other machine shops of the same character as itself; each and all of these should be able to turn out specific machinery for the manufacture of specific things...A machine shop consisting of lathes of different kinds and sizes, planers, and drills would be able to turn out machinery for making guns, engines, agricultural implements, clocks, etc. In a large country like China...they would need many primary or fundamental machine shops but after they had one...they could make it the mother shop for reproducing others....[5]

After hearing this proposal, Tseng felt that a judgment on its correctness was beyond his competence. He gave implied approval, however, by empowering Yung Wing "to go abroad and make purchases of such machinery as in the opinion of a professional engineer would be the best and the right machinery for China to adopt."[6] Tseng's concurrence with Yung Wing's views on the type of machinery that China should acquire is further substantiated by a statement made in a letter to Li Hung-chang of December 5, 1863: "We are planning to establish a machine shop and employ machinery-making machinery. It must be bought from the West."[7]

Tseng arranged funds for the purchase of machinery.[8] Yung arrived in the United States in early 1864 and placed the order with the Putnam Machine Company, Fitchburg, Massachusetts, which completed the order in early 1865. It was shipped directly to Shanghai, arriving in November or December 1865. Between one and two hundred pieces of equipment were included.[9] There is little likelihood that Tseng Kuo-fan grasped the far-reaching potential of his decision to introduce capital equipment to the Chinese economy. Nevertheless, when presented with the option of establishing machine production broader than the purely military production so important at that moment, he chose to do so, for reasons that he did not commit to writing. Had he perhaps sensed the desirability, at least in the long run, of a basic change in the mode of production?

THE SHANGHAI-SOOCHOW ARSENALS

There is no doubt that such ideas were beginning to take shape in the mind of Tseng's lieutenant, Li Hung-chang. After the recapture of Anking in September 1861, Tseng adopted a new anti-Taiping strategy, which provided the opportunity to employ Li in the position of great responsibility for which he had been grooming him. Tseng evolved a three-pronged attack plan in which forces under Tseng Kuo-ch'üan would press down river toward the Taiping capital at Nanking from Anking in the west. Armies under Tso Tsung-t'ang, newly appointed governor-general of Fukien and Chekiang, would move up from the south. And the crucial task of stemming the Taiping onslaught in the east, where it was again threatening Shanghai, was entrusted to Li who, on Tseng's recommendation, was named acting governor of Kiangsu.[10] The decision to send Li to Kiangsu was actually triggered in November of 1861 when Tseng received an urgent appeal from gentry leaders in Shanghai to rescue the beleaguered city from the Taiping menace. Unable to spare a sufficient number of troops from his own command, the Hsiang Army, for a relief expedition, Tseng dispatched Li to his home area in northern Anhwei to recruit a new force, which he was to bring back to Anking for training. Tseng augmented the 3,500 troops which Li recruited with two thousand from the Hsiang Army and together they comprised the original nucleus of the Anhwei, or Huai, Army. In March of 1862 this force was transported from Anking down the Yangtze through the Taiping lines to Shanghai on seven British steamers rented for this purpose by the gentry of Shanghai.[11]

In early April 1862, Li reached Shanghai with the first contingent of the Huai Army. Practically from the moment that he arrived, Li was deeply impressed by the effectiveness of the foreign ordnance which he saw there and by the woeful inadequacy of

Chinese efforts at ordnance production. At the time, in addition to some three thousand British, British-Indian, and French troops defending Shanghai, there were also about three thousand Chinese troops of the Ever Victorious Army officered by Western volunteers under the command of an American, Fredrick Townsend Ward. All were equipped with foreign ordnance. Unlike earlier Chinese commanders in Shanghai, who had urged the foreigners to assume greater responsibilities for defense of the city, Li was quick to recognize the long range threat that foreigners and their superior weapons posed to China. He held to the general policy lines laid down earlier by Tseng Kuo-fan, attempting to minimize the intervention and influence of the foreigners while at the same time seeking to obtain and to reproduce their superior ordnance. In both respects he was notably successful. The Ever Victorious Army was brought under effective Chinese control and strategic direction, and by early October 1862 Li had gained the agreement of Ward to act for China in hiring foreign technicians to produce ammunition and in purchasing small arms.[12]

Subsequent to an edict received at Li's headquarters in November 1862 directing commanders to appoint Chinese to study the production of foreign munitions, Li engaged British and French military personnel experienced with ordnance to duplicate their production. He ordered Colonel Han Tien-chia and a party of Chinese artisans to study with them and requested the transfer of Ting Jih-ch'ang, an official experienced in the production of domestic ordnance, to be in charge of production in Shanghai. However, diminution of local government customs income in Shanghai subsequent to the opening of the customs house in Hankow, coupled with the high cost of production in Shanghai and the high cost of imported raw materials, delayed the beginning of production and forced prolonged reliance on the foreign supply of ammunition. But continued contact with foreign forces deepened Li's respect for the effectiveness of their arms and strengthened his determination to produce them. In early 1863, when he established an institute for the study of foreign languages (Kuang-fang yen-kuan) in Shanghai, he observed that this would enable Chinese to understand fully the techniques involved in the production of firearms and steamships. On February 2 he wrote to Tseng that he had visited British and French vessels and was deeply impressed with the excellence of their arms and ammunition. He urged his officers to study Western techniques and felt that the blame would be great should this opportunity to learn slip by. That spring Li estimated his requirements for munitions production at twenty thousand taels each month; he was purchasing foreign arms, recruiting foreign technicians, and buying arms production equipment in Hong Kong. In October his efforts bore fruit; the artisans under Han Tien-chia began producing explosive shells and fuses, funded from Li's military budget.[13]

Meanwhile, Li was receiving encouragement and assistance from another source. In the spring of 1863, Dr. Halliday Macartney, a physician, had left the British forces in China and joined Li's staff as an adviser. He urged Li to produce his own ammunition because of the excessive cost of foreign purchase. Once Macartney demonstrated that he could successfully produce explosive shells with Chinese labor, Li authorized him to hire fifty workers and begin production in a temple in the Sungkiang area near Shanghai. This arsenal was part of the arms depot of the forces that Macartney commanded for Li. His equipment was crude; the iron smelting furnace was built with earth.

After Li's forces captured Soochow, the capital city of Kiangsu, in early December 1863, he shifted his headquarters there and directed Macartney to follow with his small arsenal. While the move was in progress in January 1864, Macartney persuaded Li to purchase a set of arsenal machinery which had been brought to China with the gunboats of the ill-fated Lay-Osborn Flotilla. By April 1864 this machinery, the first steam powered production equipment employed in China, was installed in a former Taiping temple in Soochow.[14] The Soochow Arsenal entered production under the direction of Macartney and a Chinese, Liu Tso-yu. It was manned by a Chinese staff and four or five foreign technicians; the latter drew salaries of one to three hundred yüan each month. Although steam powered machinery was employed, production was limited to explosive shells. About four thousand of varying sizes were produced each month.[15]

By this time two other arsenals were operating in the Shanghai area: one under the direction of Ting Jih-ch'ang who had joined Li's staff in 1863, and the other under Han Tien-chia. The work force in these arsenals was entirely Chinese and numbered more than three hundred persons. Here foremen received a modest twenty to thirty yüan each month and other workers five to ten. Native style furnaces were used for casting shells. Monthly output was six or seven thousand explosive shells and six or seven small guns. Percussion caps and fuses were also produced, but quality was not up to that of foreign products. Coal, iron, sulphates, and nitrates required for production all had to be bought from abroad. None of the three plants could produce gunpowder of the quality required for use with foreign ordnance. Since the price of high quality foreign powder was reasonable and it was difficult to obtain the equipment and ingredients for foreign-style powder, there were no plans for the initiation of powder production.[16]

At this time the Huai Army, which Li headed, consisted of about fifty thousand men. Among this number, thirty to forty thousand were equipped with foreign small arms or cannon which fired explosive shells. In addition to this, there were pacification units headed by P'an Ting-hsin, Liu Ping-chang, Lo Jung-kuang, and Liu Yü-lung, all of which were equipped with foreign style artillery. The cannon and shells employed by these forces originally were purchased from abroad, but eventually the three arsenals took over the complete responsibility for supply. Shells from these arsenals were used successfully when Li's forces retook Soochow, Ch'ang-chou, Chia-hsing, and Hu-chou. Li was well pleased with the functioning of the three plants; in late 1864 he memorialized that shells made under Macartney's supervision had been instrumental in retaking Soochow. On the basis of Li's recommendation, Macartney was awarded the cap button of the third grade of imperial officials.[17]

In the spring of 1864 the Tsungli Yamen asked Li for a report of the progress that had been made in the arsenals under his supervision. Li's reply outlined the facilities, production, personnel, and costs of his arsenals and went on to state that production of arms should be expanded through the acquisition of machinery capable of producing other types of machinery and that the skills involved should be disseminated:

> I consider that if China wishes to make herself strong, then there is nothing more important than study and practice with the excellent weapons of the foreign nations. To learn about these foreign weapons, there is no better way than to seek the machines which make machines and learn their way [of making them] but not employ their personnel.

> If we wish to seek machinery for making machinery and the personnel to make machinery then we should establish a special course and select scholars. The scholars for the rest of their life should have a goal through which they will become rich and famous, then, this undertaking can be successful, the skill can be perfected and the talent [necessary to do it] also can be assembled.[18]

The suggestion was clearly that there should be an avenue for social ascent for scientific and engineering personnel aside from that offered by the civil service examination system, and that there should be material rewards for their accomplishment, not merely the incentive of bureaucratic position. As a first step, he proposed that troops from the Artillery and Musketry Division at Peking be trained in the production of Western arms.[19]

The study and production of arms were already under way at Peking, but, as at Anking, there were neither foreign technicians nor foreign machinery. Interest in the production of Western-style weapons in the North dates from 1859 after the forces of Seng-ko-lin-ch'in, the Mongol commander of the Ch'ing Armies, turned back the British forces in their initial attempt to reach Peking and coerce ratification of new treaties. Impressed by the excellence of the weapons that had been captured, Seng-ko-lin-ch'in ordered the Artillery and Musketry Division to study and reproduce them. By the autumn of 1862, troops under the superintendence of Northern Commissioner Ch'ung-hou were continuing this effort. They were trained with Russian rifles and had cast and successfully test-fired at least ten cannon and had produced six gun vehicles of Western design.[20]

In the spring of 1864, after receiving Li's report on the arsenals in Kiangsu, Prince Kung of the Tsungli Yamen presented it to the throne with a preface that incorporated his own suggestions for the development of arms production. He commended the achievements that had been made in Li's arsenals and endorsed the purchase of machinery to produce other types of machinery. He went on to state that the troops from the Artillery and Musketry Division at Peking had not progressed because they lacked proper technical instruction. To remedy this, he proposed to dispatch eight officers and forty men from this division to Li's arsenals to study the production of foreign munitions and machinery-making machinery. He anticipated that they could later be dispersed to the banners to serve as instructors. These personnel arrived in Shanghai in July 1864 and were sent on to the three arsenals for training. In December 1865 Li reported favorably on their accomplishment in mastering the production of explosive shells. In 1867 some of these officers and men were assigned as part of the initial personnel complement of the first modern arsenal established in North China, at Tientsin.[21]

By 1864 there was a growing recognition among self-strengthening leaders of the need for foreign technical assistance in the production of modern ordnance and of the necessity for incorporating technical and scientific training in China's educational system; but the way that these problems would be resolved was far from settled. The training of personnel from the Artillery and Musketry Division was an important first step but fell far short of the large-scale educational adaptation that Feng Kuei-fen had advocated. During the spring of 1865 Prince Kung proposed a different approach for China to learn the production of Western-style arms. The Tsungli Yamen addressed a confidential letter to Li soliciting his views on the advisability of sending bannermen abroad to study arms production. Li felt that there was nothing to fear in such a mission but that the results could not be foreseen. He recommended instead that a bureau be established in China equipped with foreign machinery and staffed with foreign and Chinese instructors. Once students had shown some progress they could possibly be sent on for further study. This way, he reasoned, the undertaking could be more closely supervised, the results would be quicker and more certain, and the cost would be about the same.[22]

He dismissed Prince Kung's fears that China might not attract really capable technicians or first rate equipment. If good salaries and high positions were offered, Li argued, the good men would come and they would bring with them the first rate machinery. Even if those who came were not highly skilled, he felt that there was much that Chinese personnel could learn from them. He urged that China take this opportunity of temporary peace with the West to establish its maritime defense. To undertake, at this time, to send students to the foreign centers of technology would be a complicated and time consuming task. The temporary opportunity for defensive strengthening could be lost. It would be wiser, he reasoned, to learn what could be learned from the technicians whom China could get and proceed on that basis.[23] There is a pragmatic ring to this reply. Li discouraged Prince Kung's grandiose suggestion for transforming the ordnance industry through overseas education of bannermen in favor of a step-by-step approach, which he foresaw would bring more rapid, if more limited, results in improving ordnance production for the immediate task of pacification while laying the foundations for long-range strengthening against the West.

The general guidelines which Li favored for the employment of foreign technical assistance and the development of technical personnel for the production of ordnance were becoming clear by early 1865. By this time, also, Chinese contacts with the West were broadening and the urgency of reform in the critical area of ordnance production was becoming even more apparent. A forceful statement of such views from the pen of Wang T'ao, a maverick Chinese scholar residing in Hong Kong, reached one of Li's arsenal directors, Su-Sung-Tai Taotai Ting Jih-ch'ang, during 1864. Wang T'ao's observations were included in his preface to a volume on ordnance production entitled Huo-ch'i shuo-lüeh (A Discussion of Firearms), compiled and translated by Wang and a friend who had traveled in the United States. The book contained materials dealing with smelting iron, making molds, setting up furnaces, boring guns, making powder, surveying, small arms, and the first discussion in Chinese of the principle of wind resistance. In his preface to this work, Wang pointed out that firearms techniques were one special aspect of Western affairs that China would do well to master promptly before relations with the West went from bad to worse. He observed that good weapons were essential for pacification of the rebels. To continue to rely on foreign supply was an insecure policy. And to continue to conduct military examinations in archery and rock hurling, as was being done, revealed a grave shortcoming in the system. He saw the production at the small arsenals in Shanghai as a ray of hope in understanding Western methods and called for further development of the production of Western-style ordnance and the training of personnel as a means to put down the Taiping Rebellion. He even went so far as to set forth a proposed plan for a combined artillery and naval bombardment of Nanking. But Wang also reminded his readers that arms were not exclusively for rebellion suppression. They had the additional value of intimidating potential rebels and making China less vulnerable to foreign intrusion. Firearms, he observed, should be an instrument to effect just rule in the hands of a wise ruler and not an aid to oppression. "Therefore," he concluded, "I say that firearms are one aspect of planning for pacification at present and intimidating potential enemies in the future. Can we fail to make urgent efforts?"[24] Ting Jih-ch'ang's views on self-strengthening expressed in 1864 echo Wang T'ao's sense of urgency and unqualified commitment to military modernization.[25]

Meanwhile, in early 1864 a similar expression of the importance of ordnance production originating from a high bureaucratic source reached Li. A memorial of Court Historian Chen Ting-ching calling for the establishment of arsenals at Canton and Shanghai and the employment of foreign technicians was forwarded to his headquarters and to that of Tseng Kuo-fan for comment. In the wake of these expressions of the importance of modern ordnance production during 1864, Li stepped up his production effort. From August 1864 to July 1865, production of modern ordnance in the three arsenals was the most important form of military production carried on by his forces. A total of 110,658 taels, about one-sixth of total military expenditures during this period, was devoted to support production in these plants whereas only 69,311 taels were used for the production of traditional-style weapons.[26]

THE KIANGNAN ARSENAL

Though Li was pleased with the production in the three arsenals, he needed larger guns which these plants could not produce. In the spring of 1864 he made up his mind to purchase the foreign machinery required for such production.[27] His initial contacts with foreign ordnance machinery supply firms were made through Dr. Halliday Macartney who arranged for Colonel George Gordon, the new commander of the Ever Victorious Army who was returning to Great Britain, to purchase machinery to produce one thousand rifles per month from a British firm. Li was prepared to make payment when apprised of the total cost. However, when Macartney subsequently determined through direct correspondence with the firms that the price for such equipment would run between ₤50,000 and ₤100,000, Li was shocked and issued directions through Macartney

for Gordon to hold off on the purchase.
    Li was, no doubt, wary of entrusting such a sum to a foreign purchasing agent in view of the recent bitter experience which he and other Chinese officials had suffered as a result of this practice. More than 150,000 taels had been advanced to Frederick Ward's brother to purchase ships in America. Of this sum, only 20,000 taels was acknowledged by Ward's executors, the rest having been lost through poor management and currency exchange. Moreover, several years had elapsed since Li had given 10,000 taels to a French agent for the purchase of machinery and to date nothing had been received. These disappointments were quite apart from the disastrous Lay-Osborn Flotilla affair, the ill-fated plan to purchase British gunboats which miscarried during 1863 because of disagreement over how the British-manned vessels were to be controlled. The net loss to China was more than 700,000 taels. While these bitter experiences induced a judicious caution in Li, others in the government were soured on dealing with foreign firms and actively opposed Li's plan to purchase machinery.[28]
    Accordingly, he adopted an approach designed to eliminate some of the expense and the unreliability of overseas purchase through foreign purchasing agents and to rebuff official objections to this scheme. He directed Ting Jih-ch'ang to investigate the availability of machinery already in China where on-the-spot bargaining could be conducted. Time wore on and, by the spring of 1865, Ting still had not located suitable machinery. Meanwhile, he had read Wang T'ao's Huo-ch'i shuo-lüeh, which no doubt deepened his understanding of the complexities of ordnance production. Li's understanding of the problems involved in establishing machine production of modern ordnance was also sharpened during the intervening months. In the spring of 1865 he wrote to Prince Kung that the requirements for ordnance production would be great, greater for example than those for shipbuilding. He felt that the thirty thousand taels which Yung Wing had at his disposal would be inadequate to buy all that was needed. Nor did Li have the funds in Kiangsu to purchase a complete set of the required equipment from abroad. In any case he was more convinced than ever that this would be an impractical and imprudent course. He continued to search for the right equipment at the right price among the foreign firms in Shanghai.[29]
    In the spring of 1865 Li's prolonged search for production machinery among the foreign firms in

the treaty port finally met with success. Ting Jih-ch'ang reported that he had reached agreement with the foreign owners for the purchase of machinery in a site later known as Hunts Wharf in the Hung-k'ou section of Shanghai. Forty thousand taels of the total price of sixty thousand were supplied by the donations of three cashiered officials who sought to regain their positions--one of whom was instrumental in negotiating the sale. The remaining twenty thousand taels for the initial purchase of materials was raised by Ting himself. The purchase was concluded sometime in the spring of 1865, and in late May or June of that year the plant began operating under Chinese management. Li changed its name to the Kiangnan General Manufacturing Bureau (<u>Chiang-nan chih-tsao tsung-chü</u>) but, from that time on, it has been known to foreigners as the Kiangnan Arsenal.[30]

Although it is perhaps impossible to catch the exact connotation which Li attached to the use of the Chinese terminology, "general manufacturing bureau," a term that subsequently became one of the synonyms for arsenal, he used these words, as he said in his report to the throne, "to rectify the name and distinguish the thing" (<u>cheng-ming pien-wu</u>). This was a clear allusion to the Confucian philosophical tenet that things should be given names that denote their reality and distinguish them from other things.[31] One reason for changing to this name was, as Li explained, to make clear that the machine shop was no longer foreign-owned. His rationale seems to have gone beyond this, however. It most probably related to the broad mission that he foresaw for the new machine shop and the catalytic role that he believed machine production would play in China's economic development. He reflected on these considerations also in his report to the throne:

> ...what we have is machinery-producing machinery; no matter what type of machinery it can be reproduced step-by-step following the [right] method; then, it can be employed to make that type of product; there are no limits to what can be produced; all things can be mastered. At present we are unable to do everything at once; it is most important that we still produce iron ordnance to meet our military needs...foreign machinery can produce machinery for plowing, weaving, printing, ceramics and tile making, which will benefit the daily needs of the people; originally it

47

was not just for munitions...I predict that in several decades there certainly will be wealthy Chinese farmers and great traders who will imitate foreign machine manufacturing for their own profit.[32]

Ting Jih-ch'ang also foresaw that, when circumstances permitted, the capital equipment at Kiangnan should be employed to produce other types of machinery for use in the textile industry, agriculture, and river conservancy. In his correspondence with Li, Ting stressed the need for a change in traditional attitudes toward industrial occupations. He saw that successful operation of machine industries would necessitate the cultivation of scientists and engineers. He called for government encouragement through increased material rewards and the award of official status to those who mastered Western sciences and their industrial applications. Ting considered these changes the natural consequences of the establishment of Kiangnan and necessary measures if China was to control its fate in an era of increasing foreign pressures.[33]

The two smaller arsenals headed by Ting and Han Tien-chia were merged with the new arsenal. The personnel from the Artillery and Musketry Division from Peking who were stationed at these two plants were transferred to Kiangnan to continue their training. Ting was placed in charge of planning and supervision while Han Tien-chia, Feng Chün-kuang, Wang Te-chün, and Shen Pao-ching were appointed managers. Operating funds were initially provided by Li from his military budget. The machinery, which Yung Wing purchased in the United States, arrived in China in late 1865 and was subsequently installed in the Kiangnan Arsenal.[34]

The equipment that Li and Ting purchased had previously been employed primarily for the construction and repair of steamships. Developments in the Nien Rebellion during 1865 dictated that the newly acquired facilities be quickly converted to the production of arms and ammunition. In the spring of 1865 the imperial forces campaigning against the Nien in Shantung were badly defeated at Ts'ao-chou. The commander, Prince Seng-ko-lin-ch'in, lost his life. Gravely alarmed, the government in Peking moved to revitalize its forces in North China. In late May 1865 Liangkiang Governor-General Tseng Kuo-fan, who had recently concluded the campaign that had crushed the Taiping Rebels in the Yangtze Valley, was transferred to the command position left vacant by the death of Seng-ko-lin-ch'in, and Li Hung-chang was named acting governor-general of the Liangkiang provinces. Li was ordered to provide troops armed with modern weapons to bolster the forces in the north and to send ordnance and munitions from the arsenals of Kiangsu. More than ten thousand explosive shells were shipped immediately, and Li reported that there was still a large number on hand at the Shanghai and Soochow Arsenals, which could be supplied as required.[35]

THE NANKING ARSENAL

This turn of events proved to be of enormous consequence for the establishment of additional facilities for the production of modern ordnance in China. Li had founded his first modern arsenals in the Shanghai-Soochow area where they were conveniently located to supply the Huai Army forces, which he commanded against the Taipings. Now that the Nien had replaced the Taiping Rebellion as the foremost domestic threat, North China also replaced the Yangtze Delta area as the most critical theater of military operations. This meant that the Kiangnan Arsenal was hardly established before its location proved unsuitable for supplying the government units under Tseng Kuo-fan battling the Nien in North China, a large number of which units were detached from Li's Huai Army. Furthermore, in his new headquarters at Nanking, the administrative capital of the Liangkiang provinces, Li found himself far removed from the Shanghai-Soochow logistical base that he had worked to establish during the past several years.

Responding to this situation, Li moved to insure his control over supply of modern arms and ammunition to Huai Army units in North China; he directed Macartney to remove the small Soochow Arsenal which had begun production of small guns to Nanking. There, under Li's watchful eye, it was reestablished as the Nanking Arsenal (<u>Chin-ling chih-tsao-chü</u>) outside the southern gate of Nanking. Its initial operating funds were supplied from the budget of the Huai Army. Beginning in 1867 these funds were augmented by an annual allocation from the income of the Kiangnan Arsenal for the purchase of foreign materials needed for production. By 1870 facilities had been expanded to include an iron smelting furnace, a boiler house, a brick kiln, and a branch arsenal for the production of rockets at Shen-mu-an outside the

Tung-chi Gate. Early production included guns of various calibers, gun mounts, gun ammunition, gingals, small arms, small arms ammunition, percussion caps, and fuses.[36]

THE TIENTSIN ARSENAL

Although the production of the Nanking Arsenal eventually made an effective contribution to the pacification of the Nien, the reestablishment at Nanking was not completed until June 1866. In the meantime, the burden of logistical support for the forces battling the Nien fell squarely on the newly established Kiangnan Arsenal. Kiangnan with its new plant of foreign machinery could hardly be removed from the Shanghai area, for the foreign advice essential for its operations was most readily available there. Consequently, no sooner had the Shanghai plant opened its doors than it received appeals to help establish a comparable facility in North China. The same edict which directed Li to send troops, arms, and ammunition to North China in the summer of 1865 also called upon him to assist in the establishment of another arsenal to facilitate supply in that region. The Court asked that, if Ting Jih-ch'ang could be spared, Li send him north with the troops to establish production in Tientsin. Li replied that Ting could not be spared from the arsenal in Shanghai, but he instructed P'an Ting-hsin, the commander of the relief forces which he sent to Tientsin, to assess the situation. If P'an felt an arsenal could be established, Li said he would send Ting, but Ting was never sent.[37]

The Tsungli Yamen, however, was determined that Li should assemble a set of machinery such as that at Kiangnan and send it on to Tientsin where Northern Commissioner Ch'ung-hou would use it for the establishment of a second arsenal. Li showed little enthusiasm for this venture. In January 1866, in response to an inquiry from Ch'ung-hou, Li stated that the machinery from the Kiangnan Arsenal could not be delivered to Tientsin until the spring of the following year. He explained that the technical and personnel difficulties being experienced in the initial operation of Kiangnan made it impossible to fulfill this requirement any earlier. Furthermore, Li suggested that Ch'ung-hou recruit his own foreign technicians and Chinese artisans so that personnel would not have to be sent from Shanghai.[38]

As it became clear in North China that Li was

carefully husbanding his meager production resources in Kiangnan, in the spring of 1866 the Tsungli Yamen commissioned Sir Robert Hart to purchase machinery in Great Britain. Thirty-three crates of munitions machinery purchased by Hart arrived in Shanghai in September 1866. The Tsungli Yamen directed that these be sent on to Ch'ung-hou pending instructions as to their further disposition. In the meantime, during the summer of 1866 the Tsungli Yamen proposed to the throne the idea of establishing an arsenal equipped with foreign machinery and employing foreign technicians at Tientsin to provide for the logistical needs of the northern armies. It was suggested that financing be provided from the provincial portion of the maritime customs income by Northern Commissioner Ch'ung-hou. Although imperial approval was given to this plan, Ch'ung-hou hedged, objecting that the demands placed upon the customs income were already excessive.[39]

At about the same time, the Board of War and Governor-General of Chihli Liu Ch'ang-yu made a separate proposal for an arsenal to produce six hundred traditional "mountain splitting" guns, three hundred gun carriages, accessory parts, powder, and ammunition, all urgently needed to equip the new armies which had been recruited for the defense of Chihli; the cost was estimated at 69,000 taels. Before the end of 1866 Ch'ung-hou gained imperial approval for a plan to finance the production for Chihli from the Ch'ang-lu salt revenue. An arsenal was established, and in mid-March 1868 Ch'ung-hou reported the production mission completed and distribution accomplished at a cost slightly above the original estimate.[40] It is unlikely that foreign machinery or modern methods were employed in this undertaking. In fact, the arsenal may have been at cross-purposes with the Tsungli Yamen's intention to bolster logistical potential in North China through the establishment of a modern machine-operated arsenal since it drew from the fiscal resources of this area at a time when the arsenal proposed by the Tsungli Yamen was encountering grave financial obstacles.

Though Northern Commissioner Ch'ung-hou was unable to provide establishment funds for a modern arsenal in Tientsin from the maritime customs income, he supported the Tsungli Yamen's proposal for such a plant and looked elsewhere for financing. However, information which he received on the availability and price of foreign machinery from the Danish consul in Tientsin, an Englishman named Meadows, convinced him that the original plans for a large, modern arsenal would have to be scaled down considerably. Consequently, in the fall of 1866 he came up with a more modest alternative proposal. This plan eliminated the immediate purchase of ordnance machinery because of the great expense involved and suggested instead that Meadows be commissioned to purchase powder-making machinery valued at about eighty thousand taels. The required funds would be derived from the liquidation of the steamships of the Lay-Osborn Flotilla. Additional costs of establishment, estimated at several tens of thousands of taels, Ch'ung-hou would raise himself. For the regular operating expenses of the arsenal after establishment, Ch'ung-hou proposed the allocation of part of both the Tientsin and the Chefoo customs income that was regularly forwarded to the Board of Revenue. The funds for the purchase of machinery were promptly approved, but the Board of Revenue succeeded in influencing the court to veto the use of the imperial government's share of customs funds on the conventional grounds that no alternative arrangement for supplementing imperial revenue had been made.[41]

Ch'ung-hou went ahead with the establishment of the arsenal despite the uncertainty about regular operating funds. Meadows was commissioned to purchase powder-making machinery and hire technicians from Great Britain. Te-ch'un, a taotai of Fengtien province, experienced in maritime defense affairs, was named to head the establishment of the arsenal. A location was selected at Chia-chia-ku Tao about six miles east of Tientsin and work was formally begun in May 1867. The site was low and considerable filling had to be accomplished before construction could begin. Channels in the river approach also had to be dredged. Some of the troops from the capital who had formerly trained at Li's arsenals in Kiangsu were appointed to the arsenal for further training and Meadows was named director. In the fall of 1867, Ch'ung-hou forwarded another 33,333 taels from customs and opium taxes to Great Britain to cover shipping, purchase of coal, and other expenses associated with the acquisition of the powder machinery. But the question of operating capital, after the machinery arrived, remained unsettled. This was the Tientsin Powder Bureau (<u>Huo-yao chü</u>), subsequently referred to as the East Arsenal.[42]

By late 1867 Ch'ung-hou had purchased iron casting equipment and machine tools from Shanghai and established another arsenal at Hai-kuang Szu south of Tientsin. This was known as the West Arsenal. Its mission was to produce machinery and parts for the powder plant, when that was established, and to make ordnance parts and steamship fittings. Mr. Stewart, an Englishman, was placed in charge. In January 1868 Ch'ung-hou reported that he had spent 22,000 taels in the establishment of this plant. He predicted that expenses would increase steadily, especially after the arrival and installation of the powder machinery, and he took the opportunity to reiterate his request for an allocation from the imperial government's portion of the Tientsin and Chefoo customs.[43]

INITIAL OPERATIONS OF THE KIANGNAN ARSENAL

The establishment of arsenal industry at Tientsin had been delayed during late 1865 and early 1866 when Li resisted the Tsungli Yamen's efforts to have him ship machinery from the Kiangnan Arsenal to Tientsin, pleading that technical and personnel difficulties experienced in the initial operations at Kiangnan made such support temporarily impossible. Indeed, the initial operations at Kiangnan were far from smooth. From May 1865 until November 1866 Li supervised the Shanghai plant from his new post as acting Liangkiang governor-general in Nanking; operating costs of 15,000 taels each month came from the military budget, which he raised from the revenues of the Liangkiang provinces. The new Chinese management retained the foreign foreman and eight technicians from the staff of the foreign machine shop, their first task being the construction of forty odd pieces of machinery necessary to convert the plant to ordnance production.[44] By the spring of 1866 technical and personnel problems reached a critical stage. Director Shen Pao-ching reported that small arms production machinery had been inoperative during a week-long period in the middle of February due to a loss of boiler pressure. Though repair of the boiler had been accomplished, the lining of the furnace proved defective and could not withstand the temperatures necessary for the production of small arms. Machinery for the manufacture of musket stocks was incomplete. Rather than wait any longer for this equipment, Shen proposed to go ahead and make the stocks by hand so that they would be available when small arms production began. Several thousand gun shells had been produced and these were sent to Li's headquarters during March and April, but it was well into the spring of 1866 before the machine production of ammunition for small arms began. Available information indicates that no more than two thousand rounds were ever produced. Gun production had been delayed awaiting delivery of a British four-and-one-quarter inch caliber twelve-pounder cannon to serve as a model.[45]

Li expressed extreme dissatisfaction with the arsenal's attempts at small arms production. Many months had elapsed and enormous sums had been spent, still nothing had been accomplished. He felt that Feng Chün-kuang had placed undue reliance on the foreign foreman who in turn shifted the blame to inadequacies in the equipment. Li directed that the furnace be rebuilt so as to deprive the foreman of further opportunity for making excuses. He warned that if the arsenal was not turning out foreign-style small arms within one month after the furnace was completed, the officials would be deprived of their salaries and the foreign foreman would be paid what was coming to him and deported with a letter to his consul explaining the unsatisfactory nature of his employment. Li advised the arsenal officials to eliminate the manual labor in the production of small arms and find a more economical and productive method of making them; otherwise, he feared that they would be unsatisfactory when completed, if that day ever came. Meanwhile, small arms needed for the forces battling the Nien under Liu Ming-ch'uan and Tseng Kuo-fan were to be purchased.[46] In the summer of 1866 Li wrote to the Tsungli Yamen that the small cannon produced at the arsenal were comparable to foreign models but that few small arms were being turned out and these were of poor quality.[47]

Aside from the technical and personnel difficulties that hampered production at Kiangnan during its first year of operation, there was another matter of serious concern to Li and to Arsenal Director Ting Jih-ch'ang. Kiangnan's location posed a number of problems. Ting had purchased the machinery in this plant, but the buildings remained under foreign ownership. The arsenal was paying six to seven thousand taels per year rent for their use, a figure that Ting regarded as exorbitant. Furthermore, the buildings were fast becoming inadequate for the rapidly expanding plant of machinery. In addition to the more than one hundred machines which Yung Wing had purchased, thirty to forty more had been built at the arsenal. The site was in a section of Shanghai heavily populated by foreigners and well-

known for its gaiety and bustle. Ting felt the
environment would affect the morale of the work force,
and he feared that incidents might occur between the
Chinese artisans and the foreign residents of the area
who objected strenuously to the presence of the
arsenal. Li himself regarded the Hung-k'ou site as
unsuitable for long-range planning. He favored a
move to Nanking along the banks of the river where
it would be more convenient for him to exercise
personal supervision.[48]

THE NIEN REBELLION AND THE TIENTSIN ARSENAL

Despite its many problems and its poor location,
Kiangnan was the only domestic arsenal producing for
the forces campaigning against the Nien during 1865
and until the Nanking Arsenal opened in May 1866.
This campaign was not going well. By the fall of
1866 the court was growing impatient with the anti-
Nien strategy employed by Tseng Kuo-fan; after almost
eighteen months in command, Tseng seemed a long way
from bringing the campaign to a successful conclusion.
In December 1866 he was summoned to the capital and
Li Hung-chang was appointed to replace him in command
of the forces fighting the Nien. Although the production of arms and ammunition from the Kiangnan and
Nanking Arsenals played an increasingly important role
in the supply of the forces which Li commanded against
the Nien, the overall military situation went from
bad to worse during 1867 for the government forces.
By early 1868 Peking was in a state of alarm. The
Western Nien had advanced from Shansi and reached
the environs of Peking. The Eastern Nien, which had
reportedly been wiped out during December by Li's
forces in Shantung, reappeared in Chihli during January
and penetrated to within a few miles of Paoting.[49]

It was against this background of events in
January 1868 that Northern Commissioner Ch'ung-hou
reiterated his request for an allocation from the
portion of the Tientsin and Chefoo customs regularly
forwarded to the Board of Revenue for the support of
arsenal operations in Tientsin.[50] In 1865 Li and
Ting Jih-ch'ang had been hesitant to establish an
arsenal in Tientsin fearing that it would drain
resources from the Kiangsu arsenals. Now the military
situation in North China had deteriorated markedly
and Li was charged with command responsibility for
suppression of the rebels. It was not long before
a sharp change in his attitude became apparent. In
late January 1868 Li wrote to the Tsungli Yamen

forwarding Ting Jih-ch'ang's recommendations for an arsenal in Tientsin and expressing his own concurrence:

> Machine shop establishment should be expanded to include Tientsin so as to provide for guarding the capital. Tientsin is not far from Peking and it is on the seacoast; the purchase of material for production will not be difficult; we should quickly establish another machine shop in this strategic spot to facilitate study close at hand by the troops at the capital in order that we may consolidate our base. After this has been successfully done, we should also establish additional machine shops at the ports along the coast 51

With this strong backing, final obstacles to the establishment of machine production of modern arms in Tientsin were overcome; Ch'ung-hou's request for 40 percent of both the Tientsin and the Chefoo customs to support the arsenal received imperial approval. Starting in February 1868, the Tientsin Arsenal began receiving regular annual income from these funds.52

Foreign technicians for powder production began arriving in the spring of 1868. The machinery purchased from Great Britain was shipped in and installed in the summer. In August and September several shipments of arsenal equipment were sent from the Kiangnan Arsenal to the Tientsin Arsenal, the equipment which Li Hung-chang had promised to Ch'ung-hou in 1865, including fittings for casting guns and ammunition as well as a large iron and brass casting furnace. Part of this equipment was purchased while another part was made at the Kiangnan Arsenal. Kiangsu province stood the expense, which amounted to something less than ten thousand taels.53

Although the crisis caused by the Nien offensive in North China loosened the imperial purse strings, resulting in the provision of customs funds for the operation of a modern arsenal at Tientsin, establishment of the Eastern Arsenal was not completed until 1870. Meanwhile, the Western Arsenal began production in 1868 but on an extremely limited scale. This plant, under the direction of Mr. Stewart, consisted of an iron foundry, a gun casting shop, and woodworking shop; a staff of about fifty Chinese artisans was employed. During 1868 the arsenal produced twelve 450 pound brass cannons which threw a twelve pound ball and by 1870 some seven thousand pieces of ordnance and steamship equipment had been produced.[54]

CONCLUSIONS

The 1860s witnessed the establishment of modern arsenal industries at Shanghai, Tientsin, and Nanking. All grew directly from the urge for self-strengthening of Li Hung-chang, a Confucian pragmatist, who bore the command responsibility for pacification of the Taipings and the Niens and saw close at hand the irrefutable evidence of the superiority of Western ordnance technology. All three were established for the immediate purpose of supplying ordnance and ammunition to ground forces engaged in rebellion suppression. Still it is certain that Li, Tseng Kuo-fan, Ting Jih-ch'ang, and Prince Kung also saw the importance of modern arsenal industries in strengthening China against foreign pressures. Li, in particular, was constantly vigilant lest the infant industries provide opportunities for unscrupulous Westerners to victimize China even further. He sought technological independence for the new ordnance plants which, for the present, he felt could be best achieved through short-term production-oriented educational reform. Though constantly overwhelmed by urgent demands for military products, Li never lost sight of the transformational effect which machine industry introduced in the arsenals could have on China's socio-economic structure. In a few short years, a handful of innovating Chinese leaders had imported the machine age, but the adjustments and accommodations necessary for machine industry to take root and thrive in China's preindustrial soil had just begun.

IV. The Arsenals of Li Hung-Chang Enter Production, 1868-1875

The 1868 production of cannon at Tientsin was hardly of an order to have influenced the outcome of counterinsurgency operations against the Nien, which were successfully concluded that year. Indeed, the most important effect on the development of strategic industry resulting from the last gasp of the Nien Rebellion, from 1866 to 1868, was not the rebellion's immediate stimulus for arsenal establishment at Tientsin but the change of command that brought Li Hung-chang to North China in 1867 and returned Tseng Kuo-fan to Nanking as Liangkiang governor-general and southern commissioner. The long-range consequences of this shift would have an influence on the development of China's new arsenals. In the decentralizing power structure of China in the late 1860s, who held the reins of local government was a matter of great consequence in determining the direction of the development of strategic industry. The imperial government frequently made appointments to the arsenals at the recommendation of the northern and southern commissioners who supervised arsenal operations, but the commissioners themselves were transferred about at the discretion of the throne, usually to meet the requirements of crisis management and rebellion suppression.[1]

THE KIANGNAN ARSENAL

As a result of the divergent ideas of China's industrial needs held by Tseng and Li, Kiangnan started off on a zigzag course of development. Tseng Kuo-fan from the early 1860s on had favored the domestic construction of steamships as a basis for long-range self-strengthening against aggression by the West.[2] Li, on the other hand, foresaw the enormous demands for human and economic resources that a large-scale shipbuilding program would create and attached far greater importance to the pressing problem of producing arms and ammunition for the forces combating the rebels. Li's views were shared by the Tsungli Yamen. As long as the provision of arms for rebellion suppression remained critical, plans for the construction of steamships were held in abeyance. This had been the case from the time the Kiangnan Arsenal commenced operations in May 1865 until July 1866. During this period Li, as acting governor-general of the Liangkiang provinces, drove Kiangnan to produce war materials for Tseng's pacification campaign in North China. Despite repeated urgings from Kiangnan Arsenal Director Ting Jih-ch'ang to begin production of steamships to counter the growing maritime power of Japan, Li insisted that the arsenal's newly acquired machinery and its foreign technicians be employed solely for the production of field guns and small arms. Production of the latter, however, was notably unsuccessful. Consequently, in July 1866 when sources for the purchase of small arms opened up, Li decided that this type of production should be temporarily discontinued and the arsenal should be relocated where it could undertake the construction of small gunboats for harbor and river defense.[3]

Planning for the move had just begun in December 1866 when Li was transferred to relieve Tseng as the commander of the North China pacification campaign. Tseng was moved back to the Liangkiang governor-generalship and named southern commissioner.[4] Finding the arsenal's affairs in an unsettled condition, Tseng moved to remold Kiangnan in accordance with his own conception of China's strategic industrial needs. During early 1867 he assayed the resources available for strategic industrial development. These included the original machinery purchased for the arsenal, most of which was for shipbuilding; thirty to forty additional machines for ordnance production; and more than one hundred items of general machine shop equipment which Yung Wing had ordered in the United States several years earlier.[5] Human resources were scanty; management was in the hands of enthusiastic but inexperienced Chinese officials. The only trained technicians on the staff were a handful of foreign shipwrights hired at the time of establishment who showed very little expertise in ordnance production and had little or no effect on improving the technical competence of their Chinese coworkers.[6] Financial resources were also limited; production costs were allocated from the Huai Army supply accounts at Li's disposal.[7] Material resources, fuels, metals, and the like were purchased from foreign supplies in Shanghai or directly from abroad.[8]

Despite the limited resources at his disposal, Tseng determined to push ahead with his plans for shipbuilding. In his judgment the only critical shortage was lack of funds. In an important memorial to the court of May 1867, several months after taking office, he pointed out that the revenue of the Liangkiang provinces was insufficient for him to discharge the two most urgent military duties at hand: establishment of shipbuilding and provisioning of the forces fighting the Nien rebels in North China. As a temporary solution he requested that 20 percent of the proceeds of the Shanghai maritime customs income be deducted from the 40 percent that was regularly forwarded to the Board of Revenue in Peking and that this amount be retained in the Liangkiang provinces. One half, or 10 percent of the total proceeds, would be used for support of the forces combating the rebels and the remaining 10 percent would be used for steamship building. Tseng's proposal gained prompt approval, and in June 1867 the Kiangnan Arsenal began receiving regular support for steamship building from the maritime customs income.[9]

Once imperial approval had been given to augment the arsenal's income with 10 percent of the Shanghai maritime customs proceeds, Customs Taotai Ying Pao-shih, who was also a director of the arsenal, purchased a new ten acre site south of the city at Kao-ch'ang Miao on the banks of the Huang-p'u River. During the winter of 1867-1868 buildings were erected and equipment set up for the production of machinery and ordnance, and a plant for the construction of steamships was established including a dry dock.[10]

The construction of steamships began promptly and by August 1868 the first vessel, a paddle wheel steamer, was completed.[11] From 1868 to 1875 production at Kiangnan reflected Tseng Kuo-fan's overriding concern for the domestic construction of steamships. Six or seven British and French technicians directed construction. All materials employed were purchased from abroad.[12] Some noteworthy advances were made during these years. The propeller propulsion system introduced on the second vessel was moved to a protected position below the waterline on the third. The first three vessels were armed with smoothbore brass cannon; beginning with the fourth, rifled steel ordnance purchased from abroad was installed. The construction of small, twin propeller, armor plated gunboats was initiated. These craft, first produced in the West in the 1860s, had a shallow draught and were well-armed and highly maneuverable, excellently suited for harbor and river defense. By 1875 construction of China's first ironclad had begun. This type of vessel had dominated construction in the West since the 1860s.[13] (See Appendix I Table 1.)

Despite the considerable number of ships built at Kiangnan and the technological improvements they embodied, it was not long before the shipbuilding program encountered determined opposition. At the root of most of the criticism was official dismay at what was considered the excessive cost of the new program. The first attack came in early 1869 when Ma Hsin-i, who had replaced Tseng Kuo-fan as Liangkiang governor-general and southern commissioner in September 1868 following the pacification of the Nien, discovered that the Kiangnan shipbuilding program was in financial difficulty. Fiscal reorganization following the suppression of the Nien had deprived the arsenal of the Huai Army funds used to support production of arms and ammunition. Consequently, beginning in 1869 it became necessary to borrow from the 10 percent of maritime customs proceeds allotted for shipbuilding to support arms production and capital construction.[14] At the same time, production costs for the second and third vessel were mounting due to the increased purchase of foreign materials for propeller propulsion systems. In early 1869 Ma submitted a memorial explaining the cramped financial situation at Kiangnan and requesting that the other 10 percent of customs proceeds, which had been allotted for rebellion suppression, be assigned to the arsenal.[15] A memorial in opposition was submitted by the Board of Revenue and the request was disapproved. The board, under the leadership of Lo Tun-yen, an official known for his opposition to modernization, argued that these funds were badly needed at the capital. It relied on the formalistic rationale that Tseng Kuo-fan's original memorial had stipulated that the allocation of 10 percent of customs proceeds for rebellion suppression was only a temporary measure and that the funds would revert to the Board of Revenue after the emergency was terminated.[16]

This rejection did little to deter officials who supported Kiangnan's shipbuilding program. During the second quarter of 1869--possibly before official notification of the disapproval of Ma's memorial had been received in the Liangkiang provinces--Acting Customs Taotai Tu Wen-lan forwarded the entire 20 percent of the customs proceeds to the arsenal despite the lack of imperial authorization to do so.[17] By August 25, 1969, official notification of the disapproval had reached the Liangkiang provinces. On that date the arsenal petitioned Kiangsu Governor Ting Jih-ch'ang (who also supervised the affairs of the arsenal from his capital at Soochow after leaving the directorship) to memorialize the matter once more.[18] Ting personally inspected the arsenal and in October submitted a memorial lauding the production taking place there, observing that additional funds would be needed, and pointing out the necessity of planning ahead for the cost of vessel maintenance and operation.[19]

In October, at Ting's urging, Ma submitted a second memorial requesting allotment of the additional 10 percent of customs proceeds. This document, which also bore the cosignatures of Tseng Kuo-fan and Li Hung-chang, stressed that additional funds were needed for other arsenal operations, such as capital construction, machine building, and ordnance production.[20] In the interim Tung Hsun, a member of the Tsungli Yamen known for his progressive views, had been appointed president of the Board of Revenue.[21] Ma's second memorial was referred to the Tsungli Yamen where it received sympathetic consideration; after careful study approval was recommended. Consequently, in December 1869 the Kiangnan Arsenal was assigned a permanent annual income of 20 percent of the proceeds of the Shanghai maritime customs, commencing retroactively from the beginning of 1869.[22]

The annual income of the Kiangnan Arsenal grew steadily from 1867 to 1875, reaching almost 550,000 taels. Of this amount, 97 percent was allotted from the Shanghai maritime customs; the remainder comprised payments for services and munitions provided to local governments, return of deposits, and other miscellaneous income. (See Appendix I Table 2.) Only the maritime customs income was reported to the throne in the arsenal's periodic financial accounting which the southern commissioner submitted to Peking. These statements broke down expenditures according to categories of production. From 1867 to 1875, 44 percent of customs funds expended were devoted to steamship construction and upkeep; costs associated with establishment consumed another 22 percent, munitions production 9 percent, and machine building 8 percent.[23]

Although shipbuilding clearly occupied the most important place in the arsenal's operations during these years, great strides were also made in capital construction, establishment of production facilities, and production of ordnance and ammunition. By the end of 1867 the basic facilities for construction of steamships and production of ordnance and machinery were operational at Kao-ch'ang Miao. Included were boiler, machine, wrought iron, small arms, and carpentry shops, a foundry, and a shipyard. A rocket plant was established at Ch'en-chia Kang. Warehouses, coal bins, and living quarters for Chinese and foreign employees were built, as well as administrative buildings which included business, documents, counting, disbursing, and purchasing offices. In 1868 an institution for the translation of Western books was established; the following year the language school which Li Hung-chang had established in Shanghai in 1863 was moved to the arsenal. By 1870 a technical training program had been established with a view to development of technical competency among personnel at the arsenal.[24]

In 1869 expansion began with construction of a separate building to house the small arms shop. A steam hammershop was begun, though it was not completed until at least 1872. In 1870 at the direction of Tseng Kuo-fan a parcel of land of about twelve acres was purchased at nearby Lung-hua. Facilities for the production of powder, percussion caps, and fuses were established at this site. A black powder plant and a cartridge plant entered production at Lung-hua in 1874 and 1875 respectively. Meanwhile, by 1872 the dry dock begun five years earlier in connection with the shipyard was completed. In 1874 a gunnery school was established at Kao-ch'ang Miao. By 1876 the arsenal there occupied more than sixty acres. Twelve or thirteen large buildings had been completed, but the quality of construction in some was questionable and they had not been positioned to facilitate the production process. Foreign technicians and about two thousand Chinese workers were carrying on production of arms, ammunition, and steamships. The branch arsenal at Lung-hua occupied about twelve acres. It was headed by a foreign technician and employed, in addition to the Chinese work force, twelve foreigners. The Ch'en-chia Kang rocket plant occupied about one acre and was also under the direction of a foreigner.[25]

The production of machinery, ordnance, and ammunition at Kiangnan was sustained and in some ways improved during the period from 1867 to 1875. Materials employed were for the most part purchased from abroad. More than one hundred pieces of equipment, including lathes, planers, boilers, engines, brass and iron smelting furnaces, ordnance machinery, and engine parts, were produced. Most were for use at Kiangnan but in 1869 approximately twenty machines were forwarded to the Tientsin Arsenal. Maintenance of the machinery and tools retained at Kiangnan was haphazard, however. Cleaning was performed only once each year, with the result that tools were sometimes so dirty that exact work could not be accomplished with them.[26]

The most important advances in ordnance and ammunition production were made in the fields of small arms and cartridges. Initially, muzzle-loading 11.0mm caliber Mausers based on British and American models were produced.[27] Seventy-nine hundred of these had been turned out by 1871, when Kiangnan artisans under the direction of four new foreign technicians began machine production of Remington breech-loading rifles, a model that had come into use in Europe and the United States only several years earlier.[28] By 1875 output topped 3,500 rifles annually--about twelve completed weapons each working day. These rifles had iron rather than steel barrels. Though strong and fairly serviceable they were not uniformly made; parts were not interchangeable. Furthermore, 250 to 300 workers were employed in rifle production. With this manpower and Kiangnan's machinery, Western observers estimated that production should have reached at least fifty rifles per day. Remington cartridge machinery and more technicians arrived in 1872 but production of metallic cartridges essential for the effective operation of the breech loaders did not begin until a new plant was established at Lung-hua in 1874-1875.[29] Machine production of the black powder required for Remington and other types of modern ammunition began in a new powder plant at Lung-hua in 1874.[30] Production of small arms ammunition surpassed 580,000 rounds in 1875. (See Appendix I Table 3.)

There was very little progress in the production of heavy ordnance. Light smoothbore brass cannon for infantry use were turned out in considerable numbers, and at least 40 smoothbore brass guns of about 1,300 pounds weight suitable for shipboard use were made. It was not until 1874, however, that one twelve pounder muzzle-loading rifled gun with a steel barrel reinforced with wrought iron was produced under the supervision of a foreign technician, the first of its kind to be made in a Chinese arsenal. The first production of shot and shell for use with heavy ordnance took place in the machine shop on an emergency basis during the 1874 crisis with Japan. By early 1876 800 70-pound shells for use in shipboard Krupp guns were being turned out weekly.31 (See Appendix I Table 3.)

Most of the arms and ammunition produced at Kiangnan were distributed to ships and units subordinate to the southern commissioner. After 1870, however, a broader pattern of distribution became apparent. Between 1870 and 1876 about one quarter of the small arms, one-third of the gun ammunition, and lesser amounts of other war materials were delivered to units under the control of the northern commissioner, a post that from 1870 was held by Li Hung-chang. Kiangnan also made large-scale emergency distribution of arms and ammunition to the forces fighting the Nien and the Northwest Moslem rebellions, as well as to ships and units arming for the confrontation with Japan on Taiwan in 1874.32 (See Appendix I Table 4.)

Although the accomplishments at the arsenal in the first decade of operations were in many ways remarkable, there were areas of real concern regarding Kiangnan's viability as a self-strengthening institution. The first and most crucial of these was the high cost and unreliable supply of materials employed in production. Most materials were unobtainable in China and had to be purchased from abroad. Prices were inflated by the cost of shipping and insurance and consumed more than half of all funds spent prior to 1875. (See Appendix I Table 5.)

Since such a large part of Kiangnan's resources were used for purchasing, Tseng Kuo-fan had wisely instituted a system for handling expenditures designed to guard against the development of abuses in this area. By his procedures, the director and three separate offices were involved in each transaction.33

After Tseng's death, however, the situation appears to have deteriorated. In 1873 it was reported that the arsenal was making its purchases through a German purchasing agent, a Mr. Muller who was a confidential agent of Director Feng Chün-kuang. Unscrupulous foreign purchasing agents in China such as Muller were known to charge high commissions which they split with their Chinese confederates who directed the business to them. One foreign firm was reported to pay a 20 percent commission to any official at the arsenal responsible for placing an order with them. In addition, a levy was paid to the director. In early 1876 the British Consul in Shanghai estimated that financial abuses in purchasing doubled the actual cost of materials and machinery at Kiangnan.34

Personnel and administration were other areas in which costs were high, occupying more than one third of total expenditure. (See Appendix I Table 5.) One reason for this was Kiangnan's continued reliance on a cadre of highly paid foreign technicians. The technical training program and on-the-job instruction available at the arsenal could not quickly develop the essential skills that foreign technicians provided. Though the management of Kiangnan had made every effort to minimize foreign influence at the arsenal, in 1875 foreign technicians were still essential to production. The cumulative expense that the arsenal had incurred for wages for these foreigners amounted to 6 percent of total outlay.[35]

There is not a great deal of information regarding the personnel system governing the Chinese staff or on internal administrative procedures. It is known that official personnel were transferred in and out by imperial edict, frequently at the recommendation of supervisory personnel. As in other bureaus of the Chinese government, internal administration was headed by the director who was usually a Taotai incumbent in the Su-Sung-Tai Circuit. In this capacity he was also superintendent of the Shanghai Customs House and thus was able to facilitate the flow of funds to the arsenal. Below the director served one or more assistant directors. As a link between the top-most level of administration and the various shops there was a proctor (t'i-t'iao) or, in modern parlance, a general manager. Each shop was under the direction of an official deputy (wei-yüan). The various administrative offices were distinct from this organization, directly subordinate to the director. It is not clear whether or not policies or practices relating to management officials may have affected the arsenal's personnel or administrative costs during these years, but evidence suggests that management policies toward the labor force were indecisive and contributory to higher costs. For instance, when it was disclosed that a tramway was to be installed for the transport of heavy castings, the coolie labor at the arsenal realized that their positions would be imperiled and threatened to strike until the scheme was abandoned--quite possibly China's first labor dispute in modern times.[36]

THE NANKING ARSENAL

During the years from 1867 to 1875 while Kiangnan expanded rapidly, strategic industries were beginning to put down their roots elsewhere in China. In contrast to the situation in Shanghai where Tseng Kuo-fan's interest in shipbuilding exercised a shaping influence in the development of Kiangnan, at both Nanking and Tientsin it was the strategic priorities, self strenthening zeal, and the modernizing vision of Li Hung-chang that guided new arsenals through their initial growing pains. After Li's departure from Kiangnan in late 1866, active military command of the imperial forces opposing the Nien rebels consumed his energies until 1868. Thereafter he was involved with the investigation of a series of missionary disputes and abuses by local officials, until ordered to lead units of his Huai Army against the Moslem Rebellion in the northwest in 1870. He had assembled his forces at Sian in July of that year when an edict directed him to return immediately to Chihli to bolster its defenses against an anticipated French attack in retaliation for the Tientsin Massacre, which had taken place the previous month.[37] Despite these heavy responsibilities, or perhaps because of them, Li never lost sight of the critical importance of strategic industry, maintaining effective control of the Nanking Arsenal even after his appointment as governor-general of Chihli and northern commissioner in 1870.

The Nanking Arsenal was in essence an adjunct of the Huai Army, which Li commanded. A large portion of the funds required annually for operation of the arsenal was supplied from the logistic accounts of the Huai Army, and in return the bulk of its output went to supply Huai forces. This was true not only when the Huai Army was stationed in Kiangsu but also during its campaign against the Nien in North China and after 1870 when Huai Army troops were deployed as coastal defense units. During these years Li maintained a close cooperative relationship with officials in Kiangsu, particularly Tseng Kuo-fan; beginning in 1867 the income of the Nanking Arsenal was augmented by annual allocations from the customs allotment of the Kiangnan Arsenal earmarked for the purchase of foreign materials. Li's ties with Macartney, the foreign director of Nanking, were also very close at least through the early 1870s. Macartney also enjoyed a relationship of mutual understanding with Li's successor at Nanking, Tseng Kuo-fan. As a result, after Li's departure from Nanking in 1866 there developed a close cooperative arrangement whereby the Nanking Arsenal continued to supply the Huai Army and eventually even assumed the responsibility of ordnance supply for coastal defense installations around Tientsin, where Li had his headquarters while serving as northern commissioner. With Li's approval, some ordnance was also produced for forces under the commissioner of southern ports beginning in 1873.[38]

During these years the Nanking Arsenal expanded considerably. In addition to the main arsenal outside the South Gate of Nanking and the rocket plant outside the T'ung-chi Gate, a powder plant was completed at Chiu-lung Ch'iao outside the T'ung-chi Gate in 1872. A separate arsenal for the production of fort equipment was established at Wu-lung Shan, a short distance downstream from Nanking on the Yangtze, by 1874. This, however, was quite distinct from the Nanking main arsenal in that its production was financed from river defense appropriations and it was wholly controlled by the southern commissioner. Though the rocket and powder plants were destroyed by fire in 1875, the production of the Nanking Arsenal was considerable and diversified, including cast iron guns, brass rifled guns, gun carriages, gun ammunition, small arms, percussion caps, naval mines, torpedoes, and Gatling guns, which were reportedly first produced in 1874.[39]

All was not well at Nanking, however. This became abundantly clear in January 1875 when two sixty-eight pounder iron guns cast at the arsenal and installed at the Taku Forts guarding Tientsin exploded, killing several Chinese soldiers of the gun crew. This incident focused attention on quality control of the arsenal's products, an area in which serious problems had developed, and on the related problem of management. In the late 1860s and in the early 1870s following Li's departure from Nanking, Director Liu Tso-yu, who supervised the work force, reported to Li Hung-chang that the foreign technicians were not instructing the Chinese workmen in the techniques of ordnance production. Macartney retorted that he lacked the control over the work force necessary to conduct training. The Chinese supervisors hired the workers, moved them from one assignment to another, and dismissed them without regard for his wishes. More often than not, according to Macartney, personnel shifts were made on the basis of nepotism, favoritism, or other particularistic interests. Consequently his efforts to develop technical competency among the workers were entirely frustrated. Furthermore, with the exception of a very few northerners who had been assigned to the arsenal in 1866 and had served continuously thereafter, the bulk of the work force consisted of hangers-on and favorites of the Chinese supervisors, who were uninterested and slow to learn. The result was a decline in the quality of the arsenal's products, which was apparent to Li by 1872. In that year Macartney was summoned to Li's headquarters in Tientsin to explain the decline in quality and other charges of the Chinese supervisors. Li apparently decided in favor of Macartney, for in 1873 Liu Tso-yu was relieved as supervisor.40

Unhappily, the situation continued to deteriorate. In 1874, after returning from a seven month journey to Europe during which he had ordered new equipment for the arsenal, Macartney was again called to Tientsin to explain the poor quality of the arsenal's products and the failure to develop a staff of competent Chinese technicians. Macartney admitted the shortcomings in product quality and training very candidly, attributing them to the interference and outright obstruction that he had encountered from the Chinese supervisors during the past several years. This, he said, prohibited him from developing an organization of workers competent to insure proper standards of quality. This time Li appeared less willing to extend full support to Macartney, for in late 1874 he sanctioned personnel shifts at the arsenal which placed the new Chinese supervisor and another Chinese as joint managers and relegated Macartney to the post of foreign instructor. This prompted Macartney to offer his resignation. Not only did he regard his position as untenable but he also wished to escape responsibility for the "wild, costly, and abortive attempts at manufacture" which the Chinese supervisors at the arsenal were undertaking.41

Li had not yet accepted Macartney's resignation on January 5, 1875 when the Nanking-built guns blew up at Taku and he again summoned the Englishman to Tientsin. An investigation conducted in May and June 1875 revealed that the guns had burst because of the poor quality iron with which they were cast. It was also disclosed that Macartney had sanctioned the production of the guns from this inferior grade iron (which had actually come to China as ballast rather than for industrial use) in order to provide the work force with experience in casting while awaiting the arrival of metal of the proper quality. This questionable judgment was compounded to extremely grievous error. When the guns were completed, technical conditions at the arsenal prevented the kind of test firing that could adequately prove their quality. Nevertheless, they were shipped to Taku. Though Macartney had functioned under extremely trying circumstances, Li could not excuse his actions in this instance. In July 1875 Li directed him to transfer his responsibilities at the arsenal to the Chinese supervisors and vacate his post.[42]

The tragedy of the explosion of the Nanking Arsenal guns at Taku left a deep impression on Li Hung-chang regarding the need for quality control and safety features in heavy ordnance production. Moreover, it suggests the complexity of modern industrial management problems in traditional Chinese society. Macartney was a physician entirely lacking the training or credentials of an ordnance engineer, the position that he purported to fill and for which he was handsomely remunerated by the Chinese. The explosions were, by his own admission, due to his errors in judgment. Nevertheless, Macartney had served Li well in many ways at the arsenal and had faced insurmountable obstacles in dealing with the Chinese workmen due to the dual control in the arsenal. Li, who was growing wary of the influence of foreigners in the Chinese arsenals based on experience at Kiangnan and Tientsin, wished to see control of production returned to competent Chinese as soon as feasible. Still, he was aware that some were grasping prematurely for technological independence. His solution was to restrict foreign participation to that of technical advice and instruction while management authority was vested in Chinese officials, a formula that would continue to depend heavily for success on the ability of both sides not only to perform their functions but also to coordinate them smoothly with the functioning of the other side.

THE TIENTSIN ARSENAL

Although Li attached great importance to the ordnance and ammunition production of the Nanking Arsenal, its shortcomings were clear. Foreign participation had been at best a mixed blessing. Nanking's overall production capacity was small compared to that of Kiangnan. Furthermore, it was far removed from the regions in which Li had military responsibility. Li no doubt was acutely aware of the difficulties of supply from Nanking when he led units of the Huai Army into distant Shensi province in early 1870 and then countermarched into Chihli later in the year. Subordinate to the forces under Li's command at this time were several mobile or field arsenals for the production of Western-style ammunition. These arsenals were in operation from at least May 1870 until September 1872 and appear to have been forerunners, perhaps the prototypes, of the Tientsin

Mobile Arsenal (hsing-ying chih-tsao-chü), which was operational by September 1870. From 1870 until 1872 this plant received financial support from the Huai Army, the Tientsin Arsenal, and northern maritime defense appropriations. During most of this time it was under the direction of Wang Te-chun, an official of the Tientsin Arsenal. After Li's arrival in Tientsin in 1870, however, the logistical potential of the arsenal facilities already established there monopolized his attention. The concept of a mobile or field arsenal seems to have faded in importance and shortly after 1872 the Tientsin Mobile Arsenal probably became stationary at a facility adjacent to the West Arsenal at Hai-kuang Szu. Although its production was expanded to include Winchester and Gatling gun cartridges, gun mounts and carriages, and even the construction and repair of small mine vessels, little is known about this plant other than the fact that it was originally a part of the Huai Army.[43]

Events of the summer of 1870 impressed the importance of strategic industrial development at Tientsin indelibly on Li's mind. The era of relative good feelings that had prevailed between China and the West during the 1860s faded in 1870 when the British Parliament failed to ratify the Alcock Convention, which would have greatly liberalized China's trade relations with Britain. It came to an abrupt and tragic end later in that year with the Tientsin Massacre, an ugly incident characterized by arrogance and cultural insensitivity on the part of the French in Tientsin and ignorance and superstitious fear on the part of the Chinese mob and their gentry leaders, who launched the protest against alleged abuse of Chinese children in an orphanage operated by French nuns. In the violence that erupted when the French consul unwisely fired a shot at a Chinese magistrate, killing his servant, more than a dozen foreign lives were lost. French military retaliation seemed inevitable. Li Hung-chang and the Huai Army were summoned to Chihli. China would have been subjected to further military humiliation and even more grossly inequitable treaty arrangements had France not suffered an untimely defeat in the Franco-Prussian War. As a consequence, the French were induced to accept an official apology from the Chinese Court instead.[44]

On June 28, 1870 the luckless Northern Commissioner Ch'ung-hou was named special emissary to bear imperial apologies to the French capital. Ch'ung-hou did not actually leave China until late in the year. In the intervening months his defense and diplomatic responsibilities were transferred to Li Hung-chang. Li's position in North China was initially established when he was named governor-general of the metropolitan province of Chihli late in August 1870, replacing Tseng Kuo-fan in the shift of high officials following the assassination of Liangkiang Governor-General and Southern Commissioner Ma Hsin-i. Then, upon Ch'ung-hou's recommendation, in early November an edict placed Li in charge of the Tientsin Arsenal. Less than a week later he was named to replace Ch'ung-hou as northern commissioner. His responsibilities were to include supervision of the Tientsin, Newchang, and Chefoo customs, all modernization matters, and maritime defense.[45]

The establishment of the Tientsin Arsenal had been completed only in August 1870. Expenditure reached nearly 500,000 taels, of which 80,000 represented funds realized from the liquidation of the Lay-Osborne Flotilla while the remaining 405,333 taels had come from customs proceeds. Close to four-fifths of the total expenditure, 388,178 taels, had been spent on the Eastern Arsenal at Chia-chia-ku Tao, which far outstripped the Western Arsenal at Hai-kuang Szu in size and importance. The Eastern Arsenal had one complete set of powder-making machinery, facilities for the treatment of nitrates and sulfates, percussion cap machinery, and power-driven carpentry and metal working tools. The Englishman, Meadows, was in charge of the Eastern Arsenal and controlled the expenditure of all funds other than the salaries of Chinese officials. Foreign technicians were also employed. Though production had not begun because of the high cost of material and personnel expenses, it was anticipated that unit costs for powder and ammunition might exceed that of foreign purchase. Ch'ung-hou and Meadows both favored the addition of three complete sets of powder making machinery, which they argued would greatly increase output with only a minimal increase in personnel expense, thereby reducing unit costs. The Western Arsenal at Hai-kuang Szu was much smaller. Under the direction of another Englishman, Mr. Stewart, it consisted of an iron foundry and a gun casting shop. Fifty Chinese artisans were employed turning out brass cannon as well as steamship and ordnance equipment.[46]

During the first five years of Li's incumbency in Tientsin, he rid the arsenal of foreign management, retaining only essential foreign technicians and engineering personnel, and completely restaffed the plant with his own appointees. The first foreigner to come under Li's scrutiny was Meadows, the director of the Eastern Arsenal. Li regarded Meadows' recommendations for three additional sets of powder machinery as premature and overly expansive. It would be wiser, Li felt, to repair any deficiencies in existing facilities and to begin production promptly. In Li's opinion Meadows' statements were exaggerations and Meadows himself was unreliable. Before the end of 1870 Li had replaced him with a Chinese, Shen Pao-ching, who had served as a director of the Kiangnan Arsenal since 1865. Li particularly recommended Shen as one who had proven that he could deal with foreigners without letting authority slip into their hands. Aside from Shen, Li had many other officials and artisans transferred from Kiangnan to Tientsin. Wages for the new personnel were reported to be many times those paid to their predecessors. By 1872 the arsenal was staffed largely by Li's hand-picked men.[47]

In 1872 also, a dispute arose among the foreign employees at the Tientsin Arsenal over the assignment of duties. Though this was an inconsequential matter, it exemplifies the knotty problems and great costs that resulted from the employment of foreign personnel in China's arsenals. Daniel McKensie Davidson had been employed by Meadows in 1866 to serve as a cap maker and instructor in the Tientsin Arsenal at a yearly salary of 1,166 taels plus housing and medical care. After Meadows left the arsenal, a Mr. McIlwraith replaced him as director of all foreign technicians. At that time it was stipulated that McIlwraith's position was subordinate to the Chinese director of the arsenal. Before leaving the Tientsin Arsenal, Meadows had arranged to have Davidson transferred to the powder works. There he eventually incurred the displeasure of Shen Pao-ching, allegedly for giving unauthorized orders to a Chinese employee and thereby creating a dangerous situation. Subsequently, when ordered to return to the cap factory by a Chinese <u>taotai</u> of the powder works, Davidson found that the cap factory would not accept him without the approval of Mr. McIlwraith. McIlwraith then modified Davidson's orders telling him to report to the engine shop. This Davidson refused, saying that the duties there were beyond his capabilities and that the terms of his employment called for work as a cap maker. Finally, he was discharged by McIlwraith for insubordination. Davidson, however, adamantly refused to accept this, appealing his case ultimately to the British minister to China, Sir Thomas Wade. Although Davidson performed no duties after March 20, 1872 he continued to draw full pay and occupied the quarters provided by the arsenal for more than a year, until the court of inquiry convened by Wade decided that his dismissal was justified. On June 16, 1873 Davidson signed a cancellation of contract in return for additional payment of 928 taels.[48]

This incident underscored China's financial vulnerability in contractual arrangements with foreigners in the ordnance industry. Together with the impact of Macartney's tragic blunder, this seems to have confirmed Li's determination to minimize foreign participation in the arsenals under his control. By 1875 only five foreign technicians, all British, were employed at the Eastern Arsenal advising a Chinese work force which numbered about 500. Costs associated with foreign personnel at the arsenal had dropped from about 35,000 taels in 1870 to about 14,000 in 1875.[49]

During these years while foreign influence was drastically reduced at Tientsin, the annual income of the arsenal provided by 40 percent of the Tientsin and Chefoo customs mounted steadily from less than 150,000 taels per year in 1870 to almost 300,000 in 1875. (See Appendix I Table 6.) Since neither Kiangnan nor Nanking was equipped for large-scale production of powder, Li felt that Tientsin should stress powder production. At the end of 1870 he reported that the arsenal had the capacity to produce only 300 to 400 pounds of powder per day and announced his intention to increase production facilities, a suggestion that he had belittled only a few months previously when advanced by Meadows. During the next five years Li used the expanding income from the customs proceeds to transform Tientsin into a major plant for the production of powder and ammunition. Forty-three percent of all expenditure was invested in new machinery and structures to house it, 26 percent was used for production material, most of which had to come from abroad, and 29 percent was devoted to personnel expenses which, with the exception of expenses paid to foreign personnel, increased throughout the period. In 1870 the iron casting facilities of the Western Arsenal were moved and consolidated with the Eastern Arsenal. By 1875 acquisition of new machinery, much of which came from Great Britain, and erection of new structures had completely changed the Tientsin works. Three new powder plants were complete and operational. Machinery for production of Remington rifles, Remington center-fire cartridges, percussion caps, Mauser cartridges, and breech-loading gun ammunition had been purchased. Cast iron, wrought iron, and wood cutting shops had been added and three new powder magazines built.[50]

Despite the obvious high priority that Li assigned to rapid expansion of facilities for the production of military hardware, he maintained a keen interest in the application of machinery in other sectors of the economy, actively soliciting plans and explanations on the mechanization of milk textile production from his British suppliers. Li was also quick to perceive some of the knotty problems that would arise as strategic industry expanded in China and to take steps to deal with them. Mr. Davidson of the British firm of Greenwood and Battey of Leeds, which had provided Li with much of the equipment for Tientsin, reported that Li preferred to deal directly with the home office of the British firm, thereby circumventing foreign purchasing agents who together with their Chinese confederates made a tidy profit by exacting large commissions that were ultimately tacked on to the purchase price paid by the arsenal. Li even foresaw the dangers that unregulated growth of arsenal production held for product uniformity. The production of weapons of various calibers, for example, could greatly complicate the problems of ammunition supply. As early as 1873 he acquired machinery for the conversion of breech pieces for fifty Gatling guns, which he held to the same caliber as the Martini Henry rifles with which his troops were equipped.[51]

The ultimate test of the effectiveness of Li's leadership at the Tientsin Arsenal was in production. Though Tientsin was slow getting started, by 1875 its output was quite impressive. Percussion cap production, which began in 1871, reached 720,000 per month in 1875. Shot and shell were first turned out in 1873; monthly production in 1875 was 9,600 rough items, 7,200 rounds finished and ready for distribution. Remington center-fire cartridges, friction tubes, and fuses were first produced in 1874. By the following year 96,000 cartridges, 4,000 friction tubes and 2,400 fuses were produced each month. The most striking advance, however, was in powder production. Output capacity jumped from 300 to 2,000 pounds per day with installation of the three new mills. Actual monthly production in 1875 was estimated at 38,400 pounds of various types of powder and 9,000 pounds of prismatic powder. Gun carriage production began in 1875 and 41 were completed that year. These products were already being distributed widely. In addition to supplying the needs of maritime defense units in Tientsin, the arsenal was providing munitions to Huai and Lien Army units stationed in Chihli, as well as armies stationed in Manchuria, Inner Mongolia, and Taiwan. Shipments were also made to the expeditionary forces campaigning against the Moslem rebels in the Northwest.[52]

CONCLUSIONS

By 1875 the arsenals at Shanghai, Tientsin, and Nanking were producing at full capacity. In less than a decade ordnance production had been transformed by the introduction of steam powered machinery and modern industrial methods. Rifles and ammunition produced in China were the same models introduced in the West only several years earlier, and steamships--even an ironclad, one of the indices of the big power status--were built at Kiangnan. The drive for most of these accomplishments had been led by Li Hung-chang and, until his death in 1872, by Tseng Kuo-fan. Li's guiding hand was visible in the development of a pattern of complementary production at the arsenals, Kiangnan stressing small arms, Nanking heavy ordnance, and Tientsin powder and ammunition. The exception to this was Kiangnan's steamship program, which had been conceived and promoted primarily by Tseng Kuo-fan. A pattern of cooperation is also apparent in the distribution of products from the three arsenals, evidence of coordinated strategic planning for the Yangtze Valley and North China under the overall direction of Li.

Still, the problems that had appeared in the arsenals did not augur well for the further development and modernization of ordnance production nor for the extension of machine production into nonmilitary sectors of the economy, an area in which Li continued to exhibit a lively interest. The rush to enter production had resulted in serious problems in quality control at both Kiangnan and Nanking. Related to this was the matter of foreign technicians on whom aspirant Chinese artisans and engineers depended for their knowledge of ordnance technology and for the operation, maintenance, and construction of production machinery. Foreigners were always costly and not always effective. Those who proved ineffective or troublesome could be replaced only as qualified Chinese became available. Though Li worked to reduce dependence on foreign technicians throughout this period, in some areas they remained absolutely essential. The technical training program at Kiangnan and the on-the-job training conducted by the foreigners simply had not produced the kind of Chinese talent needed. Furthermore, the bureaucrats who managed the arsenals were untrained for their roles as leaders of modern industry. Inefficiency in production methods seems to have been tolerated at Kiangnan. Financial abuses in purchasing were unquestionably serious. These problems raised Kiangnan's operating costs substantially and were, no doubt, reflected in the unit costs of individual ordnance items. There is no evidence to suggest that inefficiency and financial abuses were serious problems, if they existed at all, at Tientsin, an institution which seems to have been run by Li's chosen men under his watchful eye.

Perhaps the most important trend in the development of Li's arsenals by 1875 was their role in self-strengthening. Though all three plants had been hastily established primarily to meet the logistic needs of rebellion suppression, the change in production missions in the late 1860s and early 1870s leaves no doubt that defense against foreign threats was now assuming an equally important role. Nowhere was this more apparent than at Kiangnan, where steamship building consumed the lion's share of the arsenal's resources. Steamships were clearly not a tool primarily for pacification of rebels, nor were the coastal defense guns built at Nanking. Even at Tientsin the rapid expansion and development of powder and ammunition production after 1870 was plainly inspired, at least in part, by the threat of renewed foreign pressure after the Tientsin Massacre. Though the arsenals were dependent on foreign materials and technicians and in this sense may be called semicolonial, at the same time there unquestionably was an antiimperialist drive reflected in their production.

V. The Evolution of a National Policy for the Ordnance Industry, 1872-1875

Prior to 1875 there was no comprehensive plan for the development of strategic industry throughout China. The various plants that had sprung up to produce Western-style ordnance, ammunition, and steamships were essentially provincial undertakings resulting from the self-strengthening initiative of Li Hung-chang, Tseng Kuo-fan, and others. The imperial government usually encouraged and cooperated with provincial initiatives, but at times it had also blocked them, and it had failed to provide coordinated national leadership. In consequence, Li Hung-chang moved into the vacuum and established a system of arsenals in the Yangtze Valley and North China. The production missions of these plants generally complemented one another, and they all supported the Huai Army and the maritime defense installations of North China which Li commanded.

There were clear limits to Li's influence on the development of strategic industry, however. The most important example was the shipbuilding program at Kiangnan, which consumed the bulk of that arsenal's resources. Beyond this were the arsenals and shipyards that were beginning to sprout along the southeast coast and in West China (see Appendix II), also well outside the range of Li's influence. The best known of these, the Foochow Dockyard, was not involved to any significant degree in the production of ordnance or ammunition and is beyond the scope of this study. There were, however, a small arsenal in the city of Foochow, an arsenal and shipyard in Kwangtung, and arsenals and ammunition plants established by the forces engaged in suppressing the Moslem Rebellion in West and Northwest China.

In the years from 1872 to 1875 friction developed in China's relations with Japan. At about the same time the Moslem Rebellion in the northwest gave rise to a separatist movement in Chinese Turkestan. The question of how resources were to be allocated between these two problem areas for national security became a matter of urgent concern not only to self-strengthening officials in the provinces but also to strategic planners in the Tsungli Yamen. One crucial aspect of the national security question was what types of production the various ordnance plants should undertake. Slowly the broad outlines of a policy assigning responsibility for control and development of arsenals in various areas and allocating production missions began to take shape. The first stage in this evolution was the reappraisal of the steamship program of the Kiangnan Arsenal, which monopolized resources that might alternatively be employed for the development of ordnance production. This was followed in late 1874 and early 1875 by a high level debate over national defense policy. The role of China's arsenals was reconsidered against current national needs, and ultimately a new defense policy including a new organization and new guidelines for the ordnance industry was adopted.

THE DECISION TO TERMINATE SHIPBUILDING AT KIANGNAN

Shipbuilding was the largest, most conspicuous, and most expensive category of production at Kiangnan. Not only were the vessels completed after 1870 larger, more sophisticated, and therefore more costly than earlier ones, the arsenal was also burdened with the mounting expense of maintenance and operation of completed vessels. As a result, by early 1872 the shipbuilding program, including the maintenance and operation of completed vessels, had consumed close to one-half of the 1,870,000 taels which the arsenal had received from the maritime customs.[1] A wave of opposition began to gather. On the one hand, imperial officials lodged complaints against what they regarded as a costly and ineffective program of the Liangkiang provincial government; on the other, Li Hung-chang began to question the practical advisability of further steamship building at Kiangnan.

The initial response to these pressures came during 1871. In a move to silence growing opposition to the high cost of the steamship program at Kiangnan and to place shipbuilding on a sound financial basis, the Tsungli Yamen advanced a proposal for the rental of Kiangnan ships to Chinese merchants who would bear the cost of operating and maintaining them, thereby relieving the arsenal of this burden. Both Tseng Kuo-fan and Li Hung-chang were consulted. In January 1872, while the Tsungli Yamen's proposal was under discussion, the shipbuilding program at Kiangnan and the arsenal itself were the subject of a new and potentially ruinous attack. A memorial of Sub-Chancellor of the Grand Secretariat Sung Chin recommended that the customs allotment of the Kiangnan Arsenal and a similar one made to support shipbuilding at the Foochow Dockyard be halted and that the funds revert to the imperial government where they could be put to better use for disaster relief. Sung observed that the threat of naval attack from the West was no longer imminent. In any case even if an attack should come, he judged that Chinese-built vessels would be no match for those constructed in the West. The traditional water forces, he argued, could cope with local pirates, and traditional junks were better suited for commercial carrying, particularly the transport of grain, which would be twice as costly if accomplished with steamers.[2]

Southern Commissioner Tseng Kuo-fan was asked to respond to Sung's memorial as to whether or not operations at the Kiangnan Arsenal should be halted. Tseng died on March 12, 1872, before making a formal reply to Sung Chin. On February 24, however, less than a month before his death, he wrote to the Tsungli Yamen expressing firm support for Kiangnan's shipbuilding program and for the idea of renting Kiangnan vessels to Chinese merchants.[3]

After Tseng's death the court sought the advice of Li Hung-chang on Sung Chin's proposal. Over the years Li's relationship to the Kiangnan Arsenal had become obscure. Although his status as cofounder of Kiangnan assured him a voice in the arsenal's affairs, with the passage of time his influence waned. Supervisory authority over the arsenal became confused. In 1869 Kiangsu Governor Ting Jih-ch'ang advocated that technological matters (yang-wu) come under the joint control of the governors-general of Liangkiang and Chihli while financial dealings with the maritime customs should be handled by the Kiangsu governor. Presumably, the reason for including the Chihli governor-general in the proposed hierarchy was that Tseng Kuo-fan actually exercised supervisory control over the arsenal from 1868 to 1870 while occupying the post in Chihli. In any case, late in 1870 when Li assumed the governor-generalship of Chihli he observed that he had not exercised direct control over the Kiangnan Arsenal for some time. During 1871, while incumbent in the Chihli post, he was primarily involved with local matters at Tientsin. Tseng Kuo-fan, on the other hand, was back in the Liangkiang provinces and as southern commissioner was very much absorbed in supervising the affairs of the Kiangnan Arsenal. Tseng's influence was clearly preponderant.[4]

After Tseng's death, cofounder Li resumed an active role in the overall guidance of the arsenal from his position as governor-general of Chihli and northern commissioner, assuming also an advisory capacity in technological matters such as operations and personnel. Primary responsibility for the latter, however, remained with the Liangkiang governor-general the southern commissioner. Two considerations were no doubt of enormous importance in aiding Li to renew a degree of influence over Kiangnan: first, his close personal relationship with high officials at the arsenal such as Feng Chün-kuang, who had been appointed during Li's earlier incumbency in Liang-kiang; and second, the strategic sensitivity of Li's post in Chihli and his concurrent responsibilities as northern commissioner. These offices carried with them the responsibility for defense of the capital, Chihli province, Manchuria, and Inner Mongolia. The imperial government quite naturally turned to Li for advice in reaching important decisions regarding the largest arsenal in the Empire.[5]

Since Li's departure from Kiangnan, his views on shipbuilding and closely related problems had undergone a gradual evolution. With respect to shipbuilding Li had long harbored serious doubts about the program that Tseng had initiated at Kiangnan. In 1866 before leaving the arsenal, he stated that it was his intention that Kiangnan should build only small gunboats. In June 1869 after the launching of the second vessel, Li wrote to Tseng that the ship was far below the standards of Western warships, and in 1871 he again wrote to Tseng, observing that Kiangnan-built vessels conformed to neither commercial nor military standards. Subsequently, he suggested that the arsenal switch to the production of foreign-style sailing ships, which he regarded as better suited for commercial use and more economical. Finally, in 1872 Li wrote to a fellow official that he had felt for a long time that Kiangnan's shipbuilding program would not strengthen China against the West and that it was excessively costly.[6]

From this growing awareness of the shortcomings of Kiangnan's ships, Li came to appreciate the inadequacy of the arsenal's technical manpower resources. The functioning of the on-the-job training program is unclear, but it was clear to Li that neither this program nor the tradition-bound formal training in the arsenal school would provide the first class Chinese engineers and technicians needed to augment and replace the foreign advisors in the shipyard. It was undoubtedly with this in mind that Li reversed his stand on technological training in 1871 and joined Tseng Kuo-fan in sponsoring the China Educational Mission to send Chinese youth to the United States for schooling. It was anticipated that when these students returned some would take positions in arsenals and shipyards.

　　Li's early preference for the production of ground forces, rather than naval, armament was strengthened by his years of service as a ground forces commander. After his appointment as governor-general of Chihli and northern commissioner in 1870, he hastened to build a logistical base for the Huai Army, the forces through which he would discharge his new defense responsibility. In the area of military-industrial development, his efforts were directed chiefly to the small arsenals in Tientsin, which he transformed into a major industrial complex for the production of gunpowder and ammunition.[7]

　　After receiving an imperial invitation to memorialize in reply to Sung Chin, Li corresponded extensively with officials of the Kiangnan Arsenal and the Foochow Dockyard before submitting his views to the court in June 1872. His memorial, which bears the title "Steamship Construction Cannot be Halted," was an impassioned plea for the continuation of industrial modernization to save China from foreign encroachment. On the subject of steamship building at the Kiangnan Arsenal, however, Li expressed serious reservations. He felt that a country with land area as great as China's should give priority to the development of ground forces. Though he admired the ironclads of the West, he observed that their draft was too great for most of China's harbors. Nor were they entirely suitable for the purely defensive naval strategy that he advocated. He favored the construction of small, shallow-draft, armor-plated, harbor-defense gunboats. Li also noted that he had already directed Kiangnan that military vessels constructed in the future should not exceed the size of the fifth major vessel, the <u>Hai-an</u>.[8]

If these guidelines for ship construction were followed Li felt that the arsenal could continue operation within the limits of the income from customs, provided that a separate plan was worked out to defray the costs of steamship maintenance and operation. Li's thinking on this problem was greatly influenced by the ideas of Feng Chün-kuang, director of the Kiangnan Arsenal and an outspoken advocate of steamship building and balanced industrial development. Feng recommended steamship rentals to merchants combined with a grant of monopoly rights for the transport of tribute grain from South to North China to assure Chinese merchants a profitable carrying trade in the face of well-developed competition by Western steamers. In Feng's judgment, the only two Kiangnan steamers that could be converted for commercial rental were the fourth vessel, the Wei-ching, and the Chin-ou, which was just then in the planning stage. The remaining ships were of purely military design. Feng recommended that these be assigned to patrol the coast with costs of maintenance and operation to be borne by the provinces in which they patrolled. If the rental of the Wei-ching proved profitable, he felt that future construction at Kiangnan should emphasize commercial vessels.[9]

Li's memorial reiterated Feng's plan of assigning military vessels to coastal provinces for patrolling and support and recommended that this could be accomplished economically by concurrently eliminating traditional provincial water forces. Though Li later used Feng's idea of granting a monopoly on tribute grain to cultivate commercial steam navigation, he felt that discussion of ship rentals to merchants for the purpose of hauling grain could be delayed for the time being, since there were no vessels that had the required specifications.[10]

Feng did not confine his suggestions to the immediate problem of easing the burden of steamship maintenance. He saw that this was only a symptom of the economic backwardness that was undermining China's efforts to strengthen itself. Failure to exploit natural resources and to develop basic industries was the underlying reason for the outflow of funds which left the Empire unable to solve fundamental defense problems such as steamship maintenance. To correct this situation he advanced a series of proposals for the modernization of the extractive, refining, and transportation industries. He advocated the introduction of Western pumping, refining, and processing machinery and the use of privately-rented steamships to move basic fuels and raw materials to and from production centers and markets. This would help to free Kiangnan from the burden of steamship maintenance and upkeep and at the same time would bring down the cost of fuels and basic raw materials. He advised that the financial basis of this development plan could be sustained by the sale of coal and iron produced in excess of government requirements and by the reinvestment of profits in machinery, which in turn would increase the quantity of production and reduce the unit price. As the next step of industrialization he advocated investment in textile machinery and machine production of fabrics suitable for China's various regions.[11]

Feng's analysis of the steamship maintenance program brought him to grips with the most basic problem limiting development of the Kiangnan Arsenal, the high cost of imported fuels and raw material. By the end of 1873 Kiangnan had spent over 1.5 million taels, approximately 52 percent of all funds expended, for imported materials, the cost of which included not only transport and insurance charges but the profits of several foreign middlemen as well.[12]

Li's memorial echoed Feng's arguments for the introduction of Western machinery and methods in the coal and iron industries, but Feng's views were presented in toto to the Tsungli Yamen by Liangkiang Governor-General and Southern Commissioner Ho Ching, who attached a strong negative statement. There is no indication that they were given further consideration at this time.[13]

The Tsungli Yamen's final recommendations to the throne strongly supported the continuation of strategic industrial development and steamship building. Specific proposals for reducing the financial burden created by the steamship program were limited to the areas of vessel operation and maintenance, however. It was suggested that Li Hung-chang develop a scheme for rental of steamships to Chinese merchants and that military steamers be assigned to the coastal provinces for patrol and support if requested by the concerned provincial officials. Li's proposal for halting construction of junks for the traditional water forces so as to save funds for the maintenance of steamships was ignored, however. Nor was any mention made of modernization of the coal and iron industries or the use of steamships to promote industrial development. In August 1872 an edict approved these recommendations.[14] Both the rental scheme and the plan for the assignment of military steamers to provinces were conceived as a solution to the pressing financial problem caused by steamship maintenance. Neither offered a solution to the basic problem of economic underdevelopment, which underlay the high cost of steamship construction, arms production, and general industrial development. Though Feng Chun-kuang had recognized this problem and attempted to deal with it, his suggestions did not prevail. This being the case, even if the ship maintenance problem at Kiangnan could be solved, the development of production at the arsenal was headed for further financial difficulties.

Though the shipbuilding program at Kiangnan was nominally continued by the edict of August 1872, an abrupt slowdown in construction took place. Major vessels begun in 1872 were completed but no new ones were started. New construction was limited to a pair of small harbor-defense vessels of the type that Li favored and several miscellaneous craft. (See Appendix I Table 1.) The reasons for this slowdown stem from the financial problems at the arsenal and the influence of Li Hung-chang's strategic priorities.

Neither of the two plans designed to reduce the burden of steamship maintenance on Kiangnan's budget provided any relief. The ship rental plan ran into complications before the end of the year. Though Li established a steamship line--the China Merchants' Steam Navigation Company--for the transport of tribute grain with the anticipation that it would rent Kiangnan steamers, when the company began operations no Kiangnan vessels were ready for commercial service. Furthermore, the construction cost for new commercial vessels at Kiangnan was far greater than the purchase price of comparable foreign-built vessels. Insurance costs were correspondingly higher, and in some instances the foreign insurance companies flatly refused to insure Chinese built vessels at the actual construction costs, thereby making it extremely risky to employ Chinese ships. In addition to these difficulties, monopolistic pressures from foreign steamship companies forced the China Merchants' Company to rely largely on the transport of tribute grain for its business. Consequently, after it had acquired a fleet of five foreign vessels it found that there was no need for additional Kiangnan-built ships. By 1874 no Kiangnan vessels had been rented to merchants and both Li Hung-chang and Southern Commissioner Li Tsung-hsi expressed grave doubts about the feasibility of building commercial vessels for rental at Kiangnan.[15]

At about the same time, the plan for assignment

of military vessels to provinces for patrolling and
upkeep failed completely. This scheme clearly required
the backing and direction of a supraprovincial authority. The imperial government, however, looked to the
coastal provinces to take the initiative to request
the ships. The provinces hesitated to assume additional defense expenditures and to reorganize their
naval forces at a time of relative peace. Consequently,
no naval vessels were assigned and the Kiangnan Arsenal
continued to bear the full expense for maintenance
and operation of the ships that it had built.[16]

As it became increasingly clear that neither of
the plans to finance steamship maintenance and operation could relieve Kiangnan's budget of this expense,
Li Hung-chang began openly to advocate the curtailment
of further construction. In June 1873 he advised
Southern Commissioner Li Tsung-hsi that Kiangnan
should not undertake too many diverse types of production lest it do none of them well. He regarded Feng
Chün-kuang's idea of building ironclads as excessively
costly and of doubtful outcome. In January 1874 Li
brought up the underlying problem of the high cost of
production with foreign materials. In a letter to
his counterpart, Southern Commissioner Li, he noted
that construction costs for the Hai-an and the Yü-yüan
were enormous and that the financial burden created
by vessel upkeep was still onerous. "My idea," wrote
Li, "is that if expenses exceed income, we should
temporarily stop shipbuilding, wait until there is a
surplus, and then resume." The only qualification in
Li's mind was the construction of small, shallow-draft
ironclads of the Monitor class. He maintained a
genuine, though cautious, interest in the Chin-ou, an
experimental vessel of this type then under constructio
at Kiangnan.[17]

From 1872 to 1874, as a result of the reassertion
of Li Hung-chang's influence at Kiangnan, the cost
effectiveness of the shipbuilding program had been
called into question. By the summer of 1874, after
the failure of the various proposals aimed at reducing
costs, it seemed likely that Kiangnan shipbuilding would
be drastically restricted, if indeed it was to survive
at all. Although there had already been a noticeable
shift of resources to ordnance production, all of the
implications that the cutbacks in shipbuilding would
hold for the development of ordnance production were
far from clear. Furthermore, the whole question of
allocation of resources for strategic industrial
planning at Kiangnan and throughout the Empire was
enormously complicated in 1874-1875 by the development

of the most perilous defense crisis that the Ch'ing
dynasty had faced since the Anglo-French invasion of
North China in 1860.

THE NEW MARITIME DEFENSE POLICY OF 1875

By 1874 the campaign against the Moslem Rebellion,
which had raged in Northwest China since 1862, reached
the threshold of a new stage. A decision had to be
made as to whether or not the Ch'ing government would
attempt to extend its control into the Central Asian
region of Chinese Turkestan. By November 1874, forces
under the command of Governor-General Tso Tsung-t'ang
which had been battling the Moslems in Shensi and Kansu
completed the pacification of those two provinces.
Tso (who was also a pioneer in the field of strategic
industrial modernization, having established the
Foochow Dockyard and small arsenals at Sian and
Lanchow) looked forward to a hard-won opportunity to
test his skills as a peacetime administrator. But
the problem of Moslem dissidence was far from a final
solution. Concurrent with the rebellion in Shensi
and Kansu there had been a series of uprisings in
remote Chinese Turkestan. During the late 1860s the
Chieftan Yakub Beg was successful in establishing a
Moslem Kingdom, which by 1873 embraced all of the Tarim
Basin from the Pamir Mountains to Lop Nor, with a
force also stationed north of the Tien Shan at Urumchi.
Meanwhile, in 1871 Tsarist Russia had occupied the
rich Ili River Valley under the pretext of maintaining
the orderly conditions necessary for trade. In 1872
and 1873 Yakub's Kingdom received international recognition in one form or another from London, St.
Petersburg, and Constantinople. It seemed that the
entire area was about to slip permanently from
Chinese control. Indeed, as early as 1865 there were
those who contended that Chinese Turkestan was not
worth defending, but these arguments had always been
dismissed by the throne. Until 1874 the question of
whether or not to defend Chinese Turkestan was quite
academic; there were always more pressing problems
closer to home--the Taipings, the Nien, and the Moslems
in Shensi and Kansu. But in 1874, with the victorious
armies of Tso Tsung-t'ang poised in western Kansu,
the question of whether or not to launch what
promised to be an extremely costly and extended
campaign to secure this vast region was no longer
academic but a very real strategic option lying
before the Chinese throne.[18]

It was in 1874 also, while the Chinese Turkestan

campaign was hanging fire, that a conflict flared in China's relations with Japan, underscoring the need for strengthened maritime defense against the newly unified and expansionist Meiji state. Farsighted Chinese strategists such as Ting Jih-ch'ang had advocated naval preparedness against the potential Japanese threat as early as 1867. But the Sino-Japanese Treaty of Friendship and Commerce concluded in 1871 seemed to belie the urgency of such warnings; Article I provided for mutual nonaggression in each other's territories. The absence, however, of clearly defined boundaries and the ambiguous relationship between China and some of its traditional tributary states in a sense invited aggression, and certain former Samurai elements in Japan's ruling oligarchy needed no invitation. In the spring of 1874 the British minister in Peking brought to the attention of the Chinese government the fact that Japan was preparing to launch an expedition to eastern Taiwan to punish the aboriginal inhabitants of that area for atrocities that they had committed against ship-wrecked Ryukyuan and Japanese fishermen in 1871. Japan's position was that the aborigines were beyond the pale of Chinese administration and that the expedition involved no intrusion on Chinese territory. China maintained that the aborigines were Chinese subjects and that all of Taiwan was Chinese territory. China also contended that the Ryukyus were a Chinese not a Japanese possession and that the Ryukyuans should bring their complaint to the Chinese throne.[19]

Despite China's protests the Japanese landed a force in eastern Taiwan in May 1874. Shen Pao-chen, formerly the director of the Foochow Dockyard, was imperially appointed to lead a defensive expedition to Taiwan. Prosper Giquel, head of the French technical advisory group at the yard, served as Shen's advisor. Shen and Giquel made a feverish effort to round up all sorts of armament, breech-loading rifles, guns, ammunition, and mines. Sixty-five hundred troops of Li Hung-chang's Huai Army stationed in northern Kiangsu were also dispatched to Taiwan but did not arrive until October due to transport and communication problems. Meanwhile, during the summer of 1874 it became increasingly clear to the Chinese side that legal and historical arguments would not induce Japan to withdraw from Taiwan. Nor did China relish the prospect of a military showdown with the Japanese. Presumably, the most important consideration here was the impending campaign against the Moslems in Chinese Turkestan. The prospect of a debilitating struggle on two fronts no doubt worried the ministers of the Tsungli Yamen as they pondered the proper strategy to induce Japan's withdrawal. More specifically, from the standpoint of military preparedness both Shen and his advisor Giquel counseled the Ch'ing government to avoid a test of arms with Japan. Giquel observed that China had insufficient infantry equipped with foreign-style arms in the Fukien area and that Chinese gunboats and wooden battleships were no match for Japan's two ironclads.[20]

Actually, from the standpoint of military materiel alone, it is highly questionable whether China suffered from any real disadvantage. A recent study has revealed that Japan's two ironclads were not prepared for combat operations and that, in number of vessels and tonnage, China's navy outstripped that of Japan. In the judgment of one foreign observer, China's navy would probably have been quite capable of coping with Japan. With respect to domestic ordnance production capabilities, it is also doubtful that Japan surpassed China by very much if at all. Although Western-style smelting and casting of iron ordnance had begun in the feudal domains of Saga, Satsuma, and Mito, as well as in the Tokugawa Shogunate domains, during the 1850s, it was probably not until the 1860s, or perhaps even later, that Western-style machinery was employed for the production of such items as rifles, ammunition, and gunpowder. By 1875 six plants had entered production: the Kanko Factory in Tokyo, taken over from the Tokugawa, which repaired artillery and produced small arms; the Osaka Factory where heavy ordnance was produced; the Itabashi Gunpowder Works in Tokyo; the Kagoshima Artillery Factory inherited from the Satsuma feudal domain; the Naval Ordnance Factory in the Ishikawashima Shipyard in Tokyo; and the plant that would eventually be known as the Yokosuka Naval Factory, the output of which is uncertain. Although precise information regarding the quality and quantity of arms and ammunition produced by these plants is not available, the scant number of plants and the fact that none of them had a production history extending back more than one or two decades suggest that the Japanese industry, taken as a whole, was perhaps not far ahead of that in China. We know, furthermore, that both nations were far from self-sufficient; both looked abroad for foreign purchases to supplement domestic production of ordnance.[21]

By the same token, some important contrasts between the experience of the two countries in ordnance production tend to support the notion of Japan's relative superiority. At least one of the major arsenals in Japan, the Osaka Factory, was operating completely without foreign advisors by 1874, a claim that no major Chinese arsenal could make. The most striking difference was in the area of centralized planning and control. From the inauguration of the restoration government in Japan in 1868, there was a sustained drive for military unification. The Ordnance Office of the Military Affairs Authority established in 1868 was charged with all matters pertaining to ordnance production and specifically with planning ordnance unification. By 1872 the Military Affairs Authority had evolved into ministries of the Army and Navy, which between them controlled all of Japan's arsenals.[22] In China the situation was quite different. In the absence of vigorous leadership for the industry in the imperial government, responsibility devolved upon provincial leaders; industries developed in East China, the Northwest, Fukien, Canton, and even Yunnan, with no formal agency for nationally coordinated planning. (See Appendix II.)

Be this as it may, the Tsungli Yamen in 1874 lacked both the hindsight and the intelligence data for such a comparative analysis (which even today is far from conclusive). Relying heavily on the counsel of Shen Pao-chen and Li Hung-chang, the Yamen maneuvered frantically to avoid a showdown with Japan. But it was dealing from a position of weakness, real or imagined. The settlement that was eventually reached through the mediation of British Minister Sir Thomas Wade provided that in return for the Japanese departure from Taiwan, China would reimburse the costs of the expedition, about 400,000 taels, and indemnify the families of the Ryukyuans about another 100,000 taels. Ultimately this led to China relinquishing its claim to suzerainty over the Ryukyus in favor of Japan.[23]

On November 5, 1874, just five days after the settlement with Japan, the Tsungli Yamen, recoiling from the humiliating terms of the agreement, memorialized a series of suggestions for the strengthening of basic aspects of national defense. These were grouped under six headings: troop training, weapons, naval vessels, finance, personnel, and long-range planning. The court immediately directed Northern Commissioner Li Hung-chang, newly appointed Southern Commissioner Shen Pao-chen, and other governors and governors-general of coastal and Yangtze riparian provinces to respond to the Tsungli Yamen's suggestions within a month. Hardly had the process been set in motion when Acting Kwangtung Governor Chang Chao-tung forwarded a six-point plan for naval development drawn up by Ting Jih-ch'ang, then living in retirement in Kwangtung. This plan, originally conceived by Ting in 1867 while serving as governor of Kiangsu and pigeonholed by Liangkiang Governor-General Tseng Kuo-fan, contained specific proposals dealing with steamships, ports, troop training, government personnel, naval command and administration, and industrial development. In some areas Ting's ideas were already outdated, but in others they broached subjects that were not covered by the Tsungli Yamen's earlier memorial. Accordingly, pursuant to a request from the Tsungli Yamen the same provincial officials were sent a copy of Ting's plan and directed to include a discussion of its feasibility in their reply. Copies of both plans were also delivered to Governor-General of Shensi-Kansu Tso Tsung-t'ang for his comments.[24]

In the wide-ranging policy debate which these moves precipitated during the next several months, the memorialists expressed diverse views on the aspects of national defense raised by the Tsungli Yamen and Ting. Although the considerations which they discussed extend far beyond the purview of this study, what developed into the central issue in their discussion had a direct bearing on the future of the ordnance industry. Most simply stated, the question was whether to give first priority and first claim upon national resources to frontier defense in Chinese Turkestan or to maritime defense along the East China coast.[25] Related to this was the question of continued allocation of national resources to naval development. Specifically, should the problem-ridden shipbuilding program at the Kiangnan Arsenal be continued or suspended? Regardless of which way the debate on maritime versus frontier defense was decided, it was clearly time to take another long, hard look at Kiangnan shipbuilding. If fiscal priority was assigned to frontier rather than to maritime defense, the need to reevaluate the shipbuilding program at Kiangnan would be just that much more urgent. If the arsenal was not to continue building ships, there would have to be a new determination of the way resources would be employed to improve ordnance and other forms of production. The future employment of resources for ordnance production was an issue not only at Kiangnan but at other arsenals as well. The Tsungli Yamen and Ting had both raised this question as a matter of vital national concern involving all Chinese arsenals. Even if they had not, it is only logical to assume that the production patterns in China's arsenals would be influenced by a fundamental policy decision to emphasize either frontier or maritime defense. These three issues--frontier versus maritime defense, the future of shipbuilding, and the future of ordnance production--all of which would directly influence the development of the ordnance industry, were raised, discussed, and basically decided during the policy debate over national defense at the close of 1874 and in early 1875.

The key issue of whether to give priority to frontier defense or coastal defense was decided in favor of frontier defense. Predictably, Tso Tsung-t'ang emerged as the foremost spokesman for frontier defense and Li Hung-chang as the chief protagonist of maritime defense. Though the positions of both sides contained strong arguments as well as contrived and exaggerated claims, it was clear that Li and the advocates of maritime defense perceived that the changes in the international configurations of power resulting from the use of steam navigation and modern firearms had shifted the focus of primary concern in China's foreign relations from the northwest to the east coast. Furthermore, their thinking included Japan among China's potential enemies. Tso and the exponents of frontier defense, on the other hand, remained tied to the position, axiomatic in earlier strategic thought, that the primary threat to China's security came from Central Asia. The court was persuaded by the advocates of frontier defense, presumably for reasons stemming from traditional strategy and the unwillingness to abandon to the barbarians lands acquired by an imperial ancestor. In 1875 an edict approved the campaign to retake Chinese Turkestan and appointed Tso Tsung-t'ang to command. From the beginning of 1875 until 1878, when this great and costly campaign succeeded in pacifying all but a few pockets of Moslem resistance in Chinese Turkestan, some 26 million taels were expended. The cost of mopping-up operations and reconstruction from 1878 through 1881 raised the total to 51 million taels, straining national resources to the limit at a time when the total annual budget for maritime defense was 4 million taels, of which only about one-fourth was actually appropriated.[26]

The decision to emphasize frontier rather than maritime defense in a sense foredoomed marginally

effective programs for naval development such as the
faltering shipbuilding effort at Kiangnan. It was
Li himself, however, who took this opportunity of a
general assessment of defense planning to advocate
laying to rest once and for all the costly and
inefficient Kiangnan program. Li's views proved to
be decisive, for the new maritime defense policy that
was announced in May 1875 charged Northern Commissioner
Li and Southern Commissioner Shen Pao-chen with full
responsibility for the future of shipbuilding and
the development of a steamship fleet. In his recommendations to the throne on maritime defense, Li
had stressed the futility of attempting to catch up
with the West in naval armaments quickly. Instead
of relying solely on naval power, he urged that a
combination of ground forces and select naval units
be employed to guard the most strategic points along
the coast, the approaches to Peking and the mouth of
the Yangtze. Ideally, these points would be defended
by coastal defense forts, harbor defense gunboats,
and naval mines. This defense line was to be backed
up by highly mobile infantry units, which would guard
against enemy landings elsewhere along the coast.
An outer defense perimeter of ironclads and conventional battleships would also be established. After
considering the suitability of the Kiangnan-built
vessels for use in this plan, Li determined that
only the Hai-an and the Yü-yuan could be regarded as
battleships. The remainder of the major vessels he
classified as wooden gunboats, of little value in
modern maritime defense schemes. Since construction
costs of Kiangnan vessels were more than twice the
purchase price of comparable foreign-built vessels
due to the high cost of imported materials, Li advised
that foreign purchase would be the most economical
and advantageous method for futher acquisition.[27]

Li not only regarded Kiangnan-built vessels as
inordinately expensive and ill-suited to China's
requirements, but the following year he even characterized them as "little different from foreign
purchases; all the materials coming from abroad and
all the work directed by foreigners." Though
Kiangnan's on-the-job training program had been in
operation for more than five years, the arsenal's
dependence on foreign technicians was greater than
it had ever been.[28]

Shen Pao-chen in his recommendation did not
speak directly to the problem of shipbuilding at
Kiangnan, but he placed highest priority on the
acquisition of ironclads, none of which had yet been

completed at Kiangnan. He further recommended that each of China's new defense plants should be assigned a specialized and appropriate production mission such as ordnance, ammunition, or shipbuilding. Such a division of responsibility, he reasoned, would promote excellence in production through specialization and further economy through elimination of duplication. At the time, of course, Kiangnan was engaged in all three types of production.[29]

The new maritime defense policy of May 1875 failed to offer any new solutions to the serious financial problems that had already restricted shipbuilding at Kiangnan. Although several of the memorials submitted prior to the announcement of the policy had stressed the need for modernization of the domestic coal and iron industry, the edict approved the opening of only two modern coal mines. Nor was any headway made on either of the plans adopted earlier to relieve Kiangnan of ship operation costs. Plans for the construction of commercial steamers for rental were abandoned entirely, and no mention was made of the scheme for the assignment of military vessels to the provinces to replace traditional water forces. Instead, administrative changes embodied in the new policy established regional maritime defense commands in North and South China; Northern Commissioner Li Hung-chang and Southern Commissioner Shen Pao-chen were named to head these commands and were given responsibility for maritime defense and naval development in their respective regions, Peiyang and Nanyang. To fund their operations and activities, the new policy established a maritime defense fund of 4 million taels to be paid annually by various provinces: 2 million to the southern commissioner and 2 million to the northern commissioner.[30]

With the establishment of this fund the financial prospects for the continuation of shipbuilding looked somewhat brighter. Some of the new maritime defense fund would presumably be available to the southern commissioner to finance the construction of additional ships. But this was not to be the case. Southern Commissioner Shen had made it clear that his first concern was that China should have ironclads, and the launching of Kiangnan's first small <u>Monitor</u>-type ironclad in September 1875 proved conclusively that the arsenal was incapable of construction in this class. Not only were the guns improperly positioned, the vessel itself was incapable of putting to sea. Furthermore, Shen had strongly disapproved of broad diversification in production such as that carried on at Kiangnan. If any category of production at the arsenal was to be eliminated, shipbuilding was certainly the most vulnerable from the standpoint of cost-effectiveness. Finally, in 1875 he and Northern Commissioner Li agreed that first priority should be given to building up a defense fleet for North China that would include ironclads. Since it was also agreed that the 2 million taels annual appropriation for northern maritime defense was insufficient to accomplish this objective, Shen relinquished the South's share of the maritime defense fund to Li so that the northern fleet might be quickly established. With the passage of the entire maritime defense fund to Li's control, the last hope of using the fund to finance continued shipbuilding at Kiangnan vanished, for Li had made his position clear time and time again: Kiangnan ships were too costly, technically inferior to those of the West, and ill-suited to China's strategic needs. He favored naval augmentation through foreign purchase. Shen's position was equally clear, and it was equally unlikely that he would attempt further construction with whatever remained available from the arsenal's customs income. During the next several years, under the leadership of Shen Pao-chen no more vessels were constructed at Kiangnan and the arsenal gradually converted almost entirely to the production of ordnance and ammunition.[31]

The sequence of events resulting in the cessation of shipbuilding at Kiangnan had enormous import for the future of the ordnance industry. Now the 20 percent of the Shanghai maritime customs income that supported operations at the arsenal would presumably be available for the development of ordnance production. The overall fiscal outlook for the ordnance industry at the national level was far from bright, however. As it became clear in early 1875 that the lion's share of national defense resources would go to the campaign in Chinese Turkestan, the prospects for futher modernization and increased production at the coastal arsenals dimmed. Nevertheless, the Taiwan crisis had provided a stinging reminder of the importance of maritime defense. Li and Shen, though willing to eliminate the costly and inefficient shipbuilding program at Kiangnan, were determined to strengthen defenses against naval attack. Furthermore, Li and others foresaw that domestic ordnance production would play an important part not only in strengthening maritime defense but also in equipping and arming inland defense forces. In fact, the general guidelines for the growth of the ordnance industry during the next twenty years--probably the most crucia in its entire history--are suggested in the texts of the memorials and edicts of the debate on maritime defense.

Perhaps the most fundamental decision influencing the subsequent growth of the ordnance industry, which was reached during the debate over maritime versus frontier defense, was the determination to divide defense of the coast into two commands with headquarters at Tientsin and Nanking. Each command was separately responsible, <u>inter alia</u>, for establishment of arsenals, production of arms and ammunition, purchase of war materials, development of naval weapons, opening of mines, supply of ground forces and fort ordnance, and overseas training of personnel within their respective regions.[32] The implications of this decision for the future of the ordnance industry in China were far reaching. Two authorities now existed with imperial sanction to develop all aspects of the ordnance industry within their respective regions. Close cooperation would be essential if wasteful duplication, competition, and nonstandardized production were to be avoided. Failure to achieve such cooperation would certainly weaken the industry's nationwide self-strengthening effect. It would require strong imperial leadership at the national level to offset the divisive effect that two commands could produce.

Suggestions for future production of ordnance were forthcoming from many quarters during the debate The most pertinent to understanding future developments in the industry, however, were those of Li and Shen, the officials who would hold the all-important posts of northern and southern commissioners for maritime defense. Since Li Hung-chang would serve as northern commissioner almost uninterruptedly until the close of the Sino-Japanese War and his opinions would also carry great weight at various times in the South, his views on ordnance production are especially important. Although Li pleaded vehemently for improve maritime defense, he realized the present practicality of basing this defense on ground forces, namely, strategically positioned forts and mobile infantry units. For the time being he saw a limited role for China's arsenals in supplying these forces. He advised that production capability should be concentrated on powder, ammunition, and naval mines. In Li's view, the Chinese economy was not yet ready for heavy ordnance production which would entail the acquisition of costly foreign machinery and the regular supply of iron and steel. He felt that the purchase of heavy ordnance machinery should be delayed at least until China had opened modern coal and iron mines. He noted that he had directed both Tientsin and Kiangnan to purchase Remington cartridge machinery and had recommended additional powder-making machinery for both Kiangnan and Nanking. He proposed bringing foreign instructors to China to teach the techniques of making electrically detonated naval mines to replace the crude models then being produced at Kiangnan and Tientsin.[33]

Shen Pao-chen did not make specific recommendations on ordnance and ammunition production, but some of his generalized observations bore directly on the future of ordnance production. As noted above, Shen deplored the duplication of production missions and called for assignment of specialized missions at each arsenal. Since Shen was prepared to write off the shipbuilding program at Kiangnan and Kiangnan was the best equipped of China's arsenals for rifle production, Shen's appointment as southern commissioner augured well for the production of small arms at Kiangnan. Like Li, Shen counseled that coal and iron resources be exploited to provide domestic sources of raw material.[34]

Li advanced another proposal that revealed his clear perception of the strategic setting in which the ordnance industry was developing. Recognizing the vulnerability of coastal arsenals such as Kiangnan and Tientsin to attack by foreign naval forces, he urged that the provinces in the interior provide their own ammunition needs through the establishment of additional powder and ammunition plants. In the future, counseled Li, new arsenals should be established at inland sites on navigable waterways to reduce their vulnerability while maintaining their access to water transport.[35] The establishment of inland arsenals not only made good strategic sense, it would actually become a necessity. The financial strictures placed on maritime defense by the decision to fund the campaign in Chinese Turkestan on a priority basis meant that the commissioners would have a difficult time developing production in coastal arsenals to meet maritime defense needs. The supply to provinces in the interior would prove beyond their capacity. Consequently, provincial authorities who did not receive ordnance support by virtue of their province's role in maritime defense would not be able to depend on the major coastal arsenals for supply. They would be obliged to establish their own arsenals or depend entirely on foreign purchase. Over the next several decades the strategic need for inland arsenals, together with the financial priorities of the new defense policy, operated to encourage the establishment of a number of provincially sponsored and financed plants at inland locations. These arsenals represented a new sector in the development of the industry beyond the purview of either the northern or southern commissioner.

CONCLUSIONS

In the years from 1872 to 1875, in the absence of a strong national consensus on national defense, Li emerged a champion of a maritime defense policy that included naval development through purchase and domestic production of selected ordnance and ammunition appropriate to China's present capabilities and his own strategic priorities. Shen shared Li's views and cooperated with him in fiscal and production planning. The imperial decision to fund the campaign in the Northwest limited the financial resources of the two commissioners for the development of munitions production, however. This limitation and the strategic reasons favoring inland arsenals would result during the next several decades in the establishment of provincial arsenals designed to meet the munitions needs of various localities which lay beyond the supply capabilities of either the northern or southern commissioner. The future of the industry seemed to be taking shape. Two authorities had been established to control and develop production in major existing plants. A third area in which production would soon develop was the vast interior, which until this time had known little strategic industry. If Li's views prevailed, and it seemed likely that they might, production emphasis throughout the industry would be on powder, ammunition, and mines, with the possible exception of Kiangnan, which was already equipped for the production of small-bore ordnance.

VI. Production Under the New Maritime Defense Policy, 1875-1885

The maritime defense policy of 1875 ushered in a new era in the growth of China's ordnance industry. Under the supervision of the northern and southern commissioners, the large coastal arsenals--Kiangnan, Tientsin, and Nanking--tooled up for production missions dictated by the new strategy. At the same time, the establishment of small arsenals and ammunition plants designed to supply areas beyond the support capabilities of the three major arsenals increased in number during the several decades after 1875, chiefly at secure inland sites. (See Appendix II.) Although fifteen such plants had been established by 1894, their output capacity was small and their logistical impact fragmented. The three major arsenals, all of which bore the clear imprint of Li Hung-chang's modernizing vision, remained the primary institutions for the production of ordnance under the new maritime defense policy.

THE KIANGNAN ARSENAL

Although the construction of new vessels at Kiangnan was suspended in 1875, the shipbuilding program died a slow and painful death. During the late 1870s the burden of steamship upkeep continued to constitute a serious drain on the arsenal's resources. By the end of January 1879, personnel and administrative expenses for the first five ships built at Kiangnan had consumed a total of 693,280 taels. The sixth ship had not been manned because of the lack of maintenance funds. In addition to this, the arsenal continued to defray the costs of fuel and repairs for vessels that it had built. In the late 1870s this amounted to about 85,000 taels per year. In 1878 Southern Commissioner Shen complained that despite straitened financial conditions at the arsenal, expenses for vessel maintenance and repair could not be cut back. Several months later Li confirmed that ship maintenance was consuming half the customs income; this was why he had directed the arsenal to halt building.[1]

Nevertheless, in 1878 the idea of building new vessels at Kiangnan cropped up again. Though Shen had yielded the south's share of the maritime defense appropriations to Northern Commissioner Li, by 1878 Li had not accumulated the funds necessary for the purchase of ironclads, the vessels to which he attached highest priority. From 1875 to 1878 the levies for the annual maritime defense appropriations that were forwarded by various provinces fell far short of the stipulated amounts, and during 1877 and 1878 those funds that were received were diverted to disaster relief. In 1878 also, Shen Pao-chen decided that southern maritime defense and naval development could no longer be sacrificed for northern naval development. The deficiencies that had resulted in the river defense forts and in the southern fleet were, in Shen's opinion, too dangerous to be tolerated any longer. He observed that since the funds necessary for ironclads for Peiyang could not be collected, Nanyang should have ten to twenty swift, wooden-hulled steamers for joint operations with the North in defense against foreign aggression. Shen's request that the South's share of the maritime defense funds be forwarded to the southern commissioner was approved. This marked the beginning of a gradual resurgence of southern naval development which eventually resulted in the construction of several more vessels at Kiangnan.[2]

The maritime defense funds provided no immediate relief for Nanyang since the provinces were delinquent in forwarding their allocations. By mid 1880 only 400,000 taels, about one-tenth of the scheduled amount, had been received since the resumption of payments to Nanyang in 1878. Nevertheless, in 1880 the first specific proposals were made for new naval acquisitions. In October P'eng Yu-lin, inspector of the Yangtze naval forces, proposed the addition of ten medium-sized steamers for defense against foreign intrusions in the Yangtze estuary. In early December Grand Secretary Mei Ch'i-ch'ao, prompted by the recent incursions by Japan and Russia, submitted his plans for strengthening naval forces. He favored a resumption of ironclad building at Kiangnan and the addition of seven medium-sized steamers for Yangtze defense.[3]

Both Li and new Southern Commissioner Liu K'un-i

(1880-1882) firmly resisted the suggestion that Kiangnan undertake ironclad construction on the grounds that the arsenal was too burdened with the production of arms, ammunition, and machinery and that it had already proven incapable of such construction. On the question of medium-sized steamers for defense of the Yangtze, Li favored Mei Ch'i-ch'ao's more modest proposal but reduced this even further by suggesting that no definite number of vessels be set and that none of the construction work be allocated to Kiangnan. Southern Commissioner Liu, on the other hand, favored construction of ten vessels as recommended by P'eng, and he assigned part of the work to Kiangnan. In 1881 Liu, together with the authorities of other concerned provinces, worked out a plan for the construction of the ten vessels proposed by P'eng in two increments of five each, two from the first increment to be built at Kiangnan. Financing was the major stumbling block. The estimated cost of each vessel was 160,000 taels, a total of 800,000 for the first increment. The Kiangnan Arsenal's income from the maritime customs was completely consumed by ordnance production and the maintenance and operation of steamships. Maritime defense funds, though still far below the scheduled amounts, offered some hope, as did the possibility of finance by the Yangtze provinces which would subsequently be guarded by these vessels. One steamer designed primarily for use on the Yangtze and along the coast was launched in 1881.[4]

The next southern commissioner, Tso Tsung-t'ang (1882-1884), emphasized southern naval development even more vigorously than Liu. He planned the addition of five cruisers, which P'eng had also suggested, as well as the ten medium-sized steamers. By late 1882, construction of one of the steamers was under way at the Kiangnan Arsenal. The original specifications of this vessel had to be enlarged when it was decided to install a 1900 horsepower compound engine.[5] When completed in 1885, the new vessel, named Pao-min, cost 223,800 taels, more than 50,000 over the original estimate. One hundred sixty thousand taels were provided from southern maritime defense funds; another 50,000 from the Kiangsu provincial treasury; and the remaining 13,800 taels from the arsenal's customs allotment. The Pao-min was constructed with steel plate and armed with eight Krupp guns which cost an additional 53,000 taels.[6] (See Appendix I Table 1.)

The brief resumption of shipbuilding at Kiangnan was based upon two factors: the policy of development of the southern fleet and the availability of maritime defense funds to finance construction. In 1885 Northern Commissioner Li again memorialized that he did not consider Kiangnan vessels suitable for use. Domestic shipbuilding, he stated, should be concentrated at Foochow. Shortly thereafter the new Navy Yamen was established and given responsibility for development of the northern fleet on a first priority basis. Li was named an associate controller and the maritime defense funds of North and South were centralized under the new yamen's control. Since the arsenal's own income by that time was entirely devoted to the production of ordnance and maintenance of ships, once more there were no funds to support construction of steamships at Kiangnan. The result was the second and final cessation of shipbuilding.[7]

The annual customs allotment, which provided the greatest part of Kiangnan's income during the decade from 1875 to 1885, fluctuated unpredictably from year to year. Sharp reductions in the customs proceeds during 1876 and 1877 diminished the arsenal's allotment from its 1875 high of 520,000 taels to about 333,000 taels. (See Appendix I Table 2.) At the same time, the Empire was experiencing severe fiscal strain as the result of natural disasters in Shansi and Honan provinces. In 1878 officials of the imperial government memorialized recommending that Kiangnan's income be temporarily reduced even further so that customs proceeds could be used for disaster relief. Southern Commissioner Shen Pao-chen replied that the arsenal was sinking into debt due to the decline in the customs allotment. It was unable to meet the needs of Nanyang and Peiyang and to maintain completed vessels. He warned that if uprisings occurred in the disaster area, the need for arms could become critical and Kiangnan might be unable to meet it. Furthermore, forts had been constructed along the lower Yangtze but they had not been equipped with ordnance. Shen was temporarily successful in saving the arsenal's already diminished income from further reductions. In 1879, however, the customs allotment was reduced by administrative fiat: 50,000 taels were alloted annually to support operation of the Nanking Arsenal.[8]

Nevertheless, income from the customs increased gradually after 1877. In 1880 it again reached its level of 1875, and in 1881 it soared to more than 650,000 taels. The next year it again dropped sharply by more than 125,000 taels, and in 1883 declined still further to 438,000 taels. Meanwhile, a sharp increase in miscellaneous income--a total of 747,844 taels from 1881 to 1885--augmented the customs allotment. (See Appendix I Table 2.) The exact source of these funds is uncertain; it is probable that the allocations from southern maritime defense funds and from Kiangsu province for the construction of the Pao-min during 1883 and 1884 were included in this figure.[9] At any rate, miscellaneous income received during this five-year period when the southern commissioner controlled southern maritime defense appropriations was more than five times the amount received during the previous five years, suggesting that the southern commissioner employed maritime defense funds to augment the arsenal's customs allotment. The decline in miscellaneous income after 1885 when maritime defense funds were centralized under the Navy Yamen would seem to support this suggestion. Whatever the source, the increase in miscellaneous income in the period from 1881 to 1885 resulted in a much higher, but still very unstable, overall income despite the drastic reductions in the customs allotment during 1882 and 1883.

Increases in staff and administrative personnel during this decade siphoned off some of this income. In 1881 the gunnery school established in 1874 was converted to an artillery battalion organic to the arsenal. The following year the personnel complement of this organization was increased by more than three hundred gunnery trainees. At about the same time it was reported that the number of officials employed at the arsenal had increased from the forty or fifty during the 1870s to about eighty or ninety.[10]

By the early 1880s the administrative system that Tseng Kuo-fan had devised to insure probity in the expenditure of the arsenal's funds seems to have gone awry, probably causing further leakage of financial resources. In 1883 one of the directors reported to Southern Commissioner Tso Tsung-t'ang that those who were doing the purchasing were accepting squeeze (chung-pao). Tso eliminated the purchasing office and set up a bidding office (pao-chia ch'u). When the arsenal needed materials, sealed bids were invited from merchants. Though public bidding temporarily eliminated malpractices that had crept into the purchasing system, eventually the process of bidding degenerated into an open auction. Finally, the bidding office was done away with and a bargaining office (i-chia-ch'u) was created in its place. Details of the purchasing system in the bargaining office are unclear. Malpractices associated with the purchase of materials at the arsenal appeared again, but it was several years later, during the late 1880s, before specific instances were reported.[11]

How Kiangnan's huge, unstable income would be used

was determined chiefly by the southern commissioner. Northern Commissioner Li, however, continued to exert a degree of influence due to the cooperative relationship that he enjoyed with Southern Commissioner Shen Pao-chen in the years from 1875 to 1879 and his long standing relationship with the arsenal. During this decade the imperial government also tried in several ways to strengthen its hand vis-a-vis the commissioners not only at Kiangnan but at the other major arsenals as well. In 1878 the Tsungli Yamen proposed that standards be adopted for munitions employed throughout the Empire, a measure long overdue in an era when arsenal industry was proliferating. One feature of this plan was the appointment of a special official to exercise command over China's two largest arsenals, Kiangnan and Tientsin, and insure that their operations were closely coordinated. The proposal was referred to the commissioners for comment. Northern Commissioner Li replied that the operations of the arsenals were already closely correlated, and in the future new products would be sent to the commissioners for inspection. He assured the throne that the two commissioners would be very discriminating and insist on improvement. Li felt that there was no need to appoint another official to serve as a munitions czar, a function that he saw as his own. Subsequent to Li's recommendations, there was no further discussion of this plan.[12]

In 1883 the imperial government again took steps to extend its control; this time the plan was to put arsenal expenditures under closer scrutiny through a more detailed system of financial reporting. An edict directed that the annual financial reports from the arsenals should include the costs of new equipment (which were to be reported to the imperial government for approval before purchasing), labor, and construction. Kiangnan requested a delay in making its 1883 report due to the confusion at the arsenal during the war years. The report was finally submitted in 1887. It included several new categories of expenses as directed by the edict, and it was accompanied by detailed statements of accounts which went to the boards of Revenue, Public Works, and War. Starting with the year 1883, then, the imperial government received a clear, detailed accounting of the expenditure of funds at Kiangnan. But the reports were received so late that they could not serve as a basis for any timely steps toward enforcing economy or regulating expenditure at the arsenal. The 1884 report was not submitted until 1891, and the one for 1885 was submitted only in 1892.[13]

Among the various categories of operations supported by Kiangnan's income, capital construction played only a minor role during this decade. By 1875 most of the shops required for shipbuilding and production of ordnance and ammunition were completed, excepting only those required for heavy rifled ordnance, gun ammunition, and mines. Consequently, from 1876 on capital construction was limited to supplying these deficiencies, with one important exception: the construction of a new facility for storage of the arsenal's strategic reserves. In 1876 Director Li Hsing-jui announced plans to build a magazine at Sungkiang and to store 10,000 pounds of powder as well as surplus cartridges there each month in order to offset some of the strategic weaknesses inherent in Kiangnan's location in Shanghai. The Sungkiang site offered several advantages. First, if hostile vessels controlled the lower Yangtze, distribution of powder to forts up the river via inland waterways was more feasible from Sungkiang than it was from Shanghai. Second, Sungkiang was a more secure location than Shanghai for storage of strategic reserves. The shallow water approaches to the city would not admit the deep-draft foreign naval vessels that could easily reach Shanghai. The terrain surrounding Sungkiang rendered it less exposed than Shanghai and easier to defend against infantry attacks. The Sungkiang Magazine was completed during 1876 or 1877.[14]

As Kiangnan's steamship program sputtered to a halt during the decade, the arsenal's financial resources were increasingly devoted to turning out arms and ammunition, a category of production that depended heavily on costly imported materials. This growing specialization in ordnance and munitions virtually ruled out large-scale production of machinery for civilian sectors of the economy. Machine building was for the most part limited to general purpose equipment and types essential to military production. Machine tools, metal processing equipment, water pumps, lifting apparatus, power transmission gear, and engines were built for employment at Kiangnan, as was more specialized equipment for ordnance and ammunition production such as machinery for molding, iron cutting, rolling brass and lead, testing iron, bullet production, and powder making.[15]

The modernization of heavy ordnance and gun ammunition production was by far the most important category of operations. Although gun making had been directed by a staff of foreign technicians prior to 1875, the only usable guns turned out were small, smoothbore, iron and brass cannon, which were already obsolete by Western standards.[16] Li depended primarily on the Nanking Arsenal for cast iron ordnance. He recognized, however, that the guns made at Nanking were no substitute for the steel ordnance that was being produced in the West. By 1875 he had purchased more than fifty rifled steel breechloaders from Krupp. But for strength and durability he preferred the rifled muzzle-loaders built up with wrought iron such as those made by the Armstrong Company of Great Britain.[17] In April 1875 he ordered four new Armstrong gunboats, two mounting twenty-six and one-half ton rifled guns and two mounting thirty-eight ton rifled guns, at a cost of 450,000 taels. Li bemoaned the high price of foreign guns but felt that the cost of domestic production would be even higher. He advised against it until domestic coal and iron mines could be opened and operated on Western methods so that supply costs might be reduced.[18]

The tragic explosion of the two Nanking-built guns at Taku in January 1875 created a dilemma for the advocates of heavy ordnance production in China. It was clear from the investigation that domestically produced iron or brass guns could not withstand the powder charges necessary to propel the heavy projectiles required for coastal defense fire.[19] Although this problem had been solved in the West through the introduction of steel barrels and steel built up with wrought iron, Li Hung-chang regarded the equipment and materials necessary for domestic production of these types as prohibitively expensive. During the next three years a combination of domestic requirements and external stimuli completely altered this opinion. By 1878 the production of heavy ordnance occupied the most important position in the operations of the Kiangnan Arsenal, and modernization, from that time on, was largely concerned with the improvement of gun production.

The requirements of the new maritime defense policy prevented Li from completely abandoning the idea of modern gun production. In late 1875 he memorialized that Kiangnan was considering converting to production of rifled steel-barreled muzzle-loaders built up with wrought iron. "Guns," he observed, "are more effective than rifles in countering foreign aggression. Even though ours cannot have the enormous destructive power of Western models, we should still strive for improvement and make every effort so that our ships and forts do not become useless [for want of proper ordnance]."[20]

The first steps were taken the following year when John Mackenzie, superintendent of the Armstrong Company's gun plant in Newcastle, was engaged to introduce the production of steel barreled muzzle-loaders built up with wrought iron at the Kiangnan Arsenal. When Mackenzie arrived in China he found that in the aftermath of the Taku tragedy Li Hung-chang and many other leading officials still had grave doubts that modern heavy ordnance could be produced in China by Chinese artisans. According to one Western employee, there was a mood of crisis among the Western and Chinese personnel at the arsenal based upon their understanding that Li was considering recommending to the throne that Kiangnan halt operations.[21] The old Chinese and Western employees urged MacKenzie to show results in production of the new guns as soon as possible. Even if the quality was not the best, as long as the guns did not blow up, they felt that demonstrated results would improve the chances for continued operation of the arsenal. But officials at the arsenal were pessimistic about the future of its operations and skeptical of Mackenzie's ability. They reported to the director that the Englishman talked big but was not necessarily any better than the foreigners who had preceded him. Mackenzie accepted all this as a personal challenge as well as a challenge to British expertise in the field of ordnance production. He set resolutely to work directing the Chinese artisans in the new methods involved in making built-up ordnance--determined to show results at the earliest possible date. There were several technological factors in his favor. The facilities for shipbuilding at Kiangnan already included the steam hammer and wrought-iron shop required for the production of steel barrels built up with wrought iron.[22]

Meanwhile, in 1877 the need for fort guns in Nanyang became critical and maritime defense funds were not available to the southern commissioner to purchase them. In that year, Southern Commissioner Shen reported that Nanyang forts were short twenty-one guns and more than thirty more brass and cast-iron cannon required replacement with steel ordnance. Since the southern commissioner's maritime defense allocation, from 1875 on, had been going to Peiyang, Shen requested permission to retain the remaining 20 percent of the imperial government's share of the Shanghai customs proceeds to purchase the required ordnance. But this 20 percent was already being channeled to meet crucially important needs, the maritime defense funds and support of the forces of Tso Tsung-t'ang battling the Moslem Rebellion in Sinkiang. Consequently, the plan never materialized.23

During 1877 also, production of the new type of gun at Kiangnan showed signs of progress. Before Mackenzie had been at the arsenal very long, more than ten were nearing completion. By late spring of that year production facilities for the new process were completed and artisans were trained. Against this background of critical need for fort guns in Nanyang, severely restricted availability of maritime defense funds, and signs of progress in the domestic production of Armstrongs at Kiangnan, in the summer of 1878 Li wrote to Southern Commissioner Shen that the Kiangnan Arsenal should concentrate its production on supplying the deficiencies of the river defense forts in guns and ammunition. He followed this with a memorial stating that muzzle-loading guns were more stable and durable than breechloaders and therefore better for ships and forts. He recommended the Armstrong as one of the best of these and reported that since steamship production had been halted at Kiangnan due to high cost of vessel upkeep, the arsenal would begin producing Armstrongs. In 1878 the arsenal's steam hammer shop was officially converted to a gun plant.24

Two of the new guns of six-inch caliber firing a forty pound projectile were test fired in December 1878 with completely satisfactory results. It was reported that these guns were equal to those produced in the West. The entire production process had been performed by Chinese artisans. The next year they were tested with double charges of powder and showed no weakness. Meanwhile, the arsenal's steam hammer was already at work on a larger model of the same design. This was the seven-inch caliber 120 pounder, completed and successfully test fired in the summer of 1880. In the following year, a seven-inch caliber 150 pounder was produced. By 1889 the caliber had been increased to eight inches and the weight of the projectile to 180 pounds. All of these guns were based on the Armstrong model of a muzzle loading, rifled, steel barrel built up with wrought iron.25 In 1879 a new gun ammunition plant was established and the production of shot and shell for the Armstrong ordnance was initiated.26 (See Appendix I Table 3.)

Though these new guns received lavish praise from the local British and Chinese press, in the context of the rapidly developing ordnance technology of the nineteenth century they were already obsolete. The six-inch forty pounder, for example, was short and the built up feature made it thick around the chamber. The concentration of weight in the base made it more difficult to manipulate than the breechloaders favored by most Western nations. The black powder with which it was fired had a rapid burning speed, which diminished the sustained thrust applied to the projectile and reduced the muzzle velocity. Because of its great weight it required the strength of several men to return it to firing position after recoil. In what seems to have been an overreaction to the Taku fiasco of 1875, Kiangnan had adopted production of an ordnance piece that was characterized by strength and therefore safety, but its bulk made it difficult to operate and thus restricted its fire power. Furthermore, its great weight limited its use entirely to coastal defense forts. During the war with France, Kiangnan had to resume the production of the old-style smoothbore cannon to provide guns with the degree of mobility required for ground warfare.[27]

By 1881 the Kiangnan Remington had also been outmoded by recent advances in Western small arms. Northern Commissioner Li reported that units under his command were no longer willing to accept them. In 1884 a new model of Remington was introduced, slightly longer and heavier than the previous one. The bore diameter was reduced and the muzzle velocity increased, giving the bullet greater striking force. The main improvement was a new firing mechanism and cartridge case already widely used in the West. The firing pin now struck a primer located in the center of the cartridge base rather than on the rim, thus greatly reducing the likelihood of misfire.[28] In 1890, however, it was reported that the center fire Remington, as the new rifle was called, frequently emitted a breech blast when fired, indicating that the breech mechanism or bolt was defective. Troop units had been unwilling to use it and 12,000 or 13,000 out of the 15,000 produced since 1884 were still in storage in Shanghai and Nanking. The director of the Kiangnan Arsenal recommended that these weapons be made usable by equipping each with a shield to protect the rifleman from the breech blast. The cost of work and materials required to modify each rifle was 2 taels, or 20,000 to 30,000 taels for all of those in storage. The northern and southern commissioners both approved the plans for modifying the center fire Remington, but by this time further advances in small arms technology had outmoded these weapons also. It was anticipated that the shield equipped rifles would be satisfactory only for routine peacetime training.[29]

As Chinese armies began discarding their Kiangnan

Remingtons in favor of superior imported rifles, a demand was created for new types of rifle ammunition. In 1882 Kiangnan began production of Mauser cartridges, and by 1885 cartridges for Lee and Snider rifles were also being produced. Meanwhile, the arsenal continued to make the ammunition for the Remingtons still in use. Since Kiangnan did not produce cartridge machinery itself, the diversification in cartridge production resulted in increased expenditures for new machinery beginning in 1880.[30] (See Appendix I Table 5.)

In 1881 a new mine shop was established at Kaoch'ang Miao and the production of electrically detonated naval mines was begun.[31] In 1884 it was reported that electrically activated torpedoes were made at the Lung-hua powder plant, which was still under the direction of a foreign supervisor.[32]

The largest share of the arms and ammunition distributed from the Kiangnan Arsenal during the decade from 1875 to 1885 went to ships and units subordinate to the southern commissioner. Five of the ships involved in the naval battle with the French at Ma-wei had been equipped at Kiangnan; the Kiangnan-built Yü-yüan was sunk. The remaining distribution in Nanyang went to forts along the lower reaches of the Yangtze and depots and units located in the Liangkiang provinces.[33] (See Appendix I Table 4.)

Units subordinate to the commissioner of northern ports also received arms and ammunition distributed from Kiangnan during these years, but no vessels of the Peiyang fleet were supplied with Kiangnan products.[34] (See Appendix I Table 4.) Although there was a sharp decline in shipments to Peiyang after 1880, it cannot be inferred from this that Li Hung-chang had lost his power to command a share of the arsenal's production. An examination of the shipments from Kiangnan to Peiyang prior to 1881 shows that the most important items were Remington rifles and cartridges. In early 1881 Li expressed his dissatisfaction with the obsolete Kiangnan Remington and the Tientsin Arsenal drastically cut back its production of Remington cartridges and converted to making Mauser ammunition. This type was not produced at Kiangnan until 1882, and then the quantity was only about 10 percent of that made at Tientsin. Moreover, in overall production of powder, mines, rifle cartridges, and gun ammunition, the Tientsin Arsenal was far ahead of Kiangnan. With the exception of the new Armstrong coastal defense guns, Li did not want or need the items made at the Kiangnan Arsenal. He was interested in the Armstrongs, however, and these continued to be sent to Peiyang after other distribution stopped. Eight of the forty-pounders were sent in 1880, four of the one hundred twenty-pounders in 1881, and five more of the latter in 1882.[35]

Distribution to areas other than Nanyang and Peiyang began in 1883 but reached significant quantities only in 1884 and 1885. In early 1884 Director Shao Yu-lien reported that Kiangnan was under extreme pressure to meet the demands created by the defense crisis with France. In addition to providing all the needs of Kiangsu province, the arsenal was supplying Kwangsi, Yunnan, Fukien, Chekiang, and Kiangsi provinces, Peiyang, and Taiwan, and it was equipping units that were being transferred into the war zone. Still, the production of Kiangnan as well as that of the other Chinese arsenals fell far short of meeting the requirements of the Chinese forces during the Sino-French War. After the war, Liangkwang Governor-General Chang Chih-tung, who shouldered a great part of the responsibility for supply of Chinese forces, reported that due to the scarcity of ordnance he had spent enormous sums in Europe and the United States to supply the Chinese side with good weapons. Late in 1885 an edict addressed to Southern Commissioner Tseng Kuo-ch'üan (1894-1890) and other provincial leaders observed that in the previous year a total of 840,000 taels had been spent at the Kiangnan, Foochow, and Kwangtung arsenals; still, much of the ordnance required for the Chinese forces had to be separately purchased.[36]

At the time of the Sino-French War, the most critical deficiencies in Kiangnan's production were in modern field artillery and small arms. Large-scale, modernized production of these ordnance items would have required new technicians and new equipment. The latter, at prevailing rates in the 1880s, would have cost more than 380,000 taels.[37] Despite its vast financial resources, Kiangnan was unable to meet this expense. In fact, when income increased sharply after 1880, production stagnated. The continuing costs of steamship maintenance and the notion, which died slowly on the part of the southern commissioners, that the arsenal's facilities would be used for the construction of small steamers weakened the arsenal financially during the transition to ordnance production. Furthermore, resources that could have been used for the acquisition of urgently needed ordnance machinery were swallowed up by the costs of current production. The cost of materials--most of which came from abroad--consumed the greatest portion of Kiangnan's resources, about 41 percent. (See Appendix I Table 5.) The root problem here was the underdevelopment of the domestic coal, iron, and steel industries. Li had alluded to this fact in 1874; it still prevailed in 1885. Material costs were also driven upward by purchasing malpractices among lower officials.

Another 34 percent of expenditures was devoted to personnel costs.[38] (See Appendix I Table 5.) Though high personnel costs have been observed in the early modern munitions industries in other countries, such as Japan and the United States, in these countries high costs were accompanied by high productivity.[39] At Kiangnan this was not the case. Gunnery trainees increased by more than 300 during these years. There was also a sharp increase in official personnel, though it is entirely unclear what they were doing. Official salaries almost doubled, from 38,000 taels to more than 70,000 taels per year during the decade. Foreign personnel were another important expense factor. Kiangnan still had to rely on new foreign technicians to update production, and such well established areas as powder making remained under foreign supervision. Though the arsenal paid dearly for foreign technicians (20,000 to 30,000 thousand taels annually), the foreigners did not bring the excellence in production that the arsenal's supervisors sought.[40]

The cost of current production and personnel consumed 75 percent of Kiangnan's resources. The remainder was devoted to building, equipment purchases, munitions purchases, and translation. The arsenal had been unable to concentrate its huge, unstable income to solve the technological problems involved in the production of field artillery and rifles. If every tael spent for the acquisition of new equipment during this decade (about 310,000 taels) had been used for the purchase of the rifle and field artillery machinery needed to remedy production deficiencies, the amount still would have fallen far short of the estimated cost of 380,000 taels. In addition, more funds would have been needed for new technicians, materials, and buildings. The high cost of operating a modern machine industry in an underdeveloped economic setting had sapped Kiangnan of financial strength and prevented the capital investments necessary to modernize production for maritime defense.

THE NANKING ARSENAL AND POWDER PLANT

The maritime defense edict of May 1875 also placed the Nanking Arsenal under the nominal control of the southern commissioner. Actually, until 1879 this plant was almost entirely controlled by Northern Commissioner Li, who had founded it and continued to provide a large part of the funds needed to sustain production from the budget of the Huai Army. Until 1879 also, the Wu-lung Shan Arsenal at Nanking was controlled by its founder, the southern commissioner. In that year the two plants were consolidated and a joint North-South financing plan went into effect. This provided regular annual income of 100,000 taels, 50,000 from the 20 percent of the Shanghai maritime customs proceeds that supplied the Kiangnan Arsenal, 30,000 from southern maritime defense funds, and 20,000 from the Yangchow quartermaster of the Huai Army. Of the 50,000 taels provided by the Shanghai maritime customs, 30,000 were previously designated for Peiyang. The 20,000 taels provided by the Yangchow quartermaster of the Huai Army were also Peiyang funds. The remainder was from Nanyang.[41] The definition of financial responsibilities was probably related to the return of the southern maritime defense appropriation to Nanyang which had taken place the previous year. Although support of the arsenal was shared by North and South, from 1879 until 1885 financial reports submitted to Peking were signed by the southern commissioner, signifying that formal supervisory responsibility had passed to Nanyang.[42]

In 1884 regular annual income was increased by 10,000 taels: 5,000 from local defense funds to defray production costs for munitions needed by the Huai Army units stationed in Kiangsu and 5,000 from maritime defense funds to defray production costs for ordnance required by river defense forts. In addition to this regular income, small sums were received for ordnance provided to other provinces. In 1881-1882 the southern commissioner additionally allocated 56,047 taels to the arsenal for purchase of equipment and materials necessary to increase production of mines, fuses, and percussion caps for the Kiangnan forts. Annual income for the period 1879 to 1885 ranged from 100,000 to as high as 150,000 taels.[43] (See Appendix I Table 7.)

When the arsenal first joined with the Wu-lung Shan plant, it consisted of three machine shops, two molding shops, two wrought-iron shops, and two carpentry shops. By 1885 facilities had expanded to include a small arms ammunition plant, a plant for production of rifled guns, machinery for working brass, and another carpentry shop. A branch arsenal for the production of electrically detonated mines was established in 1877 under the supervision of foreign advisors. But in 1879 when the foreigners' contracts expired, financial limitations prohibited renewal; the following year the branch arsenal was closed and converted to a school for the study of electricity. Thereafter the only foreigners at the Nanking Arsenal were those dispatched periodically from Kiangnan. Meanwhile, from 1874 to 1881 the Chinese work force at the arsenal swelled from 200 to between 700 and 800 and costs for personnel and administration rose to between 40 and 50 percent of overall expenditure annually.[44]

In the early 1880s Nanking was producing guns, mines (of dubious quality), foreign-style small arms, gingals, gun mounts, gun ammunition, percussion caps, Gatling guns, and four-barreled one inch caliber Nordenfeldts. Production depended on costly, imported coal. Distribution was to defense forces in both Nanyang and Peiyang and to river defense forts. Like the Kiangnan Arsenal, Nanking broke its normal pattern of distribution during the war years. Starting in late July or in August 1884, Nanking distributed seventy pieces of medium and light ordnance and one hundred gingals to Kwangtung, Yunnan, Chekiang, Taiwan, Hupeh, and Kiangsi.[45]

While the Nanking Arsenal supplied an assortment of ordnance items to units of the Huai Army, it produced no powder. Through 1878 Huai Army units stationed in the Liangkiang provinces were dependent on the Tientsin Arsenal for supply of 200,000 to 300,000 pounds of black powder and a million or more percussion caps annually. Shortly thereafter the Kiangnan Arsenal probably assumed responsibility for this supply. But in 1881 Southern Commissioner Liu K'un-i found that Kiangnan's powder output was inadequate for the needs of the various defense forces stationed in the Liangkiang provinces, among which the Huai Army units figured prominently. The cost of foreign powder was prohibitive. Consequently, late in that year Liu assigned Kung Chao-yüan, director of the Nanking Arsenal, and another official to establish a powder plant east of the arsenal in the vicinity of Shuang-ch'iao Gate.[46]

Machinery capable of turning out 1,000 pounds of black powder daily was purchased from a British firm and installed under the supervision of a Mr. Bracegirdle. Establishment was completed in 1884 at a cost of 182,895 taels, provided from local defense funds and maritime defense appropriations. The southern commissioner had complete control. From the beginning of production in June 1884, regular operating funds of 40,000 taels were provided annually from local defense funds. (See Appendix I Table 8.) Initial production was intended for forces stationed in Kiangsu. It is uncertain whether the powder produced at Nanking beginning in June 1884 ever reached Chinese units in the Sino-French War.[47]

The record at the Nanking Arsenal was far less impressive than that at Kiangnan. Income was small, production limited, and logistical importance marginal. While Kiangnan had converted to heavy ordnance production, at Nanking the transition had been from foreign to Chinese management and from northern to southern control. Overhead was even higher than that at Kiangnan and at Nanking the commitment to excellence in production, which motivated the struggle for modernization at Kiangnan, seemed to be missing. The reasons for this do not emerge easily from the record. It is probable, however, that one factor was the withdrawal of foreign advisers in 1879; thereafter, the management and staff seemed to lose touch with the requirement for continuous modernization of production. The result was the simultaneous production of outmoded gingals and Gatling guns. The one ray of hope at Nanking was the powder plant, which tooled up quickly with new foreign machinery in the mid 1880s to produce the powder requirements for the Huai Army and other defense forces in the Liangkiang provinces.

THE TIENTSIN ARSENAL

The maritime defense edict also confirmed Northern Commissioner Li Hung-chang's exclusive control over the Tientsin Arsenal. While Nanking turned out a variety of small and medium caliber guns, the Tientsin Arsenal was an important producer of powder, ammunition, and mines. Operations at Tientsin during this decade reflected the strategy that Li had expressed in his maritime defense memorial of late 1874--that the purchase of expensive ordnance machinery should be delayed until sources of domestic raw materials had been developed so that operating costs might be kept down.

The mainstay of the arsenal's income was 40 percent of the Tientsin and Chefoo customs proceeds. After the 1873 establishment of China's first commercial steamship line, the China Merchants' Steam Navigation Company, income was augmented by an allocation of 40 percent of the tax levied on the foreign trade carried by these ships. But, as Li explained in 1878, this was no real increase. China Merchant ships did not carry much foreign cargo until 1876, when the company bought the vessels of the Russel Steamship Line and took over their trade. The taxes on cargoes carried by the line disappeared from the customs income and reappeared in levies on China Merchants' cargoes. Even with the levies from the China Merchants' Company, the total annual income from maritime commerce taxes in 1878 was only 160,000 to 170,000 taels. Customs income was supplemented from maritime defense funds from 1876 through 1881, and subsequently from northwest frontier defense appropriations and munitions sales to various provinces. The total annual income of the Tientsin Arsenal rose from less than 250,000 taels in 1876 to more than 350,000 taels by 1885.[48] (See Appendix I Table 6.)

The most important fact about the income of the Tientsin Arsenal was its size. The operating funds available to China's second largest arsenal were only one-third to one-half as great as those available to the largest. Second, Tientsin drew its support from diverse sources. Though the maritime customs of Tientsin and Chefoo provided income to the arsenal each year, in order to maintain total annual income at 300,000 taels it was necessary for Li to raise more than 100,000 taels from other sources.

This income supported both regular production and modernization of facilities at the Tientsin Arsenal. By 1876 production facilities were complete and the arsenal entered a four year period of what might be termed "normal" operations. That is, from 1876 through 1879, Tientsin employed an average annual income of 236,440 taels derived from customs income and Peiyang maritime defense funds chiefly for the production of powder and ammunition. Annual output, from 1876 through 1879, averaged 1,443,500 rounds of small arms ammunition, 36,265,000 percussion caps and other firing devices, 69,000 pounds of gun ammunition, and 609,000 pounds of powder. A total of 520 rifles and 650 mines were also produced during the four year period. These munitions were regularly distributed to Peiyang maritime defense depots, to elements of the Huai and Lien armies in Chihli and Shantung, to forces transferred to other provinces for defense, and to expeditionary forces in Jehol, Chahar, Fengtien, Kirin, and Heilungkiang provinces. Until 1879, 200,000 to 300,000 pounds of black powder and one million percussion caps were shipped annually to Huai Army units in the Kiangnan provinces. Each year the arsenal also supplied provincial governments with small amounts of munitions upon request, for which it received separate compensation.[49]

Modernization continued during these years, but

it was characterized by adjustments or improvements rather than sweeping changes. Production of rifle ammunition began to replace percussion caps, a natural consequence of the increased use of breechloading small arms. Production of Remington rifles was halted in 1879 because production cost was much higher than purchase price. A facility for the production of electrically detonated mines was established in 1876 under the supervision of foreign instructors. The mines that were turned out were usable. Other electrical devices were also made--the first such production in China. In 1879 a sulphur reduction plant was added.[50] The cost of carrying out these improvements was not great; nothing was spent for new equipment. Building costs consumed less than 5 percent of total expenditure, but 59 percent was used for purchase of materials, slightly more than half of which came from abroad. Personnel costs consumed the remainder, about 36 percent. Domestic personnel expenses continued to increase, while those for foreigners showed a slight decrease. This trend continued during 1880 and 1881.[51]

From 1876 through 1879, for the existing income and technological conditions, the arsenal was producing at full capacity. After 1880 Li Hung-chang attempted to increase income and improve technological conditions in order to increase output, expand distribution, and modernize. In October 1880 the arsenal was granted additional income of 10,000 taels each month from the northwest frontier defense funds in order to produce munitions for Pao Ch'ao's Ting Army, which was deployed from Tientsin to the Shan-hai-kuan against a threatened Russian invasion following the Chinese rejection of the Treaty of Livadia. When the Ting Army was disbanded in the winter of 1881, the monthly allocation was continued to support production of ammunition for border defense at Ku-lun and in Chahar and Jehol. In 1882, in addition to its regular supply to Peiyang maritime defense units and the Huai and Lien armies, the Tientsin Arsenal sent large shipments of powder and ammunition to the Chinese forces occupying Tarbagatai in the northwest and to a Chinese military advisory group in Korea. Twenty lathes were built for the small arsenal established by the Peking Field Forces. The next year Li was successful in obtaining some of the frontier defense funds to support production of munitions for the new ships of the Peiyang Navy. This allocation continued when production of munitions for Peiyang units and the provinces was stepped up in 1884 and 1885 in preparation for a threatened French attack in the north.[52]

While this struggle to increase production and expand distribution was in progress, several important steps were taken to update the facilities for powder and ammunition production. By 1881 a nitric acid soaking plant for the production of guncotton was built. This new explosive was twice as powerful as that produced earlier, and it would facilitate future production of slow burning powders. The following year a new plant for the production of acids was added. The arsenal also conducted or promoted modernization activities in related fields. In 1881 the study of electricity at the Mine Bureau resulted in the establishment of specialized schools for the study of mines and telegraphy and in that year a naval academy designed to meet the manpower needs of the new Peiyang Navy was holding classes at the arsenal.[53]

Li attempted to increase domestic raw material supply through the use of machinery to extract natural resources in North China, though it is not clear how much of this, if any, was financed by the arsenal. As early as 1874 Tientsin began buying coal domestically. In 1883 Wang Te-chun of the Tientsin Arsenal introduced pumping machinery to the coal mines at I-hsien in Shantung. This site was located about twenty-five miles from the Grand Canal, and Li anticipated that the high grade coal, extracted after the water was removed from the mines, could serve the arsenals and steamships of both Nanyang and Peiyang. In 1882 Li encouraged the use of pumping machinery to restore the copper veins at P'ing-ch'uan in Chihli in order to fill the arsenal's needs from there rather than by foreign purchase. This was to be a government supervised enterprise financed by merchant capital. Supply of copper from P'ing-ch'uan had not been developed by late 1884, however, when it was reported that the arsenal's wartime production was adversely affected by the stoppage in copper movement from South China due to the war. Other metals were purchased from abroad at least until 1881 and probably thereafter.[54]

There was also a very limited shipbuilding program at Hai-kuang Szu. In the early 1880s the first vessel, a dredge, was completed. Subsequent reports indicated that its operation was quite effective. By 1882 two 82-foot mine layers with 130 horsepower engines had been completed.[55]

Production at Tientsin seems to have been relatively successful, though output figures are lacking after 1879. Under the watchful eye of Northern Commissioner Li, limited financial resources were concentrated on production of the powder and ammunition that supplied forces from Korea to the far northwest. Small arms production was halted; heavy ordnance production was never begun; and costs for foreign advisers were reduced. A beginning was made in production of electrical equipment, and modern industrial techniques were introduced by arsenal personnel to related sectors of the economy. It seems fair to say that the soundness of the strategy, which Li Hung-chang had advocated in his maritime defense memorial of 1874, to concentrate on powder and ammunition production and to delay the production of heavy rifled ordnance until domestic raw material industries had been modernized was demonstrated by the achievements of the Tientsin Arsenal.

CONCLUSIONS

In the decade prior to the Sino-French War, production in the arsenals subordinate to the northern and southern commissioners had developed unevenly. In 1885 Kiangnan was the only plant in China producing modern ordnance; the annual output included a few usable but obsolescent coastal defense guns and several thousand partially defective rifles, but Kiangnan did not produce modern artillery suitable for use by ground forces. This area of production was covered by the Nanking Arsenal, where a variety of nondescript small and medium caliber guns as well as the relatively new Gatling gun and the premodern gingal were turned out. Powder, various types of cartridges, and gun ammunition were successfully produced at the giant powder factory of the Tientsin Arsenal and at the Lung-hua plant at Kiangnan. The Nanking Arsenal, with its newly established powder plant, turned out black powder, percussion caps for muzzle-loading small arms, and various types of gun ammunition.

As the arsenals took on discrete production missions and came under the separate control of the northern and southern commissioners, the need for overall coordination in the industry became more critical. At the beginning of the decade Li seemed entirely up to the task of planning arsenal operations with the southern commissioner, as seen in the arrangement for joint financing at Nanking. This changed somewhat as Kiangnan and Nanking went their separate ways more and more in the 1880s. The results in the Nanyang arsenals were far from encouraging. Furthermore, the related problem of standardizing munitions and munitions machinery throughout China was potentially important. Li had recognized this and attempted to deal with it a decade earlier at Tientsin, but he and the southern commissioner now sidestepped the imperial government's efforts to enforce uniform standards between Nanyang and Peiyang. Nonstandardization in the armed forces had already necessitated the production of several types of cartridges at Kiangnan and would become a problem internal to the arsenals, involving both equipment and ordnance, plaguing the industry well into the twentieth century.

VII. The Modernization of Ordnance and Ammunition Production, 1885-1895

The inadequacy of China's military preparations became obvious during the Sino-French War, giving rise to a spate of reform proposals. Representative of these was the memorial of Hanlin Compiler Chu I-hsin submitted in October 1884. Chu urged that new arsenals be established at secure inland sites on navigable waterways to avoid repetition of the disaster that had occurred several months earlier when the French fleet bombarded the Foochow Dockyard. Partly as a result of this suggestion and other similar ones, the establishment of inland arsenals proceeded during the next decade but still with no great impact on China's logistical potential.[1] (See Appendix II.)

Chu's memorial involved another precedent-shattering suggestion, however. He proposed that capital for arsenal development could be raised by allowing wealthy private individuals to form companies after the fashion of Krupp or Martini-Henry but with strict government supervision and no private sales. The idea was referred to Governor-General of Hunan and Hupeh Pien Pao-ti for comment, since Chu had suggested that Hupeh might be a suitable location for such a plant. Pien sought the counsel of his colleague Tseng Kuo-ch'üan, who had been appointed southern commissioner and governor-general of the Liangkiang provinces earlier in 1884. Tseng was entirely opposed to the use of private capital, expressing the view that since there was no market for arms in China other than the government, private capital could easily be wasted. More significantly, he feared that it would be difficult to insure that private sales would not be transacted and that arms would not reach the hands of unlawful elements. Finally, he cautioned that the greed of the merchant community would likely result in slighting quality for the sake of profit, which could have disastrous results in time of emergency. Pien succumbed to this reasoning and no more was heard about private financing in the ordnance industry until China had endured the shock of a far more devastating defeat in 1895.[2]

For the next decade, reforms were guided by less revolutionary impulses. The imperial government, recoiling from the crippling naval defeat inflicted by the French at Ma-wei in August 1884, moved to centralize control over naval operations and logistics by establishing the Navy Yamen in 1885. It was headed by Prince Ch'un, father of the Emperor. To finance the establishment of a new navy, the maritime defense appropriations were taken from the control of the commissioners and centralized under the Navy Yamen. Northern Commissioner Li Hung-chang was appointed to serve concurrently as associate controller of the Navy Yamen; the maritime defense funds of both North and South once more came under his direction. Furthermore, an edict of May 1887 stipulating that all purchases of machinery or allocations of funds by provinces for purposes related to maritime defense should have the prior approval of the Navy Yamen had the effect of restoring Li to his old position as cosupervisor of the Nanyang arsenals.[3] Plans for modernization were again sent to Li as well as to the southern commissioner for approval, and, pursuant to naval regulations, Li recommended arsenal personnel to the throne for awards.

In the provinces, jarred by the inability of China's arsenals to meet logistic needs during the war and exhorted by imperial decree, the northern and southern commissioners and other leaders introduced modernization measures calculated to stimulate production and reduce dependence on costly imported materials in the arsenals under their supervision. The most striking development in this respect was the giant Hanyang Arsenal, plans for which began to take shape in 1885. Hanyang represented a new concept of strategic industrialization involving the balanced development of raw material industries, personnel, and ordnance production--and a new arsenal builder, Chang Chih-tung. But the Hanyang Arsenal belongs to another era for it did not enter production until 1895 and made no logistical contribution to the Chinese side during the Sino-Japanese War (1894-1895). Although the struggle to get Hanyang into production was part of China's self-strengthening efforts prior to the war, it was essentially the prologue to a new chapter in the development of China's ordnance industry, a chapter that unfolded after the war.[4] In the decade prior to the war, the Kiangnan, Nanking, and Tientsin arsenals remained the main force of China's ordnance industry.

KIANGNAN ARSENAL

The production problems that Kiangnan inherited from the previous decade in regard to rifles, coastal defense guns, and light field artillery stemmed from the arsenal's inability to modernize and expand its production facilities. The lingering expense of the steamship program, the high cost of imported materials, and the support of a large staff of Chinese personnel and some highly paid foreign technicians had prevented this. In addition to these developmental difficulties there was the latent problem of strategic vulnerability. Though the Sungkiang Magazine provided an alternate route for strategic supply, the most convenient route to and from Kiangnan could still be imperiled by hostile naval vessels in the lower Yangtze. Furthermore, defense of the arsenal, with its exposed maritime location in Shanghai, became a constant source of concern to defense planners after the French bombardment of the Foochow Dockyard.[5]

In the decade from 1885 to 1895, the officials who supervised and directed the Kiangnan Arsenal attempted to solve two of the three major production problems. Most of the activity at the arsenal was centered on the modernization of coastal defense guns and rifle production. The third production problem, guns for use by ground forces, never figured in the planning at Kiangnan. This challenge was taken up elsewhere by Governor-General Chang Chih-tung, who established China's second modern ordnance plant, at the Hanyang Arsenal, where guns were first produced in the summer of 1895. The authorities who controlled Kiangnan attempted to deal with one of the arsenal's major financial problems--dependence on imported materials. China's first steel refinery was established at Kiangnan in a move designed to eliminate the need for costly imported steel for ordnance and ammunition production. But the same authorities seemed to close their eyes to the serious financial problem caused by the high cost of domestic and foreign personnel serving at the arsenal. Though there was increased awareness of the strategic weakness of the arsenal's site in Shanghai, nothing was done about this either. During the war with Japan Kiangnan's vulnerability was a keen source of worry to the southern commissioner, and from that time on it became an actual rather than potential problem, affecting all future plans for the arsenal.[6]

Before discussing the development of production, it is appropriate to consider briefly the arsenal's financial basis, some of the internal factors affecting production costs, and the overall control of operations. The 20 percent of Shanghai maritime customs proceeds remained the largest component of Kiangnan's overall income during the decade. (See Appendix I Table 2.) Year-to-year fluctuation continued to be great, but a general increase was noticeable after 1889. Prior to that time, the customs allotment varied between 400,000 and 600,000 taels annually; thereafter the variation was generally between 600,000 and 800,000 taels. Miscellaneous income also showed a marked increase from 1889 on, totaling 526,082 taels. The result was an overall income of more than 800,000 taels in 1890, 1894, and 1895. An investigation of the arsenal's financial status conducted by the southern commissioner after the war revealed that some of this miscellaneous income was from loans that were later paid back, and some was received from other parties for the arsenal to use in making purchases of machinery or materials. A record of receipts and expenditures of these funds was kept separately from the customs income, and no irregularities were noted. But it was noted that over the years, sale of scrap from the arsenal had resulted in a total income of 34,000 taels that should have been reported as regular income but was not.[7]

The arsenal's large miscellaneous income and the fact that it was not reported to the imperial government are positive indications of the high degree of autonomy Kiangnan enjoyed under the supervision of the southern commissioner. Arsenal authorities began to abuse this autonomy by malpractices in purchasing and laxity in personnel policies in the 1870s and early 1880s; there appears to have been an intensification of these problems during the decade from 1885 to 1895. An examination of the office of director of the Kiangnan Arsenal and of the background of the two individuals who directed operations and administration during most of this decade sheds some light on these problems. As noted previously, the office of director was customarily held by the taotai who supervised the Shanghai Customs House. Li Chung-chio, a proctor at the arsenal just after the turn of the century, suggested that there was another informal qualification: "In the past," Li observed, "directors were usually from Hunan Province; therefore, the officials at the arsenal also were mostly Hunanese."[8] From 1879 through 1895 the southern commissioners who recommended the directors for appointment all were Hunanese. Furthermore, on the arsenal grounds was a temple dedicated to the Hunanese founder, Tseng Kuo-fan. Here Tseng's tablet was hung and incense was burned continually. Each year on the anniversary of Tseng's death the officials of the arsenal, from the director on down, gathered at the temple for memorial services. Such evidence, together with Li's statement, suggests that favoritism was shown to officials from Hunan for the post of director and for other posts at the arsenal. It was also reported that even the workmen and military personnel were predominantly Hunanese.[9]

One of the important directors of Kiangnan during this decade was Nieh Ch'i-kuei. Nieh, a native of Heng-shan in Hunan and son-in-law of Tseng Kuo-fan, entered official life without ever passing a civil service examination. In 1882, at age twenty-seven, he held a minor post in Nanking when a distinguished son of Hunan and old comrade-in-arms of Tseng Kuo-fan, Tso Tsung-t'ang, was named southern commissioner. In his initial interview with Tso, Nieh impressed the senior statesman with his ability to correct Tso's mistakes as the latter recited passages from the Huang-ch'ao ching-shih wen-pien (Collected Documents on Statecraft) memorized more than twenty years before. Subsequently, Tso appointed Nieh to his military staff and the two frequently dined together--the quick-witted Nieh humoring the aging commissioner while finessing Tso's efforts to share his dog-meat lunches with his new staff officer. It was not long before Nieh was named assistant director of Kiangnan, but this was only after his wife had dropped a hint to Tso's daughter-in-law regarding the Nieh family's straitened finances. During the Sino-French War, Nieh supervised for Tso the production of traditional ordnance at Kiangnan and effectively covered up a scandal involving Director Li Hsing-jui. Li subsequently retired to mourn the death of a parent and was replaced by P'an Ching-ju, who left office in 1884 when Tso was succeeded as southern commissioner by Tseng Kuo-ch'üan (1884-1890), a younger brother of Tseng Kuo-fan. After the brief and unsuccessful tenure of Chung Yün-ku as director, Tseng appointed his nephew by marriage, Nieh Ch'i-kuei, to the directorship at an unprecedented monthly salary of 200 taels.[10]

The Nieh household was known to stick to a strict budget, and during his term as director Nieh was also successful in putting Kiangnan on a sound financial footing. His concern with frugality seems to have been carried to the extreme, however, resulting ultimately in irrational and wasteful personnel practices at the arsenal. Specific instances of inept personnel administration were first reported in the late 1880s. By that time, a technical training program had been in operation at the arsenal for more than ten years. Students in this program, as well as those in the language institute, had no fixed graduation dates, no fixed stipends, and no definite positions to go to after they left the school. One who was accomplished in both mathematics and mechanical drawing was assigned to the machine shop to keep work accounts. It was recommended that another student who had been studying for over ten years and had shown technical competence be taken off his student's stipend, put on a more generous salary of ten to twenty taels per month, and sent into the arsenal to work. The penny-wise Nieh had seen this man riding in a horse-drawn carriage and deplored his extravagance. He disapproved the change of status for the student, observing sarcastically that even if he were put on salary it would not be enough to pay his carriage fares. Subsequently, this student was reported to have accepted a position with a foreign mining engineer in which he earned 100 taels per month and gained a reputation for the highest competence in mathematics and mechanical drawing. There were apparently many such cases of disillusioned students going with foreign firms.[11]

Liu Ch'i-hsiang, who followed Nieh as director from March 1890 until September 1895, was also of Hunanese origin and a relative of Li Hung-chang. His father, Liu Jung, was a distinguished Hunanese warrior from the same town as Tseng Kuo-fan. They had studied together as boys and fought together during the Taiping and Nien rebellions. But Liu brought more than family connections and a notable Hunanese lineage to Kiangnan. His background included experience in negotiations with Western nations that provided him with a realistic appreciation of the sophistication and power of Western military forces. In 1880 he had served as secretary of the legation that Tseng Chi-tse (married to Liu's sister) led to Saint Petersburg to renegotiate the dispute over Ili. Included in this group were foreigners with long experience in Chinese military industry--

Halliday Macartney and Prosper Giquel, formerly of the Foochow Dockyard. In 1883 Liu served as second secretary of Tseng's legation in Paris. The following year he was appointed to assist Tseng Kuo-ch'üan in the Liangkiang provinces; subsequently, at the request of Tso Tsung-t'ang he was transferred to Fukien.[12]

During Liu's administration Nieh's parsimonious personnel policies were reversed and carried to the opposite extreme. Official personnel increased in number from about 80 to about 180; two-thirds of these, critics charged, did nothing more than draw their pay. The lowest officials had previously received 20 to 30 taels each month, clerical personnel 6 to 8. Some of these salaries were raised to as high as 80 taels per month and the lowest was at least 20. Overstaffing was not a problem that developed suddenly during Liu's administration, though it appears to have intensified at this time. It was reported that the number of menial laborers, guards, and porters employed at the arsenal had tripled since the time of its establishment. An official investigation of personnel practices conducted after the war revealed that with each change of directors it was customary for the new one to bring in 30 to 40 of his personal friends as officials and deputies without making any reduction in the existing staff. By the end of Liu's tenure the number of officials was close to 200. The work force was reported to consist of a few highly skilled artisans; the rest were old servants, unable to work but drawing high wages. The artillery battalion had increased to 600. The total cost of salaries and wages each month was set at about 30,000 taels, roughly 360,000 taels each year. This was approximately 45 to 60 percent of the customs allotment.[13] Personnel practices during the administrations of Nieh and Liu seem to have resulted in a waste of the arsenal's meager technical manpower resources and a depletion of its financial resources due to overstaffing with highly paid personal favorites and coprovincials of the director.

Wages for foreign technicians tapered off a bit between 1886 and 1889, totaling 61,622 taels over the four-year period. Figures for the years after 1889 are not available. If there was any change, it is likely that it was an increase, for several new products were introduced after 1889 and new technicians were hired to introduce the production processes. In 1889, for example, Nieh agreed to a wage of 300 taels per month for one technician, 100 taels per month more than the director himself received.[14]

The deterioration of purchasing procedures which began in the previous decade became noticeably worse during the administrations of Nieh and Liu. During Nieh's tenure the arsenal was reportedly victimized by fraudulent deliveries from merchant houses. When Kiangnan ordered and paid for iron of stipulated quality required for production, it received instead ordinary British iron valued at only three-eighths of the price paid. The ordinary iron was of no use at the arsenal and remained unused until at least 1902. This type of leakage of funds was reported to have been widespread. The orders on which fraudulent deliveries were made were initiated by the director's office rather than the bargaining office, the regular purchasing agency.[15]

Under Liu Ch'i-hsiang the function of the bargaining office was further reduced; it did no more than make occasional purchases of miscellaneous materials. All the coal, iron, copper, lead, and other regularly required materials were purchased by the director through the comprador of a certain foreign firm with whom he was very close. Competitive bidding was abandoned. It was also charged that Liu bought up materials required by the arsenal at a low price and had a third party resell them to the arsenal at a high price. After the director's office took over the functions of the bargaining office, anyone who wanted to do business with the arsenal had to prepare the way through servants and officials before they could reach Liu. Personal fees were discussed first and then the actual price. Prices were inflated to cover the fees, and the amount of the arsenal's expenditure actually applied to the cost of goods purchased was very small.[16] Though some of these charges may be exaggerated, there can be little doubt that laxity and malpractices in purchasing during Liu's administration made the high cost of foreign materials even higher and sapped Kiangnan's financial strength.

The potential problems stemming from the need for strong centralized leadership in the industry materialized during this decade as the Navy Yamen proved ineffective in coordinating Kiangnan's production with that of other arsenals. Li, while serving as associate controller, approved plans for the simultaneous development of production of two rifles of different bore diameters. In May 1889 he wired

Liangkwang Governor-General Chang Chih-tung, assuring him that the Navy Yamen would secure imperial approval for Chang's proposal to purchase machinery to make the 11 mm. caliber Mauser rifle. Then, in the fall of 1890, Li introduced the 7.9 mm. caliber Mauser and the Austrian Mannlicher rifle to Kiangnan as models for improvement of their production. Chang subsequently changed his order to 7.9 mm. caliber rifle machinery, but Kiangnan developed its own model of 8.8 mm. caliber, which it began producing about 1891. As a result of this failure to coordinate production, in 1895 when Chang's new Hanyang Arsenal began production China had two rifle plants producing two different caliber rifles requiring different sizes of ammunition. In contrast, in 1886 Japan had adopted the Murata rifle produced at the Tokyo Arsenal as the standard weapon for all ground forces.[17]

Despite these serious problems in the management and supervision of Kiangnan, the arsenal experienced a decade of furious activity both in production and in modernization of facilities. Operations included the maintenance and operation of steamships, construction of new production facilities, and production of machinery, arms, and ammunition. Although the maintenance and operation of steamships continued to consume a noteworthy portion of the arsenal's customs allotment--135,900 taels from 1886 through 1889--it did not constitute an important activity during this decade. New operations were confined to the repair of provincial steamers, and use of the drydock gradually declined.[18]

Work at the arsenal was predominantly concerned with the production of new types of arms, ammunition, and machinery and the construction of plants to house the new production. (See Appendix I Table 3.) Material continued to come largely from abroad. The initial stimulus to improve production was provided by an edict of June 1885 which directed Southern Commissioner Tseng Kuo-ch'üan to take extraordinary measures to improve production of ordnance and to reorganize the arsenals under his command. Changes began the following year after Ambassador to Germany Hsü Ching-ch'eng reported to the throne on recent developments in the European ordnance industry. Hsü noted that the Armstrong process of building up the steel inner barrel with wrought-iron bands was already outmoded in Europe. Since steel and wrought iron reacted differently to overheating and cooling, after the gun had been used extensively the barrel became loose. Krupp had developed a gun with steel barrel and steel reinforcing bands. Armstrong had also recently converted to steel reinforcing bands, and, like Krupp, Armstrong was now making breechloaders rather than muzzle-loaders. Hsü recommended that the Kiangnan Arsenal convert to the production of all-steel breechloaders. In 1886 Kiangnan engaged a new ordnance technician, Mr. Cornish, who was skilled in making the latest models of Armstrong ordnance.[19]

By the middle of 1887 Nanyang had purchased eight new 800-pounder coastal defense guns and had installed them at forts at Chiang-yin and Wu-sung. In 1890 Kiangnan completed its first all-steel breechloading gun, an 800-pounder based on an Armstrong model. The ammunition for this ordnance required a new type of propellant, cocoa-brown prismatic powder.[20] The Tientsin Arsenal had already begun to produce this, but output was inadequate to supply Nanyang. In 1889 Director Nieh Ch'i-kuei proposed that Kiangnan also establish production. By 1891 the Navy Yamen had given its approval to purchase the necessary equipment and Kiangnan artisans had been selected to go to Tientsin for production training. Production of brown powder began in 1893 in a new plant at Lung-hua. The powder machinery purchased from Krupp was powered by a plant built at Kiangnan. Comparative tests with brown powder produced at Tientsin in 1893 showed the Kiangnan product somewhat inferior.[21]

In 1890, when Director Liu Ch'i-hsiang reported to the two commissioners that Kiangnan had completed its first all-steel breechloader, he announced plans for the production of four more all-steel breechloading coastal defense guns: two weighing forty-seven tons each and two weighing fifty-two tons each. When these were completed, he planned to make ten all-steel 100-pounder quick-firing guns, a model that he had observed while serving in Europe.[22] This gun had four to five times the fire power of the single shot coastal defense gun and was suitable for shipboard installation as well as coastal defense forts. Liu had already purchased the foreign steel required for the big coastal defense guns. After hearing of the plans for the quick-firing guns, Northern Commissioner Li authorized the arsenal to make the additional purchases of steel required for production and to take other necessary preparatory measures. New shops were built, and new furnaces, shrinking pots, huge boring and turning lathes, and rifling equipment were purchased from abroad for the production of the new ordnance. Both the coastal defense guns and the quick-firing model were completed and successfully test fired in early June 1893. The former was thirty-five feet long with a bore diameter of twelve inches. The quick-firing gun was about sixteen feet long with a bore diameter of 4.7 inches; it could fire twelve rounds per minute. Both had been produced by Chinese artisans under the direction of Mr. Cornish.[23]

Production of quick-firing gun ammunition began in 1891. By 1893, specialized equipment had been installed for the production of the eight hundred-pound projectiles fired by the huge coastal defense guns. Gun ammunition produced at Kiangnan then included the various sizes required for the Armstrong guns made at the arsenal, as well as Krupp and Woolwich ammunition for imported ordnance.[24]

Small arms production commanded Director Liu Ch'i-hsiang's attention almost to the extent that heavy ordnance did. In 1890 he developed a plan to salvage the defective center-fire rifles that the arsenal had been producing since 1884. But Liu recognized that these weapons were already obsolete by Western standards and that even if he was able to salvage them they would be suitable only for peacetime training. Therefore, at the same time he had foreign technicians and Chinese artisans working on plans for regular production of a new and improved rifle. Though Kiangnan lacked the equipment necessary to produce the most recent types of Western small arms, the small arms shop was successful in turning out several models of a slightly modified version of the British Lee rifle. Tests conducted at the arsenal showed that these rifles, when fired with smokeless powder cartridges, were half again as powerful as the Mauser or Hotchkiss then popular in the West and were twice as powerful as the Remington. Liu sent the models to Southern Commissioner Tseng Kuo-ch'üan for testing and announced that he hoped to begin production by adapting the machinery that the arsenal already had and by employing hand labor to make some parts. The additional machinery required would be purchased gradually as funds became available. The tests conducted by the southern commissioner revealed that the superior performance of this rifle was dependent on the use of smokeless powder ammunition. He instructed Kiangnan to investigate the production of this new propellant.[25]

Less than 2,000 of these modified Lee rifles had been produced by 1892 when the weapon was replaced by a magazine rifle.[26] The introduction of this model was promoted by Northern Commissioner Li Hung-chang and carried through by Director Liu. In 1890 Li ascertained that the modified Lee that Kiangnan

An early specimen of heavy built-up ordnance, Chinese gun crew, and foreign technician

had produced was less than satisfactory. In the autumn of that year he directed the arsenal to study the new Mauser and the Austrian Mannlicher rifles as a basis for improving small arms production. Chinese and foreign personnel set to work on the problem. During 1891 Kiangnan began test production of an 8.8 mm. caliber magazine rifle based on the Austrian Mannlicher but with considerable modification. The most significant advance was the increased fire power that could be achieved by firing a five-round clip without pausing to reload after each shot as required with the Remington. Tests conducted at the arsenal showed that the striking force of the bullet was far greater when smokeless powder was used rather than black powder cartridges. It was also observed that the rifle overheated and required cooling after two clips, or ten rounds, or black powder cartridges had been fired, but three clips, or fifteen rounds of the smokeless powder cartridges could be fired before overheating occurred. New Southern Commissioner Liu K'un-i (1891-1894) suggested that this difficulty could be overcome through the employment of a higher grade steel for production. Because Kiangnan lacked the required specialized machinery, this rifle, like its forerunner based on the British Lee, was made partly by hand.[27]

Northern Commissioner Li was greatly impressed with the new rifle. Tests conducted at Tientsin in the fall of 1892 by troop commanders and foreign instructors on Li's staff showed that the Kiangnan weapon was the equal of the new German Mauser in accuracy, ease of operation, fire power, striking force, and velocity. The following year, when General Kawakami of the Imperial Japanese Army visited Li in Tientsin, the general was favorably impressed with the Kiangnan rifle and said that the Murata rifle, which the Japanese regarded as superior to contemporary German and French models, could not compare with it. He took two back to Japan with him to serve as models. These appraisals did not stand the test of time and closer comparison, however. As new weapons were produced in China the reputation of the Kiangnan rifle began to fade. In 1897 foreign technicians conducted comparative tests with the rifle and the German Mauser model 1888 produced by the new Hanyang Arsenal. The technicians' evaluation found the Kiangnan rifle inferior in ten major respects. Production was finally halted in 1901 in order to achieve standardization in domestically produced small arms and ammunition. The next year existing stocks were declared scrap because of firing defects that appeared after prolonged use.[28]

Production of the cartridges required for the new magazine rifle added one more type to Kiangnan's variegated output of small arms ammunition. During this decade, as a result of the use of several new types of small arms, Kiangnan produced a total of six different types of cartridges as well as percussion caps, though all types were not produced each year.[29]

Subsequent to the southern commissioner's directions of 1891, Liu set to work on the problem of smokeless powder production to supply the ammunition requirements of the new magazine rifles and quick-firing guns.[30] In January 1893 he signed a contract with Buchheister and Company for a complete set of Krupp machinery capable of producing gun cotton, nitric acid, and 1,000 pounds of smokeless powder per day. The contract also provided for a new technician to instruct in the production process. The total cost was more than 100,000 taels. The machinery was expected to arrive in eight or nine months; meanwhile, the foreign plans for the required plant building were sent in advance so that construction could begin promptly. At that time the production process for smokeless powder was a secret carefully guarded by the nations which held it. After the plant was established, time wore on and the foreign technicians had no success in reproducing the process for making the powder. It was the Chinese official in charge of the new works, Wang Shih-shou, who finally struck on the proper method, but this was not until April 1895 when the war with Japan had already been decided. Output was reported at 60,000 pounds per year but quality was lacking. In 1897 Mr. Cornish stated that the smokeless powder made at Kiangnan was little more than guncotton slightly diluted with vaseline and dissolved by ether. The objection to guncotton was that it was too easily detonated.[31]

In late 1890 Director Liu reported to the two commissioners that although Kiangnan's equipment for producing all-steel guns and breechloading rifles was not complete, it was adequate to maintain production. The arsenal, however, was entirely dependent on costly foreign imports of steel for production of big guns, steel shells, and rifle barrels. To reduce costs and provide a secure domestic source of supply, Liu recommended that Kiangnan establish its own refinery. Both commissioners approved the proposal, and Liu proceeded with the purchase of a small refining furnace and equipment to roll rifle barrels. The cost was only 12,000 taels, and the expected output was 3 tons of steel and 100 rifle barrels per day. The following year, steel refined at Kiangnan from imported ore was sent to the Nanking and Tientsin arsenals for tests. Both plants reported that the Kiangnan product was the equal of high-grade foreign gun steel. By 1892 the arsenal had begun production of steel gun shells employing ore from Hunan province.[32]

The operation of a single furnace made the refining of steel an inefficient and costly process. It took two weeks to heat the furnace to the temperature required for smelting. Then the ore could be inserted. After the pig iron was removed from the furnace, a two-week cooling period was required, after which the interior had to be inspected and repaired if necessary. Finally, the pig iron could be refined. Well over a month was required to produce three tons of steel, and during the cooling period workers sat idle at full pay. Nevertheless, in 1893 domestic production of rifle and gun barrels was inaugurated at Kiangnan, an extension of the refinery was completed, and new British equipment was installed.[33]

During this period of rapid modernization of production and construction of new facilities, the production and acquisition of new machinery created a substantial drain on the arsenal's financial resources. Expense figures show a sharp increase in the amount spent for new machinery during 1893 and 1894. (See Appendix I Table 5.) Production figures also give some inkling of the position that machine building occupied in the arsenal's operations. The output of heavy machines, some of which were to provide power for newly purchased production equipment, rose from fourteen pieces in 1890 to twenty-eight in 1894. (See Appendix I Table 3.) The following year, Southern Commissioner Liu K'un-i commented that machine building was the chief activity at the arsenal.[34]

During this decade the largest portion of the arms and ammunition produced at Kiangnan continued to go to ships, units, and forts in Nanyang. (See Appendix I Table 4.) Distribution to Peiyang units was limited, and no ships of the Peiyang squadron were supplied from Kiangnan. As in the early 1880s, the only important supply to Peiyang units was heavy ordnance and gun ammunition. From 1886 through 1895, 11 of Kiangnan's big guns and 20,000 to 30,000 pounds of ammunition were sent to units and depots subordinate to Northern Commissioner Li. Other than this, the only distribution was 200 of the new magazine rifles and a total of 61,000 cartridges sent between 1892 and 1894. Kiangnan's contribution to the Chinese forces opposing Japan was made by equipping Nanyang units transferred into the war zone. During 1894 and 1895 large quantities of black-powder cartridges, rifles, guns, and gun shells were distributed to the units of the Hsiang Army transferred to Shan-hai-kuan. Shipments to areas other than Nanyang and Peiyang reached significant quantities only in 1893, 1894, and 1895. These war materials were sent to units in Hupeh, Hunan, and Taiwan, and to provinces along the southeastern coast.[35]

Thanks to an agreement reached between Japan and Great Britain in the summer of 1894 which placed the city of Shanghai outside the zone of hostilities, shipments of munitions from the Kiangnan Arsenal continued uninterrupted during the war. The arsenal was in constant jeopardy, however. In the fall of 1894 the Japanese government showed a decided inclination to renege on its promise not to attack Shanghai. At this point, powers with interests in Shanghai--the United States, Great Britain, and France--intervened. On December 13, 1894, Arsenal Director Liu Ch'i-hsiang wired Acting Southern Commissioner Chang Chih-tung that there was a persistent rumor among consuls and merchants in Shanghai that the Japanese again planned to violate the agreement. They were expected to attack the arsenal first and then move up the Yangtze. Local defense authorities had recommended that the households of Kiangnan's 2,000 artisans be moved from the arsenal to a more secure location, that the moat surrounding the plant be made wider and deeper, and that the perimeter wall be built higher. Noting that these measures would require time and financial resources, neither of which were at his disposal, Liu recommended additional deployment of troops to defend the arsenal. Japan did not attack, however, probably because of the announcement by Great Britain in early January that it would take whatever steps necessary to insure the proper observance of the neutrality agreement.[36]

After the war, Acting Southern Commissioner Chang Chih-tung memorialized that this experience had demonstrated clearly that Shanghai was strategically unsuitable as a site for China's most important arsenal. He pointed out that shipments of munitions from Kiangnan had been possible only because of the international agreement. The ease with which production materials could be supplied in Shanghai had determined the arsenal's location in that city decades before.

Strategic considerations had been overlooked. As a result, Chang observed, a dangerous situation had come about and could no longer be tolerated.[37]

Despite the fact that Kiangnan had not been attacked and its supply function had not been interrupted, munitions from the arsenal were not an important factor during the hostilities. The war with Japan was decided largely by naval battles between Japanese vessels and those of the Peiyang squadron. Kiangnan had not equipped any of the Peiyang ships. With only one unimportant exception, the <u>Tsao-chiang</u>, Nanyang vessels built or equipped at the Kiangnan Arsenal offered no assistance to the Peiyang squadron during the war. Peiyang units also bore the brunt of the ground fighting; Kiangnan had not made significant shipments of infantry arms or ammunition to Peiyang for almost fifteen years prior to the war. The largest Nanyang units transferred to the war zone, presumably those equipped by Kiangnan, arrived too late to take part in the fighting.[38] The bulk of the war materials distributed from Kiangnan from 1886 to 1895 went to areas in South China that had no direct involvement in the war. In short, Kiangnan arms were not put to an effective test during the Sino-Japanese War because of the isolation of the southern ships from the naval battles in the North and the late arrival of the ground forces equipped by Kiangnan.

Under the directorship of Liu Ch'i-hsiang, Kiangnan experienced its most rapid expansion and modernization since the establishment years from 1867 to 1875. Taking stock of the arsenal's production at the time of the Sino-Japanese War, however, it is clear that results were at best uneven. The heavy ordnance produced at Kiangnan during the early 1890s was of quality equal to that produced in the West, but only one or two of the big coastal defense guns and a maximum of twelve 40-pound quick-firing guns or six 100-pounders could be produced each year. Kiangnan still did not have the machinery necessary to produce light field artillery. (In contrast, Japan beginning in 1887 had equipped all field artillery units with a seven cm. mountain gun produced at the Osaka Arsenal based on an Italian model.) Production of smokeless powder required for quick-firing gun and magazine rifle ammunition did not begin until almost the end of the war, and then the quality was questionable. Eight hundred pounds of the brown powder used for coastal defense gun ammunition could be produced daily. Output of the obsolescent Kiangnan rifle was limited due to the lack of specialized production machinery; only five or six of these partially handmade weapons could be turned out each day. Guided by the diverse requirements of Chinese armies during the war, the arsenal divided its resources to produce percussion caps and four different types of cartridges, including those required for its own magazine rifle. Five thousand of the latter could be turned out daily, using smokeless powder purchased from abroad. The steel refinery produced rifle barrels from Hunan iron ore, but steel for heavy ordnance production required pig iron imported from Sweden. Foreign technicians and supply were required in many other areas of production as well.[39]

The Kiangnan Arsenal was unable to produce uniformly high quality modern arms and ammunition in large quantities at the time of the Sino-Japanese War, primarily because modernization of production facilities carried on during the previous six years had been incomplete, imperfect, and tardy. Production expenses during the years when facilities were being modernized were so high that they restricted the acquisition of new equipment and taxed financial resources beyond their limit. In early 1895 Kiangnan Director Liu revealed to acting Southern Commissioner Chang Chih-tung that many of the improvements that had taken place and were taking place were not yet paid for. The arsenal had accepted credit from foreign firms and then found that it was unable to meet its indebtedness. Two hundred and fifty thousand taels were owing on the price of new equipment for steel refining, powder, and ordnance production. In addition, another 150,000 taels had been advanced by foreign firms for purchase of land, building for the steel refinery and the new powder plants, and purchase of ordnance steel and constituents for powder production.[40]

Examining the arsenal's expenditures during the years when modernization was taking place, it is difficult to escape the conclusion that the costs of personnel and materials were responsible for Kiangnan's financial calamity and the incomplete status of production equipment. The arsenal's total personnel expense increased from 264,468 taels in 1890 to 349,531 taels in 1895, accounting for a total of 36 percent of all expenditures during the six-year period. Another 51 percent was consumed by purchases of material. The remaining 13 percent was devoted to purchase of munitions and machinery, and expenses associated with translation. (See Appendix I Table 5.)

Behind these cost factors were the same basic problems that had marred conversion to ordnance production in the previous decade. Kiangnan was attempting to develop modern industrial capability in an economic environment in which raw materials industries lagged far behind the required state of development. Furthermore, the officials who directed and operated the arsenal emerged from the official class of traditional society. Untrained for their positions as managers of modern industry, they permitted unbusinesslike personnel practices and laxity in financial dealings that resulted in large-scale waste of the arsenal's financial resources. In addition to these developmental weaknesses, experience during the war had shown that China could not defend Kiangnan, nor insure uninterrupted distribution of products. Though this problem came to a head in 1895, it had been present for three decades. Investment in permanent facilities at Kao-ch'ang Miao while Kiangnan was still primarily a shipyard had created a force of inertia that made removal unlikely. Further, Shanghai was probably the best location in China for the arsenal to obtain the imported materials that it needed for production; more than anything else, this had determined the arsenal's location. In this sense, adapting to deficiencies in the domestic economy had also contributed to positioning Kiangnan in a site difficult for defense and ill-suited to serve as a central distribution point during wartime.

THE NANKING ARSENAL AND POWDER PLANT

Although the operations of the Nanking Arsenal were dwarfed by those of its giant neighbor in Shanghai, Nanking continued to receive the serious attention of the southern commissioner during this decade, for it alone among Chinese arsenals stressed production of guns for ground forces. Shortly after the Sino-French War, Southern Commissioner Tseng Kuo-ch'üan memorialized that in view of the difficulties experienced in importing arms during the war, domestic production should be expanded. The Board of Revenue authorized a special appropriation of 100,000 taels from the Shanghai, Kiukiang, and Hankow Customs proceeds for expansion and modernization of the Nanking Arsenal. Work was accomplished during 1886 and the first half of 1887. With the aid of foreign technicians from Kiangnan, new machinery purchased through the American Russel Company was installed.[41]

Following the expansion of production facilities, annual income, which had been fixed at 110,000 taels (not including special allotments), was increased by 4,000 taels beginning in 1887. These funds, provided from local defense appropriations, were earmarked for production of additional munitions for the Huai Army and other defense units. In 1890 an allocation of 10,000 taels from the Kiangnan Arsenal's customs allotment was authorized to support production during the additional month in intercalary years, bringing regular annual income to 114,000 taels and 124,000 taels on intercalary years.[42] (See Appendix I Table 7.)

After modernization of facilities at Nanking and allocation of new income, production was reported to be about the same: guns, gun mounts, gun ammunition, percussion caps, fuses, and fort equipment. The production of one- and two-pounder steel guns probably also began about this time. A small vessel, the I-fu, thirty-nine feet in length with an eight-foot beam and a six-horsepower engine, was constructed in 1886 to carry production materials from Shanghai. Distribution of products was to both Nanyang and Peiyang, the latter probably reflecting Northern Commissioner Li Hung-chang's renewed influence at the arsenal due to his new status in the Navy Yamen.[43]

During the Sino-Japanese War, the Nanking Arsenal hired additional personnel and operated on overtime hours. Only a few instances in which the arsenal provided war materials to the Chinese forces emerge clearly from the record, however. Breech-loading gingals were one ordnance item that was requested by Chinese commanders and supplied from the Nanking Arsenal. Guns, described as short-range, from Nanking are also known to have reached Chinese units during the war. The anachronistic production of the premodern gingals was substantiated by a British observer, Lord Beresford, who after visiting the Nanking Arsenal in 1898 noted that "the machinery was modern and first class but it was used to make obsolete and useless arms...most of the plant was still devoted to the production of gingals."[44]

The Nanking Powder Plant had hardly been established when production facilities were expanded. In the latter half of 1885 and early 1886, new buildings were erected and additional machinery installed at a cost of 89,481 taels, provided from local defense appropriations and imperially controlled funds. Rising production was supported by an annual income, which increased to more than 50,000 taels beginning in 1887. Allocations of more than 7,000 taels for building and machinery maintenance were received from local defense funds in 1888 and again in 1893.[45] (See Appendix I Table 8.)

The output capacity of the Nanking Powder Plant was probably close to 2,000 pounds of black powder per day after the expansion of 1885-1886. Though production never reached this level, in 1886 it was reported to be approximately equal to the needs of the Liangkiang provinces, and powder was also shipped to Taiwan. At the beginning of the Sino-Japanese War, Nanking was ordered to produce 300,000 pounds of powder. A total of 310,000 pounds was produced between September 1894 and February 1896 at an added cost of 40,031 taels.[46]

The Nanking Powder Plant was involved in the relatively simple production of black powder; it benefited from a small but steady operating income as well as regular allocations for expansion and maintenance of its plant. Its production met the peacetime needs of defense units in the Liangkiang provinces, and it was able to step up output sharply under wartime conditions. The situation was far different at the Nanking Arsenal. There the management had several options as to the types of ordnance that the arsenal would turn out. To meet the request of certain Chinese field commanders during the war, Nanking's recently modernized facilities were used to produce outmoded gingals. This raises a question about the management in this plant where there was no regular foreign presence. Did the Chinese managers at this relatively isolated inland site tend to revert to familiar types of production? On the basis of the limited evidence that we have it is impossible to do more than speculate that this was so. Still, one should not discount Lord Beresford's observation in 1898 about Nanking that "the Chinese officials didn't seem to know what they were making and why."[47] Although it is difficult to say that the management was the crucial negative factor influencing production at Nanking, it is clear that the positive factor of an energetic, modernizing leader such as Liu Ch'i-hsiang of the Kiangnan Arsenal was missing.

There was also the continuing problem of high personnel and administrative costs, which depleted production funds at Nanking. During this decade such expenses typically consumed one-half of the arsenal's budget. The Nanking Arsenal's size and limited facilities, however, were plainly the most important factors limiting productivity, and there was very little that could be done to change this. As Chang Chih-tung observed after the war, Nanking's location was hemmed in on all sides by the terrain. There was simply no room for expansion or for the addition of production facilities. Though selected improvements could be made, there was no way that Nanking at its present site could be enlarged greatly so as to play a major role in China's ordnance industry.[48]

THE TIENTSIN ARSENAL

Under the direct supervision of Northern Commissioner Li Hung-chang, the Tientsin Arsenal, China's second largest, continued to expand production and modernize facilities in the decade prior to the Sino-Japanese War. It was the only major Chinese arsenal to have a direct logistical involvement in that conflict. As in earlier years, the central problem for Li was how to find additional funds beyond the allocation of 40 percent of the Tientsin and Chefoo customs proceeds (which supported regular production) to finance expansion and modernization.

In 1887 the arsenal embarked on a program of modernization designed to provide the most up-to-date types of ammunition to the Peiyang forts and navy. In that year a plant for the production of cocoa-brown prismatic powder was built with the help of German advisers. Machinery was erected by the Englishman, Mr. Stewart, who was still at the arsenal as chief engineer. Subsequently, German technicians assisted in production. The North China Herald observed that when the powder plant was completed, China would have the largest and finest gunpowder-making works in the world.[49]

Just as this modernization was beginning in 1887, the imperial government terminated the annual allocation that Tientsin had been receiving from frontier defense funds. The following year the arsenal was to receive a new allotment from the Shanghai Opium Likin proceeds authorized by the Navy Yamen. When this did not materialize, Li drew from funds designated for the support of overseas envoys to cover expenses in 1888. The regulations for the new navy also provided for an additional 80,000 taels per year starting in 1888, to be forwarded to the arsenal by provincial customs houses to support production of brown powder and steel shells for long naval and fort guns. This income also proved unreliable, however. In 1894 Li reported that it was still not being received in full.[50]

Nevertheless, in 1889 he decided to purchase

equipment and hire the technicians necessary for forging steel and producing the long projectiles. As required by the new naval regulations, he submitted this plan to the Board of War where the idea for purchasing the steel forging equipment became bogged down due to objections that the freight and insurance charges were too high. In mid-1891 the matter was still under discussion and the machinery had not been shipped to China. Meanwhile, machinery for producing this ammunition from steel forged abroad was operational by early 1890, but Li reported that production was inadequate to supply the requirements for both training and stockpiling; he requested authorization to purchase sixteen more sets of machine tools.[51] In 1891 Li finally received the approval necessary to go ahead with the acquisition of steel forging equipment. He ordered a complete plant for refining and forging according to the Siemens Martin process from the New Southgate Engineering Company of New Southgate, England. The steel works was completed and ready to begin production in May 1893. It enjoyed the services of foreign technicians in smelting, forging, and analytical chemistry. Meanwhile, since the arsenal was still not receiving the full 80,000 taels per year from provincial customs income designated to support production of steel shells, beginning in 1891 allocations from northern maritime defense funds supported this production as well as the production of cocoa-brown prismatic powder. A special appropriation from the Tientsin customs purchased additional brown-powder machinery. Production of brown powder, steel shells, and gun ammunition for Lü-shun, Wei-hai-wei, and Dairen continued in 1892, supported by allocations from northern maritime defense funds, and another allocation from the Tientsin customs defrayed the costs of additional new machinery.[52]

    The Tientsin Arsenal was not entirely specialized in the production of modern powder and gun ammunition for the new navy and coastal defense installations. Li's annual reports indicated that regular production and distribution was continuing, but he did not go into detail. In 1888 the North China Herald reported that the arsenal at Hai-kuang Szu employed about 300 workers and produced small arms, small rifled cannon, cartridges, shells, and some explosives. The East Arsenal, the main plant at Chia-chia-ku Tao, employed about 1,100 workers. In addition to its powder plant, described as one of the largest in the world, the East Arsenal turned out steam launches for which it produced the engines and boilers, rifled bronze cannon, a variety of gun ammunition, rifles, torpedoes and iron piles, and girders for bridges.[53]

Beginning in 1887 the Tientsin Arsenal tackled other types of production entirely unrelated to military preparedness. In that year Li and Shen Pao-ching planned to establish a mint for the production of copper cash, a venture which miscarried badly. After the foreign machinery had been purchased and installed, they found that it could not be successfully adapted to punch holes in the center of Chinese coins. Furthermore, the percentage of copper in the machine-made coins had to be greatly increased. The project was abandoned because of high production costs.[54]

Between 1887 and 1891 the arsenal resumed its shipbuilding program. This time the direction came from the Navy Yamen, and the vessels were destined to ply the waters of K'un-ming Lake in the palace grounds. In all, three small steam-powered craft-- two tow vessels and a luxury barge--were constructed. The two tow vessels cost more than 9,000 taels each. During 1889 and 1890 additional expense was incurred for improvements made on the palace grounds and at the summer palace. A dock was built in K'un-ming Lake. Electric lights and railroad tracks were installed in the park on the west side of the palace, and fire engines were purchased and shipped to Peking. Electric lights were also installed in the summer palace, and a railway was laid to the Outer Detachment of the Artillery and Musketry Division stationed nearby. In 1892 a small rail line was begun connecting the East Arsenal with the city. When completed, this would make possible direct, rapid shipment of munitions from the arsenal to the piers. This had been accomplished by small boat by a roundabout route.[55]

At the outbreak of the Sino-Japanese War, Li estimated the munitions on hand that had been produced at the Tientsin Arsenal to include: gun ammunition of all sizes, Mauser, Hotchkiss, and Winchester small arms ammunition, 10 million rounds; rifle powder, 600,000 pounds; gun powder, 600,000 pounds; and cocoa-brown prismatic powder, 300,000 pounds. Overtime work was begun to speed up production but Li did not place complete reliance on the arsenal. He began making arrangements with foreign merchants for the covert purchase of arms and ammunition from neutral nations. Only 250 naval gun shells were ready for resupply, and Li tried urgently to order the 1,300 that he calculated would be needed after the first battle.[56]

The poor quality and short supply of naval

ammunition was reported to have adversely affected the fire power of the Chinese fleet at the battle of the Yalu on September 17, 1894, the first full-scale naval engagement and a crushing defeat for China. On October 4 Li wired the remnants of the fleet undergoing repairs at Port Arthur that the arsenal was working day and night to make ammunition for the shipboard guns. But on November 16 he reported that Tientsin could not fill demands for gun ammunition for naval and ground forces units despite the fact that extra personnel had been hired and work was going on around the clock. Units in need of ammunition would have to wait until the arsenal's output reached adequate amounts. Supplies of Mauser and Hotchkiss ammunition were nearly used up by mid-November. Stores of rifles and guns held by Peiyang depots were exhausted before the end of 1894. By the end of the war, Tientsin had begun production of the premodern gingal, probably a desperation move to supply ordnance from a plant unequipped for modern ordnance production.[57]

The supplies of war material from the Peiyang depots were inadequate to meet the needs of Chinese forces during the Sino-Japanese War. Specifically, the munitions supplied by the Tientsin Arsenal were entirely used up or in short supply by the end of 1894. The history of production and modernization at the arsenal in the years from 1885 to 1895 suggest several reasons for this. Although output, particularly the production of powder and ammunition, was great and the progress of modernization steady, both production and modernization were keyed to a relatively small and insecure annual income. From 1888 on, increases in both areas were dependent upon Li's ability to find 100,000 to 200,000 taels additional income each year. The allocation of frontier defense funds, which supplemented customs income until 1887, went largely for increased production to meet crisis demands for munitions. The provision of additional income to support the modernization after 1887 of powder and projectile production became a vexing problem. Delays in funding brought delays in production. As a result the steel for naval gun shells was not turned out at Tientsin until one year before the war, though limited quantities were made with imported steel before that time. From 1887 on, the uncertain supply of income to the Tientsin Arsenal retarded the modernization of production facilities and eventually restricted the quantities of high grade naval ammunition supplied to the Peiyang fleet before and during the Japanese War.

Output of other types of rifle and gun ammunition was also limited by the same small and uncertain income. These products were already being spread across a broad field of distribution. To increase by amounts adequate to meet wartime demands, substantial new sources of regular income should have been provided well in advance. The management of the Tientsin Arsenal cannot be faulted for the ill-advised production policies that seem to have prevailed at Nanking. Nevertheless, the abortive attempt at minting was a costly error and the construction of pleasure boats and improvement of palace facilities, probably at imperial behest, further depleted the arsenal's small and unstable operating capital.

CONCLUSIONS

Although Japan enjoyed an advantage over China in the field of ordnance resulting from the superior accomplishments of its domestic ordnance industry, the outcome of the Sino-Japanese War was not decided by the relative fire power of the two forces. Much larger issues reaching far beyond the scope of this monograph were involved.[58] The uneven progress of modernization in the arsenals of Nanyang and Peiyang in the decade prior to the war, however, limited the Chinese logistically and forced reliance on the purchase of foreign ordnance.[59] In addition, Kiangnan and Nanking were remote from the northern theater of operations and a cumbersome command structure complicated their support of the Chinese side.

The Chinese ordnance industry was simply not yet ready to make an important contribution to the supply of China's armed forces. All three plants had undertaken major programs of modernization stimulated by experience during the Sino-French War or developments in the European ordnance industry. Kiangnan artisans quickly mastered the production of modern heavy ordnance equal in quality to Western counterparts. Tientsin's munitions works were described by foreign observers as among the largest and best equipped in the world. Though production figures are lacking, indications are that the output of powder and ammunition was improving steadily at Tientsin, retarded only by the difficulty that Li encountered in finding additional income. The management at both plants exhibited an uncompromising commitment to the highest standards of production. Both had taken the first steps toward self-sufficiency in raw materials with the establishment of steel refineries, the first in

China. Though no such progress was evident at the Nanking Arsenal, black-powder production developed quickly at the new Nanking Powder Plant to meet the needs of the Liangkiang provinces.

Still, the problems were grave and new ones appeared during this decade. Overhead expenses, inflated by the need for imported materials and the persistence of traditional practices in personnel administration and purchasing, paralyzed Kiangnan and Nanking. Educational changes in China lagged far behind the arsenal's need for technical personnel. Foreign technicians were still essential for certain types of production. This may have been the difference at Nanking where regular foreign advice was perhaps prematurely eliminated. By the close of this decade, another fundamental problem had arisen regarding the arsenals--their location. The relative weakness of China's maritime defense had exposed the Foochow Dockyard and the Kiangnan Arsenal to foreign attack or the threat of it. The Tientsin Arsenal would be destroyed by a foreign landing force a few years hence during the Boxer Uprising. The inland site at Nanking had also been poorly chosen. Postwar strategic industrial planning would have to cope with this new dilemma.

Though progress had been great, it was marred by problems of overwhelming magnitude and production fell far short of China's wartime needs. From the standpoint of the strategic industrial development in the arsenals of Nanyang and Peiyang, the Sino-Japanese War was simply the wrong war at the wrong time. It had forced upon these plants a timetable for modernization which, under existing economic and social conditions, they were unable to meet.

The Tientsin West Arsenal after the foreign bombardment in the summer of 1900.

VIII. Conclusions

The ordnance industry of the late nineteenth century was the epitome of the self-strengthening movement, the vanguard of its achievements, and the victim of its shortcomings. To catch its historical meaning and draw from the experience in the arsenals those inferences which the record warrants, a few fundamental questions regarding the arsenals' establishment and operations must be considered.

First, why were these plants established? Moreover, to what extent did they realize their mission? The establishment of modern machine production in the Chinese arsenals was motivated by multiple causes: foreign and domestic, military and nonmilitary. Although the military emergencies created by domestic rebellion provided the immediate background in which the arsenals were established, the reasoning of the various officials who brought the plants into being leaves no doubt that their ultimate purpose was to rid China of foreign influence, a concern also shared by the neo-Confucian scholars whose writings provided the font of ideas from which the founders of the arsenals drew inspiration. Beyond this patriotic rhetoric, there is irrefutable substantive evidence from the arsenals themselves. The sustained efforts made and the great expense incurred at the Kiangnan, Nanking, and Tientsin arsenals from 1867 right up to 1895 to produce the most modern ocean-going warships, coastal defense ordnance, and naval munitions cannot be rationally reconciled solely in terms of preparing to crush domestic enemies. Though the Nanking Arsenal may have faltered in this respect in the 1880s, the antiimperialist import of the Kiangnan and Tientsin arsenals became clearer with the passage of time and the growing emphasis on ordnance and ammunition for maritime defense.

But the arsenals, with their strange new machinery, should not be regarded simply as expedient departures from the traditional patterns of production prompted entirely by current military considerations. The idea of adjusting institutions to meet contemporary needs was characteristic of the nineteenth century Confucian School of Statecraft. This was the rubric of Confucian political theory under which the establishment of modern machine industry for military production was rationalized. It seems appropriate to regard these plants as examples of institutional innovation stemming from the drive for practical reform characteristic of nineteenth century Confucianism, inspired partly by a desire to protect the dynasty from domestic foes and partly by antiimperialism.

While the arsenals were effective institutions in combating domestic rebellion, ordnance and ammunition from these plants were never employed successfully against foreign foes. This has led some authors to disparage the antiimperialist significance of the arsenals. This is a simplistic view of a complex problem. It assigns to China's arsenals the primary responsibility for the dynasty's inability to resist imperialist pressures, a responsibility which should rightfully be shared with other elements of China's society and leadership. Furthermore, it fails to look beyond the simple fact of relative logistical weakness to the factors that induced this circumstance. The antiimperialist thrust of the Chinese arsenals was diminished by the prevailing condition of foreign dependency, or semicolonialism. Of the more than 25 million taels invested in the Kiangnan, Tientsin, and Nanking arsenals, more than 80 percent came directly from duties on foreign trade. Moreover, after thirty years of arsenal operation, China still had to look abroad for most of the technology and all of the specialized machinery needed to update production. The introduction of new technology and the maintenance of modernized production still required foreign technical advice. Even raw materials and fuels in many instances continued to come from abroad. Any interruption of trade occasioned either by hostilities between China and one of its suppliers or by a sympathetic embargo by a supplying nation allied with a belligerent would inevitably have had a highly disruptive effect upon the finances, the materiel, and the personnel of China's ordnance industry (as it did a few years later during the Boxer Uprising).

In short, the environment of foreign dependency in which the industry developed forced the arsenals to rely on China's potential enemies for the elements necessary to maintain modernized production. In the final analysis, this condition would have precluded the use of the arsenals to resist pressures from an imperialist power such as Britain had such been forthcoming. But China avoided direct military confrontation with Britain during these years. Moreover, in the conflicts with foreign military forces that did arise, the Sino-French and Sino-Japanese wars, production deficiencies in the arsenals themselves, rather than imperialist manipulations, weakened China logistically. Hence the tardy and imperfect progress of modernization in the arsenals was a second important factor undermining their mission of antiimperialism.

Although the motives that prompted the establishment of modern arsenal industry in China were chiefly military, the founders were aware that far-reaching changes in the economy would likely result from the introduction of steam-powered production equipment. They looked forward to the production of machinery in the arsenals for use in other sectors of the economy. But this never happened, and the reasons are instructive with respect to both the nature of China's state and society and its interaction with imperialist power. In the first place, beginning with the Tientsin Massacre in 1870 right up until the Sino-Japanese War of 1894-1895, the Empire was faced with a series of foreign threats that commanded the full attention of the few far sighted officials, such as Li Hung-chang, who favored nonmilitary production. Moreover, military pressures resulted in the concentration of financial resources on military production. Virtually all expenditures at the major arsenals were devoted to the costs of current production of military items and renewal of arms production machinery, costs that were inflated by management inefficiencies, waste, nonavailability of raw materials, and purchasing malpractices. The high priority that was necessarily assigned to military production and the cost inefficiency of the production process in the arsenals simply exhausted resources and ruled out production of nonmilitary machinery. Given the international situation, probably the only way that production in the arsenals could have been expanded to include material for nonmilitary use would have involved a large-scale reordering of the fiscal basis of the state to free resources from other sectors of the economy for investment in additional capital equipment. This was the path that Japan had followed beginning with the land tax reform of 1873. In China, it was never discussed in the context of arsenal finance.

Although the arsenals contributed to the dynasty's pacification of domestic enemies through 1895, their antiimperialist potential was undermined by foreign dependency and production deficiencies, and their direct contribution to other sectors of the economy was nil. It would be a mistake, however, to view these plants as historically unimportant simply because their missions were so imperfectly completed. From the standpoint of economic development, the introduction of steam-powered production machinery in the arsenals opened the era of mass production. This was a necessary first step in the direction of technological modernization of the economy. The use of machine tools and precision measurement and the production of interchangeable components--techniques first recognized as essential in the production of small arms--provided the technological infrastructure upon which China's light industry would develop. Other fundamental technology essential to industrial modernization, such as the production of electrical equipment and the industrial processing of chemicals, was first introduced in the Chinese arsenals.

Even more important was the indirect influence that modernization in the ordnance industry had on related sectors of the economy. The concept of balanced industrial development involving modernization of extractive and raw material industries, of personnel development, and of transport and communications took shape in the minds of officials associated with the ordnance industry by the early 1870s. Though such a plan was never systematically carried out prior to 1895 (probably because foreign threats kept resources so narrowly focused on military production and imperial leadership was lacking), piecemeal efforts were made to bring related sectors abreast of the ordnance industry. Beginning with the China Merchants' Steam Navigation Company, established in part to absorb the costs of steamship maintenance at Kiangnan, and continuing with the modernization of coal mines in Chihli, Taiwan, and Shantung and the establishment of steel refineries at Kiangnan and Tientsin, the requirements of the ordnance industry brought modernization in the Chinese economy.

Education was another area in which the indirect influence of the ordnance industry was felt. Beginning with the earliest advocates of modernized ordnance production, there was a growing awareness of the need for reform in traditional modes of education to supply technically and scientifically trained personnel for the arsenals. On the job training under foreign technicians was conducted at Kiangnan and Tientsin and until 1879 at Nanking. Kiangnan also supported a foreign language school and a formal technical training program. Chinese artisans seemed to respond to the on-the-job training, judging from the references to the excellence of their work under foreign technical direction. In a few instances Chinese personnel moved toward taking over technical direction in the production of ordnance and ammunition, as in the production of the Kiangnan magazine rifle and smokeless powder. The seminal influence of translation work supported by the Kiangnan Arsenal, which included volumes on ordnance technology and a variety of other topics, is impossible to gauge.

Aside from these indirect contributions, which introduced many of the required elements for the subsequent modernization of China's economy, the arsenals made rapid headway in ordnance and ammunition production. Production began with the crude guns and shells turned out at Anking and included smoothbore iron and brass cannon made at Shanghai, Soochow, Kiangnan, and Nanking; rifled iron imitations of Western guns and gingals built at Nanking; muzzle-loading Mausers produced at Kiangnan; and ammunition for all of these weapons plus great numbers of percussion caps, fuses, and other firing devices turned out at all of the plants. Modernized production began in 1870 with the introduction of specialized equipment for making powder at Tientsin, and it gradually replaced the earlier cruder forms, though in 1895 gingals were still in production. At Kiangnan, Remington machinery purchased in 1871 was modified in 1884 and again in 1890; in 1892 it was adapted to produce the Kiangnan magazine rifle. Heavy ordnance production improved steadily from 1878 when the first steel barrel was made until the early 1890s when the arsenal was turning out all steel breechloading quick firing guns and giant coastal defense guns. Modernized machine production of small arms ammunition began at Kiangnan's Lung-hua plant in 1874 and at Tientsin by 1875. By 1895 Kiangnan had developed the capability to produce the smokeless powder ammunition required for maximum effectiveness of magazine rifles and quick firing guns. After the Sino-French War both Kiangnan and Tientsin modernized to produce the ammunition required for the newest types of naval and coastal defense ordnance and quick firing guns. Production of the brown powder for this ammunition began at Tientsin in 1887 and Kiangnan in 1894, while the steel required for shells was first produced at

Kiangnan in 1892 and Tientsin in 1893. Meanwhile, both of these plants had begun production of electrically detonated mines: Tientsin in the late 1870s and Kiangnan in the early 1880s. Though some products were imperfect or substandard, in a scant thirty-five years, production in China's arsenals had progressed from gingals and cannon balls to the most modern types of arms and ammunition.

Finally, it must be asked what went wrong? What problems retarded the modernization of the ordnance industry and undermined its strategic potential? More than any other single factor the high costs of current production were responsible for the deficiencies in production as of 1894-1895. Production costs, especially overhead, drew resources away from investment in the new equipment needed to update and expand output of ordnance and ammunition. This was most graphically demonstrated at Kiangnan where deficiencies in the production of rifles and limitations in the numbers and types of guns produced stemmed directly from inadequacies in production equipment, equipment that should have been replaced and augmented but was not because so much of the arsenal's resources were consumed by current production costs. At Nanking, current production costs consumed almost all of the relatively small annual income, which meant that extraordinary appropriations were needed to defray the cost of expanding and updating equipment. During thirty years of operations, in only one instance was such an appropriation made. Data on current production costs at Tientsin are lacking, but it is likely they inhibited development of production there also, for the underlying problems that caused high costs at Kiangnan and Nanking were problems at Tientsin as well, though it appears that there they were not so acute.

The most important component of production costs at Kiangnan was the price paid for materials and fuel. This was a crippling expense at Nanking also and presumably a problem at Tientsin. Though precise data are lacking, costs may have been lower at Tientsin since the arsenal used domestic coal. The greatest factor determining the high prices paid for materials was that most of them came from abroad. Prices necessarily included transport charges and middlemen's profits. China's extractive and refining industry lagged far behind the state of development required to supply the rapidly increasing needs of modernized ordnance production. Lack of experience, laxity, and malfeasance on the part of the officials responsible for purchasing aggravated this problem at the Kiangnan

Arsenal.

The second important component of the arsenal's production costs was personnel and administrative expense. The practice of overstaffing seems to have reached serious proportions around 1880 at Nanking and Kiangnan, gradually increasing at the latter institution until it constituted a crippling drain on the arsenal's resources in the 1890s. Overstaffing at Kiangnan both at the administrative level and in the work force resulted, at least in part, from the influence of a clique of Hunanese at the arsenal who favored their coprovincials.

Another important element in the cost of personnel was the salaries paid to foreign technicians. China's newly established modern schools and the training programs at the arsenals fell far short of meeting the industry's requirements for scientifically and technically trained personnel. Consequently, right up until 1895 foreign technical assistance was needed to improve and even to maintain certain types of production. Though the effect of foreign personnel on production in the arsenals was uneven, their salaries were uniformly high. This was one of the reasons that prompted Li Hung-chang to eliminate foreign personnel from high management positions and to minimize the number of foreign technicians. Indications are that the Tientsin Arsenal was quite successful in this respect. Employment of highly paid foreign technicians had mixed results at Kiangnan. And at Nanking the premature withdrawal of all foreign personnel for budgetary reasons probably had an adverse effect on modernization.

Another factor that inhibited the modernization of ordnance production was the system through which the arsenals were financed. The annual operating capital of Kiangnan and Tientsin, keyed as it was to a percentage of customs revenue at certain ports, fluctuated wildly from year to year with the fluctuations in foreign trade. Long range planning was virtually impossible. At Tientsin, the customs income was limited and the production of modernized naval ammunition after 1887 was conditioned by Li's ability to draw in 100,000 taels or more per year additional income. Financial uncertainties occasioned delays in production which adversely affected the supply of ammunition during the war.

The location of the arsenals did much to undermine their strategic potential. The sites for Kiangnan and Tientsin had been chosen without adequate forethought as to their vulnerability to foreign naval attack or blockade. Both sites had been selected with the thought that they could conveniently serve as supply points for pacification forces during the rebellions of the 1860s. Furthermore, the treaty port locations facilitated the purchase of the imported raw materials and the hiring of foreign technicians essential to arsenal operations. Kiangnan was also located with the mission of shipbuilding in mind. After the Sino-Japanese War the relocation of the Kiangnan Arsenal at a secure inland site became a central concern of both the Liangkiang and the imperial governments. Tientsin was destroyed by a foreign landing force in 1900 and rebuilt in the inland city of Te-chou. The Nanking Arsenal had been positioned at the administrative capital of the Liangkiang provinces in the 1860s to facilitate supervision during the Nien Rebellion. But the site had been poorly chosen. It imposed absolute physical limitations on the possibilities for expansion of production facilities.

Perhaps the most pervasive of all problems affecting the ordnance industry was its leaders. Four different strata of leadership influenced operations: the imperial government, the commissioners who supervised the arsenals, the directors who managed them, and the foreign technicians who provided technological guidance. The arsenals had been founded under the aegis of local power during the closing years of the Taiping and Nien rebellions. They were more an expression of the innovative reform programs of provincial officials than they were the result of a conscious policy of the imperial government. The court's role was chiefly to sanction, approve, encourage, or sometimes discourage (by withholding funds) the establishment and operation of modern arsenals. Still, imperial leadership exerted a powerful and generally inhibiting influence on the development of these plants. This is best exemplified by the imperial decision in 1875 to give first priority to frontier defense in the northwest rather than to maritime defense. While millions of taels were poured into the reconquest of Chinese Turkestan, maritime defense planning operated on an austerity budget. Funds that could have been used to spur production and modernization in the ordnance industry and related sectors of the economy were used instead to extend imperial control over a vast, underpopulated wasteland. By 1895 China had won the desert and lost the war with Japan.

The lack of centralized planning and direction in the industry by the imperial government also had devastating results. Imperial officials proved incapable of enforcing standardized production in arsenals under different supervisory authorities even after the Navy Yamen was established with precisely that purpose in mind. The northern and southern commissioners managed to avoid serious nonstandardization in production in the arsenals under their supervision. In the 1890s, however, Kiangnan and the new Hanyang Arsenal, supervised by Governor-General of Hunan and Hupeh Chang Chih-tung, developed magazine rifles of different calibers, Navy Yamen regulations to the contrary notwithstanding. The imperial government also failed in its efforts to control wasteful expenditure of imperial maritime customs proceeds at Kiangnan. Worst of all, Peking's failure to insist on a uniform bore diameter in all foreign purchases of small arms by provincial governments obliged arsenals, especially Kiangnan, to divide resources to produce cartridges of as many as six different calibers to meet the variegated needs of China's armies.

Problems resulting from the leadership policies of the northern and southern commissioners were almost equally as serious. The failure of northern and southern authorities to coordinate the development of production in their respective zones posed obstacles for the growth of the industry, as in 1867 when Li balked at supporting the establishment of the Tientsin Arsenal while his responsibilities were concentrated in the south. In shipbuilding policy, the decisions of the supervisory leadership proved most disastrous. Tseng Kuo-fan's well intentioned but overly ambitious decision to concentrate Kiangnan's resources on the construction of steamships was made on the basis of inadequate understanding of the technological and economic factors involved. It resulted in the construction of highly priced and low quality vessels and consumed close to half of the arsenal's financial resources prior to 1875. Thereafter the lingering costs of the steamship program sapped Kiangnan's financial strength. In the early 1880s an ill-advised resumption of shipbuilding drew funds away from the acquisition of new rifle machinery, creating a long-term deficiency in small arms production equipment which affected rifle production adversely in the 1890s.

Even in the area of policy regarding ordnance production, supervisory leadership created grave problems. After Li had wisely decided that the most practical course for the industry would be to delay the production of heavy ordnance until production costs could be reduced through the development of raw materials and refining industries, he wavered, and, departing from this policy, approved the production of heavy coastal defense ordnance at Kiangnan. The most serious blunder, however, was the choice of a gun for Kiangnan to produce. Recoiling from the Taku disaster of 1875, Li approved production of the Armstrong muzzle-loader. Though it was the strongest and therefore the safest, it was also the heaviest and most difficult to operate. Less than a decade passed before this gun was replaced by a breechloading model that could have been adopted in the first place. In contrast, Li's adherence to the policy of concentrating production resources on powder and ammunition in his supervision of the Tientsin Arsenal seems to have brought this arsenal a moderate degree of success in at least these objectives, though detailed data to support this impression are lacking.

The provincial bureaucrats who directed operations and administration in the arsenals had neither the educational background nor the experience necessary to equip them for their roles as magnates of modern industry. Though some, such as Liu Ch'i-hsiang, showed a surprising determination and enthusiasm in their new positions, and others, such as Feng Chün-kuang, exhibited an almost visionary understanding of the problems of development, on balance the bureaucrats who managed the arsenals probably created more problems than they solved. The tendency of these officials to administer the arsenals as they would any other bureau of the traditional government, that is, without regard to cost effective management, resulted in overstaffing, misuse of personnel, laxity, and malfeasance in the handling of funds. Furthermore, the conclusion is inescapable that at the Nanking Arsenal the Chinese managers, deprived of regular foreign technical advice, used newly installed machinery to produce outdated ordnance.

Perhaps the most crucial aspect of the leadership of China's ordnance industry was the introduction of Western influence, which began with the foreign technicians. Once the arsenals had been established, the question arose could China continue to develop machine industry employing its own human resources, or would further transfusions of Western technology and personnel be required to keep these Western-style institutions alive? In this respect the Westerners who served as advisers, instructors, and technicians in China's arsenals were of enormous importance, for they were the bridge between the two civilizations. The mysteries of Western technology, the training necessary to use it, and even the scientific principles upon which it was founded came to the Chinese through the foreigners who served in the arsenals. But these advisers and technicians were at best a mixed lot, some ill-suited by temperament and background for the roles of cultural middlemen. Some, such as Mackenzie, who introduced Armstrong built-up ordnance at Kiangnan, were unquestionably highly qualified and dedicated to their mission. But the record raises serious questions about others. Halliday Macartney, the best known foreigner in the Chinese arsenals during these years, was an energetic and loyal employee of Li Hung-chang, but he was a physician without qualification or experience as an ordnance engineer, the position for which he was handsomely remunerated by the Chinese. Li Hung-chang became exasperated and bitter at what he saw as incompetence and procrastination on the part of the first foreign technicians at Kiangnan who, it will be recalled, were shipwrights doubling as ordnance technicians. Even as late as 1895 a foreign technician failed to fulfill a contract calling for the production of smokeless powder, and it was a Chinese who finally solved the problem, albeit with marginal results. In short, the foreigners in the Chinese arsenals were in many instances poorly suited to serve as transmitters of Western science and technology. The success or failure of this first phase of cultural assimilation so crucial to the survival of the Empire hinged to a large extent on the effectiveness of a small group of foreigners, which included adventurers, opportunists, and incompetents.

The record of achievement and institutional progress in the ordnance industry suggests a degree of resilience and a viability which not all writers have found in nineteenth century China. Guided by realism, practicality,and open-mindedness on the part of its leaders, the industry not only opened the era of modernized ordnance production, but it also stimulated change in education, in the economy, and, most important, in official attitudes. Still, the problems that plagued the arsenals, many of which stemmed from the traditional socio-economic and intellectual environment, were overwhelming, and what had been accomplished was only a small fraction of what remained to be done. Modernization in the ordnance industry by 1895 can be likened to a glass partially filled with water--or is it partially empty? What has been seen by some as woefully inadequate when measured against the norms of European and American counterparts reflects remarkable accomplishment when measured against the baseline of traditional ordnance production that had prevailed only thirty five years earlier. To belittle the importance of the industry because it failed to strengthen China against the onslaught of foreign power is to judge simplistically and to ignore the pervasive influence of imperialism. Imperialism made rapid modernization of the ordnance industry a survival issue for China, but rapid modernization could take place only under the tutelage of the imperialist powers and through reliance on their men, machinery, and material. This dependency, coupled with production shortcomings in the arsenals, robbed the industry of its antiimperialist potential, and Japan, the newest imperialist power, forced China to resort to arms just when the ordnance industry had taken the first difficult steps on the long road to modernized production. The result was disaster.

APPENDIX I

TABLE 1

Specifications and Cost of Vessels Built at the Kiangnan Arsenal 1867-85

Date Completed	Name	Length Beam (ft.)	Horse Power	Displacement (tons)	Description	Construction Cost (taels)
1868 Aug.	T'ien-chi	217 / 32	150	600	wooden hull paddle wheel	81,397
1869 May-June	Ts'ao-chiang	211 / 32	80	640	wooden hull propeller	83,306
1869 Aug. 25	Tse-hai	206 / 33	125	600	wooden hull propeller	82,736
1870 Sept.-Oct.	Wei-ching	241 / 38	150	1,000	wooden hull propeller	118,031
1872 May 24	Chen-an changed to Hai-an	352 / 49	500	2,800	wooden hull propeller	355,190
By 1872 July					armor plate twin propeller	5,360
By 1872 July					armor plate twin propeller	see below
By 1874 Jan.					armor plate twin propeller	13,599 including above vessel

161

TABLE 1 (cont'd)

Date Completed	Name	Length Beam (ft.)	Horse Power	Displacement (tons)	Description	Construction Cost (taels)
1873 Dec. 23	Yü-yüan	352 49	500	2,800	wooden hull propeller	318,717
1874-75	Chin-ou	123 23	200		ironclad (monitor class)	62,586
1874-75					armor plate twin propeller	8,960
1874-75					armor plate twin propeller	10,943
1874-75					motorized sampan	990
1874-75					foreign style sailing vessel	57,005
1881		160 26	650	400	twin propeller	
1885	Pao-min	264 42	1,900		steel armored	223,800

SOURCE: TWCKTK, 839-41. YWYT, IV, 33-4; 40-41; 51-52; 62. KNCTCC, 3:1-3; 55. CCKT, I, 287-90. HFT, III, 45, 60-61, 75, 83-90, 137-38. NCH, Sept. 27, 1881. Shanghai hsien hsü-chih 13:4-5.

162

TABLE 2

Income of the Kiangnan Arsenal, 1867-1895
Unit: Shanghai taels

Year	Total Income	Income from Shanghai Maritime Custom Proceeds	Miscellaneous Income	Income from Provinces for Munitions
1867-73	2,927,458	2,884,498	42,960	
1874	537,154	491,682	45,472	
1875	549,411	520,594	28,817	
1876	531,444	472,595	58,849	
1877	353,135	333,975	19,160	
1878	444,626	434,779	9,847	
1879	487,147	468,742	18,405	
1880	594,057	560,995	33,062	
1881	746,172	657,226	88,946	
1882	616,325	529,038	87,287	
1883	573,615	438,148	135,567	
1884	907,253	505,206	361,387	40,660
1885	604,999	527,132	77,867	
1886	553,390	525,468	20,135	7,787
1887	610,204	530,669	27,411	52,124
1888	568,555	556,932	11,623	
1889	631,142	502,347	128,795	
1890	895,866	793,399	96,098	6,369
1891	786,578	679,905	96,595	10,078
1892	673,311	647,834	19,108	6,369
1893	629,135	564,128	58,638	6,369
1894	817,893	662,307	126,851	68,735
1895	1,298,141	780,134 *400,000	50,783	67,224

* Special allocation from the Shanghai maritime customs (not from the 20 percent funds) to repay debts incurred from 1890 to 1895.

SOURCE: KNCTCC, 4:2-4

TABLE 3

Machinery, Arms, and Ammunition Produced
at the Kiangnan Arsenal, 1867-1895

Period	Heavy Machines	Small Arms	Guns	Mines	Powder (lbs)	Small Arms Ammunition	Gun Ammunition
1867-73	127	9,920	112			2,000	15,624
1874	35	2,500	8	44	81,200	542,000	33,450
1875	40	3,558	8	44	88,982	581,000	31,215
1876	19	2,510	1	44	115,544	1,213,400	41,739
1877	24	1,730			85,060	792,600	11,369
1878	18	1,638	4		80,920	731,850	30,266
1879	17	1,300	13		82,530	1,045,650	11,437
1880	14	2,200	6	64	224,446	1,162,000	8,235
1881	18	2,800	8		162,760	1,156,000	956
1882	21	2,400	11		171,360	1,159,900	4,681
1883	42	2,024	12	10	160,350	1,139,000	29,329
1884	9	2,327	16	22	357,250	1,177,000	33,719
1885	19	2,562	4	10	346,300	665,000	7,595
1886	17	2,250	7		235,537	1,753,880	12,080
1887	17	2,352	7	50	246,780	2,067,200	14,359
1888	14	2,450	10	52	233,516	2,012,500	32,186
1889	15	2,126	13	20	158,700	1,635,000	11,070
1890	14	825	9	82	282,000	1,964,000	41,916
1891	15	1,106	5	6	254,500	1,482,000	22,979
1892	19	860	12	91	206,960	854,500	12,216
1893	19	578	4	28	128,525	805,000	12,951
1894	28	1,224	4	40	378,249	1,494,880	10,628
1895	27	1,109	4	10	511,754	2,456,110	23,746

SOURCE: KNCTCC, 3:2-38.

TABLE 4

Distribution of Arms and Ammunition
from the Kiangnan Arsenal, 1867-1895

Year	Product	Ships and Units Subordinate to Commissioner of Southern Ports	Ships and Units Subordinate to Commissioner of Northern Ports	Other Units
1869	Guns	17	4	
	Gun Ammunition	952		
	Small Arms	40	1,524	1,000
	Small Arms Ammunition	1,000	1,000	
	Powder (lbs)	1,200	1,600	
1870	Guns	17		25
	Gun Ammunition	639		3,100
	Small Arms	310		500
	Small Arms Ammunition			
	Powder (lbs)	1,200		
1871	Guns			
	Gun Ammunition	320	4,240	4,000
	Small Arms	24	1,700	1,500
	Small Arms Ammunition			
	Powder (lbs)	50	8,480	15,000
1872	Guns			
	Gun Ammunition			
	Small Arms		900	
	Small Arms Ammunition			
	Powder (lbs)		1,600	
1873	Guns	13	10	
	Gun Ammunition	400	800	
	Small Arms	60	1,500	
	Small Arms Ammunition			
	Powder (lbs)			
1874	Guns	82	100	2
	Gun Ammunition	7,050		200
	Small Arms	3,664	100	
	Small Arms Ammunition			
	Powder (lbs)	49,482		400

TABLE 4 (cont'd)

Year	Product	Ships and Units Subordinate to Commissioner of Southern Ports	Ships and Units Subordinate to Commissioner of Northern Ports	Other Units
1875	Guns	3	2	
	Gun Ammunition	2,832	23,110	
	Small Arms	36	1,000	
	Small Arms Ammunition			
	Powder (lbs)	120,250	3,420	
1876	Guns	2		
	Gun Ammunition	1,280	10,040	
	Small Arms	2,081	1,000	
	Small Arms Ammunition	278,016	400,000	
	Powder (lbs)	80,824	80	
1877	Guns	1		
	Gun Ammunition	7,797		
	Small Arms			
	Small Arms Ammunition	12,000	200,000	
	Powder (lbs)	82,600	32,000	
1878	Guns	23		
	Gun Ammunition	3,522	22,000	
	Small Arms	575	4,002	
	Small Arms Ammunition	28,156	355,400	
	Powder (lbs)	45,373	44,000	
1879	Guns			
	Gun Ammunition	1,840		
	Small Arms	10	1,000	
	Small Arms Ammunition	38,500	350,000	
	Powder (lbs)	96,647		
1880	Guns	8	8	
	Gun Ammunition	4,302	1,200	
	Small Arms	8,039	2,000	
	Small Arms Ammunition	384,000	400,000	
	Powder (lbs)	154,979		
1881	Guns	8	4	
	Gun Ammunition	2,811		
	Small Arms	1,122		
	Small Arms Ammunition	119,500		
	Powder (lbs)	81,673		

TABLE 4 (cont'd)

Year	Product	Ships and Units Subordinate to Commissioner of Southern Ports	Ships and Units Subordinate to Commissioner of Northern Ports	Other Units
1882	Guns	6	5	
	Gun Ammunition	3,338		
	Small Arms	362		
	Small Arms Ammunition	81,600		
	Powder (lbs)	214,015		
1883	Guns	127		
	Gun Ammunition	13,100		
	Small Arms	294		
	Small Arms Ammunition	69,690		
	Powder (lbs)	79,542		
	Mines			60
1884	Guns	38		15
	Gun Ammunition	27,492	2,000	1,856
	Small Arms	15,582	140	2,000
	Small Arms Ammunition	3,566,382		2,000,000
	Powder (lbs)	472,803		
	Mines	23		20
1885	Guns	57		1
	Gun Ammunition	15,488		1,100
	Small Arms	1,089		
	Small Arms Ammunition	606,800		268,200
	Powder (lbs)	70,410		
	Mines			10
1886	Guns			
	Gun Ammunition	8,495		
	Small Arms	139		
	Small Arms Ammunition	70,200		
	Powder (lbs)	116,568		
	Mines			
1887	Guns		4	
	Gun Ammunition	5,219	630	
	Small Arms	36		
	Small Arms Ammunition	1,987,000		
	Powder (lbs)	110,982		
	Mines			

TABLE 4 (cont'd)

Year	Product	Ships and Units Subordinate to Commissioner of Southern Ports	Ships and Units Subordinate to Commissioner of Northern Ports	Other Units
1888	Guns	1		
	Gun Ammunition	2,743	10,000	
	Small Arms	250		
	Small Arms Ammunition	87,710		
	Powder (lbs)	185,896		
	Mines			
1889	Guns			
	Gun Ammunition	5,223		
	Small Arms	2		1,000
	Small Arms Ammunition	19,100		
	Powder (lbs)	304,671		
	Mines			
1890	Guns	11	2	6
	Gun Ammunition	414,283	9,000	4,000
	Small Arms	883		1,000
	Small Arms Ammunition	69,520		
	Powder (lbs)	155,079		
	Mines			
1891	Guns			
	Gun Ammunition	14,180		
	Small Arms			
	Small Arms Ammunition	48,840		
	Powder (lbs)	637,824		
	Mines			
1892	Guns	6	1	
	Gun Ammunition	1,414	20	
	Small Arms	265	200	
	Small Arms Ammunition	71,636	21,000	
	Powder (lbs)	65,247	100	
	Mines			
1893	Guns	6		
	Gun Ammunition	1,742		
	Small Arms	5,102		
	Small Arms Ammunition	562,590		
	Powder (lbs)	34,769		30,000
	Mines			

TABLE 4 (cont'd)

Year	Product	Ships and Units Subordinate to Commissioner of Southern Ports	Ships and Units Subordinate to Commissioner of Northern Ports	Other Units
1894	Guns		4	2
	Gun Ammunition	8,550	3,600	1,600
	Small Arms	7,150		
	Small Arms Ammunition	3,386,811	40,000	2,400,000
	Powder (lbs)	165,680	800	302,480
	Mines	168		40
1895	Guns	6		3
	Gun Ammunition	2,427		1,060
	Small Arms	805		2,000
	Small Arms Ammunition	2,044,393		1,400,000
	Powder (lbs)	165,680		80,274
	Mines			

SOURCE: KNCTCC, 5 1-57.

TABLE 5

Expenditure of Funds by the Kiangnan Arsenal, 1867-1895
Unit: Shanghai taels

Period	Total Expenditure	Expenditure for building, menial wages, official wages	Artisans Wages	Purchase of Machinery	Purchase of Materials	Purchase of Munitions	Translation and Cartography
1867-73	2,919,911	431,360	741,567	110,576	1,533,049	86,899	16,460
1874	567,794	50,918	129,942	46,615	303,877	29,642	6,800
1875	528,039	37,730	155,004	27,108	289,385	14,057	4,755
1876	549,628	47,789	150,965	53,835	279,371	14,288	3,380
1877	411,571	39,568	125,555	26,123	190,575	27,292	2,458
1878	348,926	84,649	106,971	5,846	66,880	80,817	3,763
1879	397,540	73,078	124,458	3,912	193,015	345	2,731
1880	588,370	63,696	133,034	60,831	312,161	16,402	2,246
1881	853,081	105,469	166,798	24,227	534,579	19,895	2,113
1882	613,770	132,389	153,128	71,304	65,565	189,658	1,726
1883	546,853	84,777	163,469	29,430	241,635	23,856	2,686
1884	983,196	76,155	243,983	32,794	294,848	133,837	1,579

Period	Total Expenditure	Expenditure for building, menial wages, official wages	Artisans Wages	Purchase of Machinery	Purchase of Materials	Purchase of Munitions	Translation and Cartography
1885	505,174	68,723	187,703	9,623	238,089		1,036
1886	491,687	73,547	160,622	16,244	240,001	771	502
1887	661,542	82,134	179,247	18,939	379,513	557	1,152
1888	487,518	72,718	153,663	25,463	233,320	1,657	697
1889	688,690	73,499	157,517	23,992	411,637	21,472	573
1890	755,717	86,740	177,728	29,034	441,962	18,674	1,579
1891	644,520	84,678	161,202	55,037	333,304	9,680	619
1892	763,154	94,154	205,248	27,936	426,110	8,750	956
1893	843,151	91,637	199,906	133,337	411,073	185	1,013
1894	859,935	93,021	231,902	222,933	308,782	22,005	1,292
1895	976,829	109,024	240,507	47,584	568,565	10,241	908

SOURCE: KNCTCC, 4:6-8

TABLE 6

Income and Expenditure of the Tientsin Arsenal, 1876-1892
Unit: taels

Period	Total Income	Income from Tientsin-Chefoo Customs Proceeds	Total Expenditure
1870) 1871)	256,080	256,080	244,988
1872) 1873)	395,269	395,269	394,700
1874) 1875)	584,617	584,287	575,494
1876) 1877)	484,119	445,608	488,364
1878) 1879)	461,542	338,910	482,539
1880) 1881)	671,667	453,999	643,757
1882	297,768	266,000*	266,969
1883	313,436	281,697*	277,078
1884	398,067	369,000*	454,468
1885	356,679*	?	294,066
1886	320,332*	?	296,212
1887	300,201*	?	345,966
1888	367,321	?	296,800
1889	358,706	?	383,074
1890	317,713	?	328,679
1891	421,572	?	316,419
1892	456,472	?	509,911

* Includes allocation from Frontier Defense Funds.

SOURCE: CKKT, I, 367; YWYT, IV, 273-76.

TABLE 7

Income and Expenditure of the Nanking Arsenal, 1879-1894
Unit: taels

Period	Income	Expenditure
1879) 1880)	202,415	199,421
1881) 1882)	256,047	257,894
1883	108,000	108,857
1884	153,076	153,116
1885	118,091	118,250
1886	210,000	210,362
1887	114,000	114,052
1888	114,000	113,545
1889	114,000	124,595
1890	124,532	124,595
1891	114,000	114,008

SOURCE: YWYT, 185-186, 193-194, 203-204, 207-217, 220-226.
Tseng Chung-hsiang Kung Ch'üan-chi tsou-i, 22:23a
CKKT, II, 440.

TABLE 8

Income and Expenditure of the Nanking Powder Plant, 1884-1891
Unit: Treasury taels

Period	Income	Expenditure
1884 June -	26,826	26,809
1885	38,589	38,450
1886	89,481	89,276
1887	54,424	54,349
1888	57,608	57,552
1889	50,178	50,158
1890	53,986	53,966
1891	49,599	49,592

SOURCE: YWYT,   IV, 196, 201-202, 205-206, 206-207, 212-213, 215, 220, 222, 224-228.

APPENDIX II

ARSENALS ESTABLISHED IN CHINA, 1860 - 1895

Year of Establishment	Plant Name	Province	Location	Establishing Official	First Director	Estimated Establishment Cost (taels)	Estimated Annual Income (taels)	Chief Products	Remarks
1861	Anking Arsenal	Anhwei	Anking	Tseng Kuo-fan				Small guns, explosive shells	
1863	Shanghai Arsenal	Kiangsu	Shanghai	Li Hung-chang	Han Tien-chia			Small guns, explosive shells	1865 merged Kiangnan
1863	Shanghai Arsenal	Kiangsu	Shanghai	Li Hung-chang	Ting Jih-ch'ang			Small guns, explosive shells	1865 merged Kiangnan
1863	Sungkiang Arsenal	Kiangsu	Shanghai	Li Hung-chang	Halliday Macartney; Liu Tso-yu			Explosive shells	1863 moved to Soochow
1863-64	Soochow Arsenal	Kiangsu	Soochow	Li Hung-chang	Halliday Mccartney; Liu Tso-yu			Explosive shells	1865 merged Nanking
1865	Kiangnan Arsenal	Kiangsu	Shanghai Hung-k'ou	Li Hung-chang; Tseng Kuo-fan	Ting Jih-ch'ang	1,000,000		Rifles, heavy coastal defense ordnance, quick firing guns, black, brown and smokeless powder, cartridges, mines, steel machine tools, steamships	1867 moved Kao-ch'ang Miao; 1867 rocket plant established at Chen-chia fang; 1871-1874 powder plant established at Lung-hua
1865	Nanking Arsenal	Kiangsu	Nanking South Gate	Li Hung-chang	Halliday Macartney		100,000-150,000	Iron ordnance and ammunition	Wu-lung Shan Arsenal established 1874 for support of Yangtze forts; merged with Nanking in 1879
1866	Tientsin East Arsenal	Chihli	Tientsin	Liu Ch'ang-yu Ch'ung-hou			69,000	Traditional ordnance	1868 stopped production
1866	Tientsin East Arsenal	Chihli	Tientsin Chia-chia-ku Tao	Ch'ung-hou	Meadows	388,178	125,000-450,000 incl. West Arsenal	Black and brown powder, cartridges, naval ammunition, steel	
1867	Tientsin West Arsenal	Chihli	Tientsin Hai-kuang Szu	Ch'ung-hou	Stewart	95,795		Small guns, machinery	
1869	Foochow Arsenal	Fukien	Foochow Shui-pu Gate	Ying Kuei	Lai Ch'ang			Ammunition, powder	1872 stopped production; resumed production 1875
1869	Sian Arsenal	Shensi	Sian	Tso Tsung-t'ang				Ammunition, powder	1872 probably moved to Lanchow
1870	Tientsin Mobile Arsenal	Chihli	Tientsin	Li Hung-chang				Ammunition	Subordinate Huai Army
1872	Lanchow Arsenal	Kansu	Lanchow	Tso Tsung-t'ang	Lai Ch'ang			Various types of ordnance, ammunition, powder	1882 stopped production

APPENDIX II (cont'd)

Year of Establishment	Plant Name	Province	Location	Establishing Official	First Director	Estimated Establishment Cost (taels)	Estimated Annual Income (taels)	Chief Products	Remarks
1872	Yunnan Arsenal	Yunnan	Kunming					Ordnance, ammunition, powder	Ceased production, date uncertain; 1880-1881 resumed production; 1885 resumed production
1873	Kwangtung Arsenal	Kwangtung	Canton; Chi-hsien fan	Jui Lin	Wen Tzu-shao	170,000		Small steamships, ammunition, mines	1885 merged Kwangtung Powder Plant
1875	Shantung Arsenal	Shantung	Tsinan Lo-k'ou	Ting Pao-chen	Hsü Chien-yin; Hsüeh Fu-chen	186,000	36,000	Rifles, ammunition, powder	
1875	Hunan Arsenal	Hunan	Ch'ang-sha	Wang Wen-shao	Han Tien-chia				
1875	Kwangtung Powder Plant	Kwangtung	Canton Ts'eng-pu	Chang Chao-tung	P'an Lu			Powder	
1877	Szechwan Arsenal	Szechuan	Ch'eng-tu South Gate	Ting Pao-chen	Hsia Shih; Hua Heng-fang	77,000	20,000-60,000	Rifles, guns, ammunition, and power	1880 Szechuan Powder Plant established nearby at Ku-chia-pa
1881	Kirin Arsenal	Kirin	Near City of Kirin	Wu Ta-ch'eng	Sung Ch'un-ao		40,000-100,000	Ammunition, powder	
1881	Nanking Powder Plant	Kiangsu	Nanking Shuang-ch'iao Gate	Liu K'un-i	Sun Ch'uan-yüeh; Kung Chao-yüan	183,000	50,000	Powder, ammunition	
1882	Chekiang Powder Plant	Chekiang	Hangchow Liang-shan Gate			100,000		Powder	1885 merged Chekiang Arsenal
1882-84	Shansi Arsenal	Shansi	T'ai-yüan	Chang Chih-tung				Ammunition	
1883	Peking Field Forces Arsenal		Peking San-chia-tien	Prince Ch'un	P'an Chün-te	200,000 300,000			1890 destroyed by fire
1883	Chekiang Arsenal	Chekiang	Hangchow	Liu Ping-chang	Wang En-hsien			Powder and ammunition	
1885	Kwangtung Cartridge Plant	Kwangtung	Canton Shih-ching	Chang Chih-tung	Hsüeh Pei-yung			Cartridges	
1885	Taiwan Arsenal	Taiwan	Taipei North Gate	Liu Ming-ch'uan	Ting Ta-i			Ammunition and powder	
1890	Hanyang Arsenal	Hupeh	Hanyang Ta-pieh Shan	Chang Chih-tung	Ts'ai Hsi-yung	1,400,000		Rifles, light artillery, ammunition, and powder	Entered production 1895
1894	Shensi Arsenal	Shensi	Sian Feng-huo Tung	Lu Ch'uan-lin				Ammunition	

SOURCES: APPENDIX II

CCKT, I, 564-566. Wang Erh-min, Ch'ing-chi ping-kung-yeh te hsing-ch'i (Taipei: Chung-yang yen-chiu-yüan chin-tai li-shih-so, 1963), 105-127. For materials on Wu-lung Shan Arsenal see YWYT, IV, 185; Hunan Arsenal see YWYT, IV, 333-335; Shansi Arsenal see YWYT, IV, 149. The establishment costs for Tientsin are based on figures from Chapter 3 of this study. The Kiangnan estimate of establishment costs includes the costs mentioned in Chapter 3 plus establishment costs through 1875, cf. Thomas L. Kennedy, The Establishment and Development of the Kiangnan Arsenal 1860-1895 (unpublished Ph.D. dissertation, Columbia University 1968), 95-96. The Hanyang Arsenal establishment costs are from Thomas L. Kennedy, "Chang Chih-tung and the Struggle for Strategic Industrialization: The Establishment of the Hanyang Arsenal, 1884-1895," Harvard Journal of Asiatic Studies, Vol. 33 (1973), 154-182.

Notes

Abbreviations Used in Notes

BPP: British Parliamentary Papers housed at the Public Record Office, London

CCKT I: Sun Yu-t'ang, ed., Chung-kuo chin-tai kung-yeh-shih tzu-liao 1840-1895 [Materials on China's modern industrial history 1840-1895], Vol. I, 2 pts. (Peking: K'o-hsüeh ch'u-pan-she, 1956).

CCKT III: Ch'en Chen, ed., Chung-kuo chin-tai kung-yeh-shih tzu-liao 1895-1914 [Materials on China's modern industrial history 1895-1914], Vol. III, 2 pts. (Peking: San-lien Shu-tien, 1961).

CS: Ch'ing-shih pien-ts'uan wei-yüan-hui ed., Ch'ing-shih [History of the Ch'ing Dynasty], 8 vols. (Taipei: Kuo-fang yen-chiu-yüan, 1961).

FO: Foreign Office files, part of British Parliamentary Papers housed at Public Record Office, London, followed by numbers indicating series, folder, and item or page.

HFT: Kuo T'ing-yee et al., eds., Hai-fang tang [Archives of maritime defense] 5 vols. (Taipei: Chung-yang yen-chiu-yüan chin-tai shih yen-chiu-so, 1957)

IWSM: Ch'ou-pan i-wu shih-mo [The complete record of the management of barbarian affairs], 260 chüan (Taipei: Kuo-feng ch'u-pan-she, 1963): 80 chüan deal with the later Tao-kuang period, 1836-1850; 80 chüan deal with the Hsien-feng period, 1851-1861; and 100 chüan deal with the T'ung-chih period, 1862-1874.

KNCTCC: Wei Yün-kung, ed., <u>Chiang-nan chih-tsao-chü chi</u> [The record of the Kiangnan Arsenal], 10 chüan (Taipei: Wen-hai shu-chü, no date).

LWCKPLHK: Wu Ju-lun, ed., <u>Li Wen-chung kung ch'üan-chi</u> (The complete works of Li Hung-chang), 166 chüan (Taipei: Wen-hai ch'u-pan-she, 1965). This refers to the 20 chüan segment entitled <u>peng-liao han-kao</u> (letters to colleagues).

LWCKTK: Wu Ju-lun, ed., <u>Li Wen-chung kung ch'üan-chi</u> [The complete works of Li Hung-chang], 166 chüan (Taipei: Wen-hai chu-pan-she, 1965). This refers to the 80 chüan segment entitled <u>tsou-kao</u> (memorials).

NCH: <u>The North China Herald and Supreme Court and Consular Gazette</u>, (Shanghai, weekly).

TWCKTK: <u>Tseng Wen-cheng kung ch'üan-chi</u> [The complete works of Tseng Kuo-fan], 5 vols. (Taipei: Shih-chieh shu-chü, 1965). This refers to vols. 2 and 3 which contain 4 chüan entitled <u>tsou-kao</u> (memorials).

YWYT: Yang Chia-lo, ed., <u>Yang-wu yun-tung wen-hsien hui-pien</u> [Collected documents on the foreign matters movement] 8 vols. (Taipei: Shih-chieh shu-chü, 1963).

NOTES: CHAPTER I

1. Chao T'ieh-han, Huo-yao te fa-ming (Taipei, 1960), p. 91.

2. Edwin O. Reischauer and John K. Fairbank, East Asia: The Great Tradition (Boston, 1958), pp. 81-90.

3. Lien-ch'in ping-kung chi-shu fa-chan chung-hsin, ed., Ping-ch'i fa-chan shih (Taipei, 1969), p. 47.

4. Ibid, p. 47; Chung-ming Chang, "The Genesis and Meaning of Huan K'uan's 'Discourses on Salt and Iron'," Chinese Social and Political Science Review, 18.1:1-52 (April 1934).

5. Wm. Theodore de Bary, Wing-tsit Chan, and Burton Watson, compilers, Sources of Chinese Tradition (New York, 1960), pp. 227-43; Chun-ming Chang, "Huan K'uan," 1-52.

6. Wang Erh-min, Ch'ing-chi ping-kung-yeh te hsing-ch'i (Taipei, 1963), pp. 10-13; Chou Wei, Chung-kuo ping-ch'i shih-kao (Peking, 1957), p. 279.

7. Chin-ting ta-ch'ing hui-tien (Shanghai, 1893), 67:44; 73:22.

8. Chao T'ieh-han, Huo-yao te fa-ming, pp. 1-20.

9. Greek fire was a flammable liquid used in warfare during the Middle Ages, particularly by the Byzantine Greeks. It was composed of such materials as sulphur, naphtha, and quicklime and gave rise to a large development of heat, taking fire spontaneously when wetted. "Greekfire," Encyclopedia Britannica, 1962, X, 820.

10. Wang Ling, "On the Invention and Use of Gunpowder in China," Isis 37:160-78 (1947); Wang Erh-min, Ping-kung-yeh, pp. 1-2; Chao T'ieh-han, Huo-yao te fa-ming, pp. 21-37, 76-77.

11. Wang Ling, "Gunpowder in China," 173; Chao T'ieh-han, Huo-yao te fa-ming, pp. 76-90; L. Carrington Goodrich and Feng Chia-sheng, "The Early Development of Firearms in China," Isis 36:114-23, 250-51 (1945-46).

12. Reischauer and Fairbank, East Asia: The Great Tradition, pp. 183-242.

13. L. Carrington Goodrich, "Note on a Few Early Chinese Bombards," *Isis* 35:211 (1944); Goodrich and Feng, "Firearms in China," 114-23, 250-51; Wang Ling, "Gunpowder in China," 178.

14. Chou Wei, *Chung-kuo ping-ch'i shih-kao*, pp. 269-72; Wang Erh-min, *Ping-kung-yeh*, pp. 2-4.

15. Chou Wei, *Chung-kuo ping-ch'i shih-kao*, p. 311.

16. Wang Erh-min, *Ping-kung-yeh*, pp. 3-5.

17. Wang Erh-min, *Ping-kung-yeh*, pp. 4-7; Fang Hao, "Ming-mo hsi-yang huo-ch'i liu-ju wo-kuo chih shih-liao," *Tung-fang tsa-chih* 40:49-54 (January 1944).

18. Wang Erh-min, *Ping-kung-yeh*, pp. 7-10.

19. Wang Erh-min, *Ping-kung-yeh*, pp. 10-13.

20. Wang Erh-min, *Ping-kung-yeh*, pp. 13-15.

21. Wang Erh-min, *Ping-kung-yeh*, pp. 16, 21-22. The explosive shell was employed as gun ammunition in the West in the early nineteenth century. The shell was a spherical casing of cast iron filled with black powder and equipped with a fuse of slow burning powder. The time of the explosion could be regulated by adjusting the burning time of the fuse. *Encyclopedia Britannica*, 1967, II, 533-34.

22. Gideon Chen, *Lin Tse-hsu: Pioneer Promoter of the Adoption of Western Means of Maritime Defense in China* (Peiping, 1934), pp. 11-18, 39-44; Gideon Chen, *Tseng Kuo-fan: Pioneer Promoter of the Steamship in China* (Peiping, 1935), pp. 8-9; Ssu-yu Teng and John K. Fairbank, *China's Response to the West: A Documentary Survey, 1839-1923* (New York, 1963), p. 35; Wang Erh-min, *Ping-kung-yeh*, pp. 21-26. For an account of the introduction of submarine mines, see *NCH*, Nov. 28, 1883.

23. Previously ammunition had been ignited by placing priming powder in the flash pan and igniting it with the spark obtained by activating flint against steel. If the priming powder was damp or for any reason failed to flash to the main propellant charge, all that occurred was a "flash in the pan." In 1842 the percussion cap was introduced in Great Britain and the United States. It was a small copper container shaped

like a cap, containing a mixture of potassium chlorate. The cap was placed over the end of a small tube which led into the bore where the main propellant charge was located. When the trigger was pulled, the hammer struck the cap and the potassium chlorate explosion was directed down the tube into the bore where it ignited the main propellant charge. Misfires resulting from action of wind and rain on the priming powder were largely eliminated through use of the percussion cap. Encyclopedia Britannica, 1967, XX, 669-93.

24. Chen, Tseng Kuo-fan, pp. 8-12.

25. Wang Erh-min, Ping-kung-yeh, pp. 28-29.

26. Chen, Tseng Kuo-fan, pp. 17-19; Wang Erh-min, Ping-kung-yeh, pp. 27-28.

NOTES: CHAPTER II

1. Liang Ch'i-ch'ao, Intellectual Trends in the Ch'ing Period, trans. by Immanuel Hsu (Cambridge, Mass., 1959), pp. 4-8, 21-22; Chang Hao, Liang Ch'i-ch'ao and Intellectual Transition in China, 1890-1907 (Cambridge, Mass., 1971), pp. 11-12.

2. Liang, Intellectual Trends in the Ch'ing Period, p. 6; Chang, Liang Ch'i-ch'ao, pp. 13-14.

3. Chang, Liang Ch'i-ch'ao, pp. 15-21.

4. Liang, Intellectual Trends in the Ch'ing Period, pp. 85-95; Fung Yu-lan, History of Chinese Philosophy (Princeton, 1953), II, 637-75.

5. Benjamin Schwartz, In Search of Wealth and Power: Yen Fu and the West (New York, 1969), pp. 10-14.

6. Chang, Liang Ch'i-ch'ao, pp. 27-30; Fredrick Wakeman, "The Huang-ch'ao ching-shih wen-pien," Ch'ing-shih Wen-t'i 1.10:8-22 (February 1969).

7. Chang, Liang Ch'i-ch'ao, pp. 28-30.

8. Teng and Fairbank, China's Response to the West, pp. 30-35.

9. Teng and Fairbank, China's Response to the West, pp. 30-35; Chen, Tseng Kuo-fan, pp. 1-12.

10. Han-yin Chen Shen, "Tseng Kuo-fan in Peking, 1840-1852: His Ideas on Statecraft and Reform," Journal of Asian Studies 27.1:61-80 (November 1967).

11. Shen, "Tseng Kuo-fan in Peking," pp. 73-80.

12. Shen, "Tseng Kuo-fan in Peking," pp. 69-80.

13. Arthur W. Hummel, ed., Eminent Chinese of the Ch'ing Period (1943-44; reprint ed., Taipei, 1964), pp. 751-55; Chen, Tseng Kuo-fan, pp. 13-23.

14. Kwang-Ching Liu, "The Confucian as Patriot and Pragmatist: Li Hung-chang's Formative Years, 1823-1866," Harvard Journal of Asiatic Studies 30:5-45 (1970).

15. Wang Erh-min, Huai-chun chih (Taipei, 1967), pp. 1-15.

16. Wang Erh-min, "China's Use of Foreign Military Assistance in the Lower Yangtze Valley, 1860-1864," Chung-yang Yen-chiu-yuan chin-tai shih yen-chiu-so chi-k'an 2:535-83 (June 1971); Immanuel C. Y. Hsu, China's Entrance into the Family of Nations (Cambridge, Mass., 1960), pp. 98-105; Masataka Banno, China and the West, 1858-1861: The Origins of the Tsungli Yamen (Cambridge, Mass., 1964), pp. 46-47.

17. Britten Dean, China and Great Britain: The Diplomacy of Commercial Relations, 1860-1864 (Cambridge, Mass., 1974), pp. 14-21.

18. Dean, China and Great Britain, p. 141.

19. Banno, The Origins of the Tsungli Yamen, pp. 203-06.

20. Banno, The Origins of the Tsungli Yamen, pp. 219-46; Wang Erh-min, "Nan-pei-yang ta-ch'en chih chien-chih chi ch'i ch'uan-li chih k'uo-chang," Ch'ing-shih chi chin-tai-shih yen-chiu lun-chi Ta-lu tsa-chih shih-hsueh tsung-shu 1.7:192-99 (1967).

21. Mary C. Wright, The Last Stand of Chinese Conservatism: The T'ung-Chih Restoration, 1862-1874 (New York, 1966), pp. 26-27.

22. Hsu, China's Entrance into the Family of Nations, pp. 98-105; Banno, The Origins of the Tsungli Yamen, pp. 207-10; Wang Erh-min, "China's Use of Foreign Military Assistance in the Lower Yangtze Valley, 1860-1864," 555-56.

23. Hummel, Eminent Chinese, pp. 241-43.

24. Teng and Fairbank, China's Response to the West, pp. 50-55.

25. Lü Shih-ch'iang, "Feng Kuei-fen te cheng-chih ssu-hsiang," Chung-hua wen-hua fu-hsing yueh-k'an 4.2:1-8 (February 1971).

26. Lü Shih-ch'iang, "Feng Kuei-fen te cheng-chih ssu-hsiang," 4; Teng and Fairbank, China's Response to the West, pp. 50-55.

27. Lü Shih-ch'iang, "Feng Kuei-fen te cheng-chih ssu-hsiang," 4; Teng and Fairbank, China's Response to the West, pp. 50-55.

28. Lü Shih-ch'iang, "Feng Kuei-fen te cheng-chih ssu-hsiang," 4; Teng and Fairbank, China's Response to the West, pp. 50-55.

29. Lü Shih-ch'iang, "Feng Kuei-fen te cheng-chih ssu-hsiang," 1-8.

NOTES: CHAPTER III

1. IWSM, Hsien-feng, 72:11-12; TWCKTK, pp. 416-18.

2. CCKT, I, 249-52; Hummel, Eminent Chinese, pp. 479, 540; Chen, Tseng Kuo-fan, pp. 82-92.

3. Tseng Kuo-fan, Tseng Wen-cheng kung shou-shu jih-chi (1909), T'ung-chih 1/5/7; CCKT, I, 249-50; CS, VII, 5469.

4. TWCKTK, pp. 549-50, 839-40.

5. Yung Wing, My Life in China and America (New York, 1909), pp. 149-51.

6. Yung Wing, My Life in China and America, pp. 151-53.

7. Chang Shih-jung, ed., Tseng Kuo-fan wei-k'an hsin-kao (Shanghai, 1959), p. 188.

8. Yung Wing, My Life in China and America, p. 154, states that the sum was 68,000 taels, half of which was to be provided by the Shanghai taotai and half by the provincial treasurer of Kwangtung; cf. Tseng Kuo-fan wei-k'an hsin-kao, p. 188, which states that Tseng directed Li Hung-chang in Shanghai to provide 10,000 taels and the governor-general of the Liang-kiang provinces to provide 20,000.

9. Yung Wing, My Life in China and America, pp. 156, 160, 164. The specifications were drawn up by an American engineer, John Haskins, and the order was filled by the Putman Machine Company of Fitchburg, Mass.

10. Hummel, Eminent Chinese, pp. 464-65.

11. Kwang-Ching Liu, "The Confucian as Patriot and Pragmatist: Li Hung-chang's Formative Years, 1823-1866," 5-45.

12. Kwang-Ching Liu, "The Confucian as Patriot and Pragmatist: Li Hung-chang's Formative Years," 13-19, 31; LWCKPLHK, 1:11b, 54a.

13. IWSM, T'ung-chih, 20:13b; LWCKTK, 3:11-13, 26:13a; LWCKPLHK, 2:45b, 2:46b, 3:3a, 3:16b.

14. Demetrius Boulger, The Life of Sir Halliday Macartney (London, 1908), pp. 79, 123-32.

15. IWSM, T'ung-chih, 25:4-8. The yüan, or Chinese dollar, was a coin issued by a provincial government and limited in use, for the most part to local transactions. Hosea Ballou Morse, The Trade and Administration of the Chinese Empire (Taipei, 1966, reprint ed.), p. 165.

16. IWSM, T'ung-chih, 25:4-8; HFT, III, 3-4.

17. Chou Shih-ch'eng, Huai-chün p'ing-nien chi 12:2 (1877); CCKT, I, pp. 254-55; YWYT, IV, 2.

18. IWSM, T'ung-chih, 25:8-10.

19. IWSM, T'ung-chih, 25:8-10.

20. CCKT, I, 343-44; IWSM, T'ung-chih, 25:1-3.

21. IWSM, T'ung-chih, 25:1-3; LWCKTK, 7:17, 9:65-66; YWYT, IV, 235-36.

22. HFT, III, 13-26.

23. HFT, III, 13-26.

24. Wang T'ao, T'ao-yüan wen-lu wai-pien (Hongkong, 1882), VIII, 8-10.

25. HFT, III, 4-5, a confidential report from Ting Jih-ch'ang to Li Hung-chang written in 1864. Ting's commitment to ordnance production is also clear from his efforts to establish the Kiangnan Arsenal in Shanghai, to be discussed below.

26. YWYT, I, 11-14; CCKT, I, 262-63.

27. IWSM, T'ung-chih, 25:8.

28. BPP, FO 17/425/81, Macartney to Parkes, 25 March 1865. On the Lay-Osborne Flotilla, see Lu Shih-ch'iang, Chung-kuo tsao-ch'i te lun-ch'uan ching-ying (Nankang, 1962), pp. 101-12.

29. LWCKTK, 9:31-35; HFT, III, 13-26.

30. LWCKTK, 9:31-35.

31. Fung Yu-lan, A History of Chinese Philosophy, I, 305-06.

32. LWCKTK, 9:31-35.

33. Ting Jih-ch'ang, Ting Chung-cheng cheng-shu, 26:76-79.

34. LWCKTK, 9:31-35; Yung Wing, My Life in China and America, pp. 160-64.

35. Stanley Spector, Li Hung-chang and the Huai Army (Seattle, 1964), p. 117; LWCKTK, 8:52-54.

36. Boulger, The Life of Sir Halliday Macartney, pp. 145-72; BBP, FO 17/425/81, Macartney to Parkes, 24 March 1865; YWYT, IV, 32, 39, 44, 46, 185; CCKT, I, 328-29.

37. LWCKTK, 8:52-54.

38. HFT, III, 21.

39. YWYT, IV, 231-35; CCKT, I, 346.

40. YWYT, IV, 232-35, 238-39.

41. IWSM, T'ung-chih, 46:18-19; CCKT, I, 348-49.

42. IWSM, T'ung-chih, 78:12-15; CCKT, I, 346-47; YWYT, IV, 237.

43. IWSM, T'ung-chih, 78:12-15; CCKT, I, 347-48, 349-50; YWYT, IV, 237.

44. Chou Shih-ch'eng, Huai-chun p'ing-nien chi, 11:9; LWCKTK, 9:31-35.

45. KNCTCC, 3:57-58.

46. KNCTCC, 3:58-59.

47. HFT, III, 27-28.

48. LWCKTK, 9:33-35.

49. Spector, Li Hung-chang and the Huai Army, pp. 117-19; Wright, The Last Stand of Chinese Conservatism, pp. 106-07; LWCKTK, 16:23a.

50. YWYT, IV, 237-38.

51. IWSM, T'ung-chih, 55:23a.

52. YWYT, IV, 239.

53. IWSM, T'ung-chih, 78:12-15; HFT, III, 45, 65-66; CCKT, I, 348.

54. IWSM, T'ung-chih, 78:12-15; CCKT, I, 349-50.

NOTES: CHAPTER IV

1. Examples of such recommendations by Li while serving as northern and southern commissioner may be found in LWCKTK, 4:44, 9:73, 17:16.

2. CCKT, I, 249-50; TWCKTK, 2:416-18, 4:839-41.

3. HFT, III, 4-5, 6, 11, 12, 27-28; LWCKTK, 9:33-35.

4. Yü Yüeh, ed., Shang-hai hsien-chih 2:28-29 (1872); Spector, Li Hung-chang and the Huai Army, p. 117.

5. LWCKTK, 9:31-35; Yung Wing, My Life in China and America, pp. 160-64; KNCTCC, 3:1.

6. LWCKTK, 9:31-35; HFT, III, 13-26; KNCTCC, 3:58-59.

7. LWCKTK, 9:31-35; Chou Shih-ch'eng, Huai-chün p'ing-nien-chi, 11:9.

8. LWCKTK, 9:31-35.

9. TWCKTK, 4:808-09.

10. Yü Yüeh, ed., Shang-hai hsien-chih, 2:28-29.

11. TWCKTK, 4:808-09. Steam was first applied to the propulsion of ships by means of the paddle wheel. The wheel was clumsy and exposed to enemy fire. Furthermore, on ships carrying ordnance it made it impossible to position a gun mount on the broadside. The propeller drive was introduced in 1838. It lay below the water line, protected from enemy fire. By the time of the Crimean War in 1854, the fighting ships of the world were normally propeller driven. H. W. Wilson, Ironclads in Action Naval Warfare 1855-1895 (Boston, 1896), II, 211.

12. CCKT, I, 287; YWYT, IV, 33.

13. HFT, III, 40, 60, 71, 75, 90-91; KNCTCC, 5:1-2; CCKT, I, 289-90; H. W. Wilson, Ironclads in Action Naval Warfare 1855-1895, II, 395; Encyclopedia Britannica, 1963, XX, 529.

14. KNCTCC, 4:12.

15. HFT, III, 51-52.

16. HFT, III, 55-57; CS, IV, 2792, 4818-19.

17. HFT, III, 57-59.

18. CCKT, I, 314-15.

19. Chiang-nan chih-tsao-chu ch'üan-an (Shanghai, n.d.), Chiang-su hsun-fu Ting Jih-chang p'ien, T'ung-chih 8/9/8.

20. KNCTCC, 4:11-13.

21. CS, IV, 2792.

22. Chiang-nan chih-tsao chu ch'üan-an, tsung li ya-men tsou, T'ung-chih 8/11/25.

23. YWYT, IV, 28-34, 37-41.

24. KNCTCC, 2:2-8; Yü Yüeh, ed., Shang-hai hsien chih, 2:28-29; Knight Biggerstaff, The Earliest Modern Government Schools in China (Ithaca, N.Y., 1961), pp. 165-76. The exact location of Ch'en-chia Kang is unclear. It may have been located with Ch'en-chia Ch'iao on the network of inland waterways just south of Shanghai.

25. KNCTCC, 2:22; Yü Yüeh, ed., Shang-hai hsien-chih, 2:28-29; HFT, III, 103; CCKT, I, 281; BPP, FO 233/85/3815, report by W. H. Medhurst, British Consul in Shanghai, 8 April 1876, p. 8.

26. YWYT, IV, 27-34, 37-41; HFT, III, 65-67, 101; BPP, FO 233/85/3815, report by Medhurst, 8 April 1876, p. 10.

27. Chou Wei, Chung-kuo ping-ch'i shih-kao, p. 316.

28. The ease of reloading the breechloader allowed the individual rifleman to achieve greater fire power. The chief obstacle to the development of the breech-loading rifle was securing the breech so that there would be no leakage of gas from the powder explosion. Such leakage diminished the force applied to driving the projectile and resulted in excessive fouling. When the breech was opened to insert the next round, residual gases would sometimes escape as a sheet of flames. Improvements in the design of breech mechanisms, the breech block, and the breech bolt helped to overcome this. Encyclopedia Britannica, 1967 XIV, 522; H. Ommundsen and E. H. Robinson, Rifles and Ammunition, pp. 91-102.

29. The most important development facilitating the use of breech-loading rifles was the metallic cartridge, which contained the propellant and was crimped to the base of the bullet. Built into the base of the cartridge was an ignition device of some type, which was exploded by the action of a firing pin. The metallic cartridge secured perfect obturation of the breech; all worries of gas leakage were eliminated.

Gases from the propellant explosion could only escape forward and increase the thrust applied to the bullet. Encyclopedia Britannica, 1967, XIV, 522; Ommundsen and Robinson, Rifles and Ammunition, pp. 91-102.

30. In 1860 it was discovered that black gunpowder, a mechanical mixture of niter, sulphur, and charcoal, could be considerably improved by compressing the powder into large grains of greater density. The increase in grain size diminished the burning surface and the increased density slowed the rate of combustion. The result was that less gas was produced at the initial explosion, but the evolution of gas continued while the projectile moved through the bore, so higher muzzle velocity could be had with less initial explosive force. Powder production was then geared to the size of the gun in which it was to be used. The fine grain powders could be used for small-caliber weapons but larger grains and eventually prismatic powders were developed to achieve higher muzzle velocities with less initial explosion force in larger guns. Ormond M. Lissak, Ordnance and Gunnery (New York, 1915), pp. 1-15. KNCTCC, 2:2; Yü Yüeh, ed., Shang-hai hsien-chih, 2:28-29; HFT, III, 103; BPP, FO 233/85/3815, report by Medhurst, 8 April 1876, pp. 8-9.

31. HFT, III, 101; NCH, February 19, 1874, July 18, 1874; BPP, FO 233/85/3815, report by Medhurst, 8 April 1876, p. 9.

32. LWCKTK, 14:42, 16:23. In early 1868 Kiangnan prepared 120 small brass cannon with gun mounts, 1,000 explosive shells, 100 muskets, 200 carbines, 100 rockets, and 100 rocket launchers for shipment to forces fighting the Nien in North China. In 1870 the arsenal shipped five 24-pounder and seven 12-pounder brass cannon along with ammunition, fuses, spare parts, and gun carriages for the cannon to units in the northwest. Three hundred 6-pound rockets, 400 rocket launchers, 10,000 pounds of powder, and 14,000 fuses were also sent. Ting Jih-ch'ang, Ting Chung-cheng cheng-shu, 2:11, 6:23-24.

33. CKT, III, 75.

34. BPP, FO 233/85/3815, Thomas Wade to W. Pitman, 8 June 1877; report by Medhurst, 18 April 1876, p. 10.

35. YWYT, IV, 31, 39; Biggerstaff, The Earliest Modern Government Schools in China, pp. 165-99. Li's observations on the limitation of foreign influence at Kiangnan may be found in LWCK PLHK, 12:2b; LWCKTK, 17:17a-b.

36. KNCTCC, 6:40-44; H. S. Brunnert and V. V. Hagelstrom, Present Day Political Organization of China (Taipei, 1963), p. 424; CCKT, III, 75; Chang Po-chu, "Shang-hai ping-kung-ch'ang chih shih-mo," Jen-wen yueh-k'an (1934), V, 5; BPP, FO 233/85/3815, report by Dunn, 8 April 1876.

37. Hummel, Eminent Chinese of the Ch'ing Period, pp. 465-66.

38. LWCKTK, 21:36, 25:45, 29:38, 37:52; YWYT, IV, 32, 39, 44, 46, 185; Wang Erh-min, Huai-chün chih (Taipei, 1967), pp. 297-98; Boulger, The Life of Sir Halliday Macartney, pp. 145-88; LWCKPLHK, 13:27b.

39. CCKT, I, 327-329; YWYT, IV, 185; BPP, Admiralty 1/6262/2, memo submitted by Admiral Shadwell, 5 February 1873.

40. Boulger, The Life of Sir Halliday Macartney, pp. 198-212.

41. Boulger, The Life of Sir Halliday Macartney, pp. 216-31.

42. Boulger, The Life of Sir Halliday Macartney, pp. 231-43.

43. LWCKTK, 2:15a, 21:32b, 23:32a, 25:42a,]7:17b,]8:4a, 29:35a, 29:38a, 32:34a, 33:29a, 34:25a, 37:53a, 40:7, 41:36, 42:37a, 48:18a, 52:36a, 55:45a, 58:26a, 58:50a, 51:14-43a, 51:17b, 61:36a, 63:17-25, 63:52a, 63:56-64, 64:20b-21a, 66:36a, 69:38a, 71:10, 73:32a, 75:34a, 76:50b, 77:42b, 79:24b; T'ien-chin fu-chih 24:7-8 (1876).

44. Wright, The Last Stand of Chinese Conservatism, pp. 279-99.

45. Kuo Ting-yee, Chin-tai chung-kuo shih-shih jih-chih (Taipei, 1963), I, 538, 543, 546, 547, 548; YWYT, IV, 243.

46. IWSM, T'ung-chih, 78:12-15; CCKT, I, 349-50.

47. LWCKTK, 17:14-18a, 36a; IWSM, T'ung-chih, 78:43a; NCH, May 4, 1872.

48. BPP, FO 17/656/233, Wade to the Foreign Office, 6 November 1873.

49. BPP, FO 233/85/3815, China Steam Navy, including a statement on the Tientsin Arsenal by Morgan, British consul in Tientsin, 31 December 1874; LWCKTK, 20:12-15a, 28:1-4. Approximate annual costs have been extrapolated from biennial figures.

50. LWCKTK, 17:36a, 20:12-15a, 23:19-22, 28:1-4, 22:8, 22:50, 24:16a; Li Hung-chang, Li Wen-chung kung ch'üan-chi (Taipei, 1965), i-shu han-kao 2:33b; Tien-chin fu-chih, 27:7-8. Some of the facilities at Hai-kuang Szu remained operational and may have been used to house elements of the Tientsin Mobile Arsenal.

51. BPP, FO 233/85/3815, W. Pitman to Thomas Wade, 18 August 1876.

52. BPP, FO 233/85/3815, Chinese Steam Navy, including a statement on the Tientsin Arsenal by Morgan, 31 December 1874; LWCKTK, 20:12-15a, 23:19-22, 28:1-4, 22:8, 22:50, 24:16a; Li Hung-chang, Li Wen-chung kung ch'üan-chi, i-shu han-kao, 2:33b. The Lien Army was a new unit established in the early 1860s in Chihli when the Army of the Green Standard proved inadequate for defense of the capital area. It was subsequently extended to other provinces. Wang Erh-min, "Lien-chün te ch'i-yüan chi ch'i-i," Ta-lu tsa-chih, 34:6, 34:10-13, 34:7, 34:22-29.

NOTES: CHAPTER V

1. HFT, III, 97; YWYT, IV, 34-41. The estimate of one-half includes most of the cost of the Hai-an, completed several months later, as well as a part of the cost of the Yü-yüan and a portion of the operating costs prorated to the end of 1871 from aggregate figures for the costs from launching each vessel through 1873.

2. LWCKPLHK, 11:31, YWYT, IV, 105-06.

3. YWYT, IV, 106-07; HFT, II, 325-26.

4. LWCKTK, 17:16, 19:44; Ting Jih-ch'ang, Fu-wu kung-tu 42:9-10 (1877); Kwang-Ching Liu, "Li Hung-chang in Chihli: The Emergence of a Policy, 1870-1875"; Albert Feuerwerker, Rhoads Murphey, and Mary C. Wright, eds., Approaches to Modern Chinese History (Berkeley, 1967), pp. 68-104.

5. Wang Erh-min, "Nan-pei-yang ta-ch'en chih chien-she chi ch'i ch'uan-li chih k'uo-chang," Ch'ing-shih chi chin-tai-shih yen-chiu lun-chi (Taipei, 1967), pp. 192-97. For examples of the primary position of the southern commissioner in personnel matters, see LWCKPLHK, 13:11, 14:38-39.

6. LWCKPLHK, 9:9, 11:7, 12:2; HFT, II, 325.

7. Biggerstaff, The Earliest Modern Government Schools in China, pp. 165-99; Li Hung-chang, Li Wen-chung kung ch'üan-chi, i-shu han-kao, 1:19-21; Kwang-Ching Liu, "Li Hung-chang in Chihli," 83.

8. HFT, II, 367-72; cf. David Pong, "Modernization and Politics in China as Seen in the Career of Shen Pao-chen (1820-1879)" (Ph.D. dissertation, University of London, 1969), pp. 249-54. Pong has examined these same documents in an analysis of Li's position on Sung Chin's proposal to close the Foochow Dockyard. He notes Li's equivocal position on shipbuilding, concluding that Li's support "was more an expression of Realpolitik than of conviction." Pong also points out that Li later stated that he felt obliged to agree with Shen Pao-chen and Tso Tsung-t'ang, who were supporters of shipbuilding.

9. HFT, II, 367-72; HFT, III, 98-110. Li was not an addressee on the report, which contains Feng's views, but the phrasing of Li's memorial leaves little doubt that he had read Feng's report beforehand.

10. HFT, II, 367-72.

11. HFT, III, 107-09.

12. KNCTCC, 4:6.

13. HFT, III, 95-98.

14. HFT, II, 385-89.

15. LWCKTK, 20:32-33; LWCKPLHK, 13:12-13; HFT, II,

486, 497. The measures taken by foreign merchants to inhibit the development of the Chinese Merchants' Company can be explained by the attitude of the foreign shipping lines toward their new competition. A report to the head of the Russel Company dated June 12, 1874 stated: "The Chinese Company are [sic] giving us a great deal of trouble--and as we reduce our tariff rates one half on the days when their steamers are dispatched our earnings are kept low. There is however no help for it." On June 13, 1874 the Shanghai manager of Butterfield and Swire wrote in his letter to London, "We are considering with Russels measures against the Chinese Company which we hope will result in their subsidence." Kwang-Ching Liu, Anglo-American Steamship Rivalry in China, 1862-1874 (Cambridge, Mass., 1962), p. 152.

16. HFT, II, 486; IWSM, T'ung-chih, 86:9-10. Here the government of Shantung declined to accept a Foochow vessel for financial reasons, a rationale which would apply to Kiangnan vessels as well.

17. LWCKPLHK, 13:10-11, 27-28. BPP, 233/85/3815, clipping from North China Daily News, September 2, 1875.

18. Hummel, Eminent Chinese of the Ch'ing Period, pp. 765-66; Wen-Djang Chu, "Tso Tsung-t'ang's Role in the Recovery of Sinkiang," Tsing Hua Journal of Chinese Studies, New Series 1.3:136-37 (September 1958).

19. HFT, III, 4-5; T. F. Tsiang, "Sino-Japanese Diplomatic Relations, 1870-1894," The Chinese Social and Political Science Review, 17.1:1-106 (April 1933).

20. T. F. Tsiang, "Sino-Japanese Diplomatic Relations, 1870-1894," 16-34; IWSM, T'ung-chih, 98:19-20. LWCKPLHK, 14:14b.

21. John Rawlinson, "China's Failure to Coordinate Her Modern Fleets," in Feuerwerker, Murphey, and Wright, Approaches to Modern Chinese History, pp. 114-15; Thomas C. Smith, Political Change and Industrial Development in Japan: Government Enterprise, 1868-1880 (Stanford, 1955), pp. 4-7, 50-52; Meron Medzini, French Policy in Japan during the Closing Years of the Tokugawa Regime (Cambridge, Mass., 1971), pp. 119-24; Tsugai Giyu, Nihon sangyō kigyōshi gaisetsu (Tokyo, 1969), pp. 10-12.

22. Tsugai Giyu, <u>Nihon sangyō kigyōshi gaisetsu</u>, pp. 10-12.

23. T. F. Tsiang, "Sino-Japanese Diplomatic Relations, 1870-1894," 16-53.

24. <u>YWYT</u>, I, 26, 29-33, 105-06, 115; <u>LWCKPLHK</u>, 5:59.

25. Immanuel C. Y. Hsu, "The Great Policy Debate in China, 1874: Maritime Defense vs. Frontier Defense," <u>Harvard Journal of Asiatic Studies</u>, 25:212-28 (1964-1965).

26. Hsu, "The Great Policy Debate in China, 1874," 218-28.

27. <u>YWYT</u>, I, 153-55; <u>LWCKTK</u>, 24:13-25.

28. <u>YWYT</u>, IV, 31, 33, 39.

29. Ko Shih-chün, ed., <u>Huang-ch'ao ching-shih wen hsü-pien</u> (Shanghai, 1888), 101:15-20; Shen Pao-chen, <u>Shen Wen-su kung cheng-shu</u> (1880), 5:22.

30. <u>YWYT</u>, I, 162-65; <u>YWYT</u>, II, 378. The discontinuation of plans to construct commercial steamers was not dealt with directly in the edict. In a memorial submitted several days prior to the edict on maritime defense policy, Hsüeh Fu-ch'eng recommended that plans for commercial construction be discontinued. See <u>YWYT</u>, I, 155-60. In a separate memorial commenting on Hsüeh's, the Tsungli Yamen indicated it had dealt with Hsüeh's suggestion on vessel construction in its memorial of May 30, which served as a basis for the edict on maritime defense policy. See <u>YWYT</u>, I, 161-62. Since in its May 30 memorial the Tsungli Yamen made no mention of further commercial construction, it is clear that it intended that there should be none. <u>YWYT</u>, I, 144-53. The edict approving this memorial officially concluded plans to build commercial vessels at Kiangnan. <u>YWYT</u>, I, 153-54.

31. <u>LWCKTK</u>, 39:30-36; <u>YWYT</u>, II, 378; <u>BPP</u>, FO 233/85/3815, clipping from <u>North China Daily News</u>, September 2, 1875.

32. <u>YWYT</u>, I, 153-55.

33. <u>LWCKTK</u>, 24:13-25.

34. Ko Shih-chün, ed., *Huang-ch'ao ching-shih wen-hsü-pien*, 101:15-20.

35. *LWCKTK*, 24:16.

NOTES: CHAPTER VI

1. *HFT*, III, 147; *YWYT*, II, 379; *YWYT*, IV, 42-45; Shen Pao-chen, *Shen Wen-su kung cheng-shu*, 7:60-61; *LWCKTK*, 32:5-7.

2. *LWCKTK*, 31:10; *YWYT*, II, 378-80.

3. *YWYT*, II, 463, 467, 489-94.

4. *LWCKTK*, 39:30-36; *YWYT*, II, 500, 508-09; *CCKT*, I, 291; *NCH*, September 27, 1881.

5. Compound engines, which were in wide use in the West in the 1860s, have two cylinders, one larger than the other. Steam is used at high pressure in the smaller cylinder and then passes at lower pressure to the larger cylinder where it is used again. The double use of the steam resulted in about 25 percent reduction in fuel consumption. In the 1870s the triple expansion engine was introduced. This achieved even greater efficiency by a third stage use of the steam. H. W. Wilson, *Ironclads in Action, Naval Warfare 1855-1895*, p. 389; *Encyclopedia Britannica*, 1963, XX, 529.

6. *YWYT*, II, 535-36; *YWYT*, IV, 51-52, 62.

7. *YWYT*, II, 567; *YWYT*, III, 1; *YWYT*, IV, 57-59, 60-62, 64-66; Li Hung-chang, *Li Wen-chung kung ch'üan-chi*, hai-chün han-kao, 1:10.

8. *CCKT*, I, 317-19; *YWYT*, IV, 185.

9. The receipt of these funds was separately reported to the throne by the southern commissioner. They were not treated as regular income and included in the regular periodic financial reports. *YWYT*, IV, 62.

10. *KNCTCC*, 2:1; *YWYT*, IV, 49; *CCKT*, III, 77.

11. *CCKT*, III, 77.

12. *LWCKTK*, 32:5, 7.

13. YWYT, IV, 51-62, 270.

14. KNCTCC, 2:1, 31-32.

15. YWYT, IV, 43, 45, 48, 57; KNCTCC, 3:6-17.

16. By the 1850s rifled guns were widely used in the West. Rifling gave the projectile a stabilizing spin which resulted in greater accuracy. Steel had long been acknowledged as the most desirable ordnance material because of its great strength, which enabled it to withstand the explosive force of greater charges of powder, but until the mid-nineteenth century no method of producing it in the quality and quantity needed for ordnance production had been evolved. The Krupp Works of Germany made the first all-steel gun about 1850. Encyclopedia Britannica, 1967, II, 533-34; 11th Ed., 1910-1911, XX, 189-218.

17. In the mid-nineteenth century in Britain and the United States, new methods were devised to strengthen the barrels of guns made from cast iron and brass, the most widely used ordnance material at that time. The most successful of these was the built-up method by which molten hoops of metal were contracted onto the barrel near the base where the force of the powder explosion was greatest. As these molten hoops cooled they would contract and place the barrel under compression. The exploding force of the powder was counteracted not only by the metal barrel but also by the force of compression created by the outer hoops. This method was employed by the Armstrong Works of Great Britain, contracting wrought-iron hoops onto a steel inner barrel in the late 1860s and early 1870s. The Krupp Works of Germany progressed still further, by contracting steel hoops onto steel barrels. As gun size was enlarged during the middle of the nineteenth century, loading from the muzzle became correspondingly slower and more burdensome. After each shot the gun had to be positioned so that a new charge could be shoved down the muzzle and rammed home in the chamber. Then the gun had to be repositioned and reaimed. During the 1860s and 1870s Krupp and companies in the United States, France, and Spain developed breech-loading systems that eliminated this delay. The Armstrong Works of Great Britain was the only major arsenal that continued to produce muzzle-loaders. Encyclopedia Britannica, 1967, II, 533-34; 11th Ed., 1910-11, XX, 189-218.

18. Kan Tso'lin, "Chiang-nan chih-tsao chü chih chien-shih," Tung-fang tsa-chih, 11.5:46-48 (November 1914); Boulger, The Life of Sir Halliday Macartney, p. 188; LWCKPLHK, 13:27b; LWCKTK, 24:14-15; John L. Rawlinson, China's Struggle for Naval Development 1839-1895 (Cambridge, 1967), p. 69.

19. Boulger, The Life of Sir Halliday Macartney, pp. 232-43.

20. YWYT, IV, 30-31.

21. This fear was probably based upon the pessimistic position on heavy ordnance production that Li had expressed in his maritime defense memorial as well as his well-known concern over the Taku tragedy. If any such plan existed--and it seems unlikely that it did--it was undoubtedly limited to eliminating the Kao-ch'ang Miao plant, for Li had placed great importance on the production of powder and cartridges at Lung-hua.

22. Kan Tso-lin, "Chiang-nan chih-tsao-chü chih chien-shih," 46-48; HFT, III, 101.

23. Liu Chin-tsao, ed., Ch'ing-ch'ao-hsü wen-hsien t'ung-k'ao (Taipei, 1965), 238:9831.

24. Kan Tso-lin, "Chiang-nan chih-tsao-chü chih chien-shih," 46-48; Feng Chün-kuang, Hsi-hsing jih-chi, p. 4; LWCKPLHK, 18:18-19; LWCKTK, 32:5-9; KNCTCC, 2:1.

25. NCH, December 28, 1878; NCH, July 22, 1879; CCKT, I, 300-01.

26. KNCTCC, 2:1; 3:1. Rifled ordnance required a new type of ammunition. When spherical shells were loaded into smoothbore cannon, the fuse was placed toward the muzzle and the shell rested on the propellant charge. Because of the loose fit of the shell, incandescent gases from the powder explosion could escape forward and ignite the fuse. Adoption of the rifled gun barrel required the use of a snug fitting cylindroconoidal shell: snug fitting so that the shell would receive the rotational influence of the rifling grooves, and cylindroconoidal because it was found that rifling did not greatly affect the flight of spherical shells. Such a shell would not allow the escape of incandescent gases forward to where they could ignite the fuse. The answer to this was

the setback fuse. This consisted of a percussion cap, a free-floating striker, and a powder train, which led to the explosive inside the shell. These components were located in the conoidal head of the shell. When the propellant explosion moved the shell forward, inertia retarded the movement of the free-floating striker, which then collided with percussion cap and ignited the powder train. The detonating fuse was the reverse of this principle. In this, the free-floating striker was located to the rear of the percussion cap, and when the flight of the shell was interrupted, inertia carried it forward so that it struck the percussion cap and ignited the powder train. All rifled ordnance required cylindroconoidal shells equipped with either setback or detonating fuses. Encyclopedia Britannica, 1967, I, 801-04; 11th Ed., 1910-11, II, 866-73.

27. Kan Tso-lin, "Chiang-nan chih-tsao-chü chih chien-shih," 46-48; KNCTCC, 3:13, 14, 16.

28. The rim fire cartridge was developed in the 1840s. It had a compound of fulminate of mercury in a cavity that encircled the rim of the cartridge base. A blow from a sharp-nosed hammer set the cartridge off. It was difficult to insure that the fulminate of mercury was evenly distributed around the rim cavity. If it was not, and the hammer struck a portion where there was no fulminate, misfire would occur. In the late 1850s and 1860s in Britain and the United States, the center fire cartridge was developed to overcome this hazard. The center fire cartridge had a depression in the base which contained a percussion cap of priming powder backed up by a small anvil. On pulling the trigger a striker, which operated through the breech bolt, would strike either of these, creating an explosion that would ignite the propellant charge. Encyclopedia Britannica, 1967, XX, 673.

29. LWCKPLHK, 20:4-5; KNCTCC, 3:1, 66-67; 7:10.

30. KNCTCC, 3:12-16.

31. Electric detonation was the most significant development in nineteenth century mine technology. When the mine was struck, a vial of acid solution was released. This became the electrolyte for a primary cell which produced current to fire an electric detonator. The advantage of this mine was that it was totally inert until struck and therefore had unlimited

life. Encyclopedia Britannica, 1967, XV, 495.

32. KNCTCC, 2:1; 3:1; NCH, March 3, 1884.

33. John L. Rawlinson, China's Struggle for Naval Development, 1839-1895, pp. 116-19.

34. For a list of vessels in the Peiyang fleet, see Spector, Li Hung-chang and the Huai Army, p. 193. This list is inaccurate in listing the Tsao-chiang as a Peiyang acquisition of 1871; YWYT, IV, 38 indicates Tsao-chiang was subordinate to Nanyang in 1878.

35. LWCKPLHK, 20:3-5; LWCKTK, 46:16-17; KNCTCC, 3:10-12.

36. YWYT, IV, 51; Chang Chih-tung, Chang Wen-hsiang kung ch'üan-chi (Taipei, 1963), tsou-i, 11:16; CCKT, II, 11.

37. Chang Chih-tung, Chang Wen-hsiang kung ch'üan-chi, tien-kao, 11:9-10.

38. I have estimated the total personnel expense for this period by adding the figures for artisans' wages (which includes foreign technicians) given in Appendix I Table 5 to the salaries for Chinese officials reported by the southern commissioner for the years 1878-1885, YWYT, IV, 44, 47, 50, 54, 58, 61. Since the figures for Chinese officials' salaries in Appendix I Table 5 are lumped together with building expenses, they cannot be isolated. This means that the overall estimate of personnel expenses for 1876-1885 does not include official salaries for the years 1876 and 1877, and is therefore somewhat lower than the actual figure.

39. Felicia Johnson Deyrup, Arms Makers of the Connecticut Valley, A Regional Study of the Economic Development of the Small Arms Industry (Northampton, Mass., 1948), pp. 206-08; Sanshi Hakumon, Gendai nihon bunmei shi, XIV, Gijutsushi (1940), p. 200.

40. YWYT, IV, 44, 47, 50, 54, 57, 61-62.

41. YWYT, IV, 185; HFT, III, 406-08. The 30,000 taels provided to the arsenal have been identified as southern maritime defense funds on the basis of their disbursement by the chiang-nan ch'ou-fang-chü, an organization which was subsequently known to serve

as a disbursing agency for southern maritime defense funds. See YWYT, IV, 62.

42. YWYT, IV, 185-86, 189-91, 193-94, 203-04, 207-10. Stanley Spector in Li Hung-chang and the Huai Army, p. 165, speculates that northern control of the Nanking Arsenal was "challenged" after Tso Tsung-t'ang became southern commissioner in 1882. Although this may have been the case, it would seem that Li's influence at the arsenal remained substantial in view of the joint financing plan. Furthermore, beginning in 1886 Li functioned as the reporting official for the Nanking Arsenal. YWYT, IV, 209-10, 213-15, 216-17, 220-22, 222-24, 225-26.

43. YWYT, IV, 189-91, 193-94.

44. YWYT, IV, 185-87, 194-95, 203-04; Boulger, The Life of Sir Halliday Macartney, p. 219; CCKT, I, 328, 332.

45. CCKT, I, 328-32; NCH, July 6, 1880; YWYT, IV, 185-86.

46. LWCKTK, 31:12a; 32:11b. See Appendix I Table 4 for totals of powder shipped to Nanyang units after 1879. For details on the various depots in the Soochow and Nanking area to which powder was shipped see KNCTCC, 5:11-24; CCKT, I, 335.

47. YWYT, IV, 188-89, 196, 200-01; NCH, April 2, 1884.

48. LWCKTK, 32:11-12.

49. LWCKTK, 31:12a; 32:11b; 33:25b; YWYT, IV, 253-60.

50. YWYT, IV, 253-60.

51. YWYT, IV, 253-60, 265-69.

52. LWCKTK, 43:15-16; 45:6; 46:21-22; 49:6-7; 58:38-39; 61:39-40.

53. LWCKTK, 42:3-5; 46:16-18.

54. YWYT, IV, 251, 268; LWCKTK, 40:46; 47:10-11; CCKT, I, 362. Financial reports from 1882 on indicate purchases involving shipping and insurance charges but do not specify the types of materials. YWYT, IV, 270-71, 273.

55. YWYT, VIII, 362; LWCKTK, 42:4a.

NOTES: CHAPTER VII

1. CCKT, I, 507-08.

2. CCKT, I, 507-09; Thomas L. Kennedy, "Chang Chih-tung and the Struggle for Strategic Industrialization: The Establishment of the Hanyang Arsenal, 1884-1895," Harvard Journal of Asiatic Studies, 33:177-78 (1973); Wang Erh-min, Ch'ing-chi ping-kung-yeh te hsing-chi, p. 146.

3. YWYT, III, 1, 52-53; Li Hung-chang, Li Wen-chung kung ch'üan-chi, hai-chün han-kao, 1:10.

4. CCKT, III, 11; Kennedy, "Chang Chih-tung and the Struggle for Strategic Industrialization," 154-82.

5. CCKT, I, 508-09.

6. Kennedy, "Chang Chih-tung and the Struggle for Strategic Industrialization," 174. On plans for the removal of Kiangnan from the Shanghai site, which first came up after 1895, see Thomas L. Kennedy, "The Kiangnan Arsenal in the Era of Reform," Chung-yang yen-chiu-yüan chin-tai li-shih-so chi-k'an, 3.1:269-346 (July 1972).

7. Liu K'un-i, Liu K'un-i i-chi (Taipei, 1966), tsou-shu, 25:32-35.

8. Tang T'o-ching, ed., Ch'ieh-wan lao-jen ch'i-shih-sui tzu-hsü (Held by the Institute of Modern History, Academia Sinica, Taiwan), pp. 272-75.

9. Hummel, Eminent Chinese of the Ch'ing Period, pp. 523, 749, 762; NCH, November 12, 1902; Shen Yün-lung, ed., Hsien-tai cheng-chih jen-wu shu-p'ing (Taipei, 1966), hsia, p. 51.

10. Shen Yün-lung, Hsien-tai cheng-chih jen-wu shu-p'ing, pp. 38048. KNCTCC, 6:42 does not specify this appointment.

11. Shen Yün-lung, Hsien-tai cheng-chih jen-wu shu-p'ing, pp. 48-51; CCKT, III, 75, 79.

12. Liu K'un-i, Liu K'un-i i-chi, tsou-shu, 25:33;

Hummel, Eminent Chinese of the Ch'ing Period, p. 855; CS, VI, 4843-44; Li En-han, Tseng Chi-tse te wai-chiao (Taipei, 1966), pp. 6, 118-19, 226.

13. CCKT, III, 77-78; Chang Chih-tung, Chang Wen-hsiang kung ch'üan-chi (Taipei, 1963), tien-tu, 28:13.

14. YWYT, IV, 65, 71; KNCTCC, 2:34.

15. CCKT, III, 77.

16. CCKT, III, 75, 77.

17. Chang Chih-tung, Chang Wen-hsiang kung ch'üan-chi, tien-kao, 11:9-10; Kennedy, "Chang Chih-tung and the Struggle for Strategic Industrialization," 172; LWCKTK, 77:1-3; CCKT, III, 265; Tsugai Giyū, Nihon sangyō kigyōshi gaisetsu (Tokyo, 1969), p. 85.

18. YWYT, IV, 66, 72; KNCTCC, 3:1; CCKT, III, 90.

19. YWYT, IV, 64, 70, 197-99; Liu Chin-tsao, ed., Ch'ing-ch'ao-hsü wen-hsien t'ung-k'ao, 238:9833; NCH, June 9, 1893.

20. In 1880 in the West a further advance in the controlled burning of gun powder was made through the use of unburnt charcoal rather than black charcoal in powder production. The resulting brown or cocoa powder burned more slowly than the black and wholly replaced it as a propellant in large guns. Ormond M. Lissak, Ordnance and Gunnery, pp. 1-15.

21. YWYT, IV, 55-56; KNCTCC, 2:1, 33-35; 3:1, 63-64, 69-70, 72; NCH, September 8, 1893.

22. Even after the breech-loading gun was perfected, there was still the problem of returning the gun to firing position after recoil. As gun size increased, the amount of human effort required to reposition and reaim was correspondingly greater. During the 1880s Armstrong and Krupp both developed devices that accumulated the force of recoil without transmitting it to the gun mount and then employed it to return the barrel to its original firing position. As soon as the gun could be reloaded it was ready to fire again. This was the quick-firing gun. Encyclopedia Britannica, 1910-1911, II, 866-73; 1967, I, 801-04.

23. KNCTCC, 3:63-64; NCH, June 9, 1893.

24. KNCTCC, 3:18-39; NCH, June 9, 1893.

25. KNCTCC, 3:65-67, 71.

26. In the late nineteenth century in the West, development of the magazine or repeating rifle brought greatly increased fire power to the individual rifleman. During the 1870s and early 1880s American and European arms companies developed mechanisms in the rifle butt which could rapidly supply cartridges to the chamber. These proved unsafe and subject to malfunction. In the late 1880s and 1890s these were replaced by magazines located below the bolt. Cartridges were loaded in the magazine under spring pressure from below. When the bolt was drawn to the rear, it would extract the spent cartridge case from the round just fired and the spring pressure would elevate a new cartridge into the void created by the rearward motion of the bolt. When the bolt was moved forward again, it would deliver the new cartridge into the chamber. Reloading could thus be accomplished in a fraction of the time required for manual insertion of the cartridge. H. Ommundsen and E. H. Robinson, Rifles and Ammunition, pp. 91-102.

27. LWCKTK, 77:1-3; KNCTCC, 3:68-70.

28. LWCKTK, 77:1-3; Tsugai Giyū, Nihon Sangyō kigyōshi gaisetsu, p. 85; Chang Chih-tung, Chang Wen-hsiang kung ch'üan-chi, kung-tu, 15:29-34; KNCTCC, 3:76-77.

29. KNCTCC, 3:19-39.

30. In 1886 smokeless powder was first produced in France. This was made by a chemical rather than mechanical process. The base was nitrocellulose or guncotton produced by treating cotton in a solution of nitric and sulphuric acids. This was mechanically mixed with metallic salts and nitroglycerine to form a colloidal jelly which was then dried and granulated. The advantage of smokeless powder was that it was almost entirely converted into gas, whereas gas evolved by charcoal powder was only about 43 percent of its original weight and part of the energy of this gas was used up in expelling the powder residue from the bore. Because of the complete combustion of smokeless powder, a smaller charge could produce greater force and impart greater velocity to the projectile. There was practically no residue left to foul the

bore. Smokeless powder was particularly well suited for use with quick-firing guns and magazine rifles, for the absence of smoke permitted rapid resighting and refiring. Ormond M. Lissak, Ordnance and Gunnery, pp. 1-15.

31. KNCTCC, 2:37; 2:37; 3:70, 76; NCH, April 26, 1895, July 16, 1897.

32. KNCTCC, 2:35-37, 3:70-72; YWYT, IV, 62-63. With the use of heavier types of armor, harder metal was required for shells. By the 1880s widespread use of steel in naval armor and fortifications had greatly diminished the usefulness of cast iron shells. Armor-piercing shells of forged steel were in common use in the West prior to 1890. Encyclopedia Britannica, 1910-1911, II, 866-73; 1967, I, 801-04.

33. CCKT, III, 78; LWCKTK, 77:1-3; NCH, May 19, 1893.

34. Liu K'un-i, Liu K'un-i i-chi, tien-tu, 11:5.

35. KNCTCC, 5:29-57.

36. Hosea Ballou Morse, The International Relations of the Chinese Empire (London, 1910-1918), III, 31; Chang Chih-tung, Chang Wen-hsiang kung ch'üan-chi, tien-tu, 19:31; NCH, January 11, 1895.

37. Chang Chih-tung, Chang Wen-hsiang kung ch'üan-chi, tsou-i, 38:4.

38. Rawlinson, China's Struggle for Naval Development, 1839-1895, pp. 167-97; Hummel, Eminent Chinese of the Ch'ing Period, pp. 686-88.

39. Chang Chih-tung, Chang Wen-hsiang kung ch'üan-chi, tsou-i, 38:4; CCKT, I, 296-97; Tsugai Giyu, Nihon sangyō kigyōshi gaisetsu, p. 85; KNCTCC, 3:34-38.

40. CCKT, I, 296-97, 319; Chang Chih-tung, Chang Wen-hsiang kung ch'üan-chi, tsou-i, 37:12-15.

41. CCKT, I, 330-32, 339-40.

42. YWYT, IV, 213-15, 220-22.

43. YWYT, IV, 213-17, 220-26; CCKT, I, 332-33, 334.

44. CCKT, I, 333; Yü-che hui-ts'un (Peking), kuang-

hsu, 21/5/2, pp. 5-6; Li Hung-chang, Li Wen-chung kung ch'üan-chi, tien-kao, 18:4a, 18:50b; 19:30a; Charles Beresford, The Breakup of China (New York and London, 1899), pp. 298-99.

45. YWYT, IV, 206-07, 213, 227-28.

46. CCKT, I, 335-37; YWYT, IV, 443.

47. Beresford, The Breakup of China, pp. 298-99.

48. Chang Chih-tung, Chang Wen-hsiang kung ch'üan-chi, tsou-i, 39:4.

49. NCH, October 27, 1887.

50. YWYT, IV, 274-78, 280-81, 282-83, 284-85.

51. Li Hung-chang, Li Wen-chung kung ch'üan-chi, tien-kao, 10:14; YWYT, IV, 275, 279-80.

52. NCH, May 19, 1893; YWYT, IV, 284-85.

53. NCH, November 23, 1888.

54. LWCKTK, 63:8a.

55. NCH, October 27, 1887; Li Hung-chang, Li Wen-chung kung ch'üan-chi, hai-chün han-kao, 4:7; YWYT, IV, 280-83; NCH, July 22, 1892.

56. Li Hung-chang, Li Wen-chung kung ch'üan-chi, tien-kao, 16:61-62.

57. Rawlinson, China's Struggle for Naval Development, 1839-1895, pp. 184-85; Li Hung-chang, Li Wen-chung kung ch'üan-chi, tien-kao, 17:38b; 18:4a-b, 40b, 45-46; 19:30a; NCH, April 19, 1895.

58. Tsugai Giyū, Nihon sangyō kigyōshi gaisetsu, pp. 84-86.

59. Wang Erh-min, Ch'ing-chi ping-kung-yeh te hsing-ch'i, p. 133.

Glossary

Chang Chao-tung 張兆棟

Chang Chih-tung 張之洞

Ch'ang-lu 長蘆

Chang Shih-ch'eng 張士誠

Chao Ti 昭帝

Chen-an 鎮安

Ch'en-chia Kang 陳家港

Ch'en Ting-ching 陳廷經

Cheng Ch'eng-kung 鄭成功

Cheng-ming pien-wu 正名辨物

Ch'i-men 祁門

Chia-chia-ku Tao 賈家沽道

Chia-hsing 嘉興源

Chiang Chung-yüan 江忠江

Chiang-nan chih-tsao tsung-chü 江南製造總局

Chiang-yin 江陰

Chien-sheng 監生

Ch'in 秦

Chin-kiang 鎮江

Chin-ling chih-tsao-chü 金陵製造局

Chin-ou 金甌

chin-shih 進士

Chin-t'ien 金田

Ch'ing 清

Chiu-lung Ch'iao 九龍橋

Cho-chou 涿州

Chou 周

Chu-hsien fang 聚賢坊

Chu I-hsin 朱一新

chü-jen 舉人

Chu Yüan-chang 朱元璋

Chuenpi 穿鼻

Ch'un, Prince 醇親王

Ch'ung-hou 崇厚

chung-pao 中飽

Chung Yun-ku 鍾雲谷

Dairen 大連

Feng Chün-kuang 馮焌光

Feng-huo Tung 風火桶

Feng Kuei-fen 馮桂芬

Fo-lan-chi 佛郎機

Hai-an 海安

Hai-kuang Szu 海光寺

Hai-kuo t'u-chih 海國圖志

Han 漢

Han Tien-chia 韓殿甲

Han Wu Ti 漢武帝

Han Yüan Ti 漢元帝

Heng-shan 衡山

Ho Ch'ang-ling 賀長齡

Ho Ching 何合

Ho-shih 合夏

Ho-Kuei-ch'ing 何桂清

Hsia Shih 夏時

Hsiang Army 湘軍

Hsien-feng 咸豐

Hsien-yang 咸陽

hsing-ying chih-tsao-chü 行營製造局

Hsü Chien-yin 徐建寅

Hsü Ching-ch'eng 許景澄

Hsü Kuang-ch'i 徐光啓

Hsü Shou 徐壽

Hsüeh Fu-chen 薛福辰

Hsüeh Fu-ch'eng	薛福成
Hsüeh Huan	薛煥
Hsüeh Pei-yung	薛培榕
Hu-chou	湖州
Hun Lin-i	胡林翼
Hua Heng-fang	華衡芳
Huai Army	淮軍
Huang-ku	黃鵠
Huang Mien	黃冕
Huang-pu	黃浦
Hung-i-ta-p'ao	紅夷大砲
Hung-k'ou	虹口
Huo-ch'i shuo-lüeh	火器說略
Huo-yao chü	火藥局
i-chia-ch'u	議價一
I-fu	奕
I-hsien	嶧縣

Jui Lin 麟真

Ju-chen 真熙

K'ang-hsi 熙

Kao-ch'ang Miao 高昌廟

Kiangnan 江南

Kuang-fang yen-kuan 廣方言館

Kuei-liang 桂良

Kuei-p'ing 桂平

Kung Chao-yüan 龔照瑗

Kung Chen-lin 龔振麟

Kung Chih-t'ang 龔之棠

kung-kuan 工官

Kung, Prince 恭親王

K'un-ming 昆明

Lai Ch'ang 賴長

Li Chih-tsao 李之藻

Li Chung-chio 李鍾珏

Li Hsing-jui 李銳成章

Li Hsiu-ch'eng 李秀成

Li Hung-chang 李鴻章

Li Shan-lan 李善蘭

Li Tsung-hsi 李宗羲

Liang-shan 良山

Lin Tse-hsü 林則徐

Liu Ch'ang-yu 劉長佑

Liu Ch'i-hsiang 劉麒祥

Liu Jung 劉蓉

Liu K'un-i 劉坤一

Liu Ming-ch'uan 劉銘傳

Liu Ping-chang 劉秉璋

Liu Tso-yu 劉佐禹

Liu Yü-lung 劉王榮龍

Lo Jung-kuang 羅榮光

Lo-k'ou 洛口

Lo Ping-chang	駱秉章
Lo Ta-kang	羅大綱
Lo Tun-yen	羅惇衍
Lop Nor	羅布泊
Lu Ch'uan-lin	鹿傳霖
Lü-shun	旅順
Lung-hua	龍華
Ma Hsin-i	馬新貽
Ma-wei	馬尾
Mei Ch'i-ch'ao	梅啟照
Ming	明
mu-fu	幕府
Nanyang	南洋
nan-yang ta-ch'en	南洋大臣
nei chün-hsieh-so	內軍械所
Nieh Ch'i-kuei	聶緝槼
Nien	捻

Ning-yüan 寧遠

Nurhachi 努爾哈赤

P'an Ching-ju 潘鏡如

P'an Chün-te 潘駿德

P'an Lu 潘露

P'an Shih-ch'eng 潘仕成

P'an Ting-hsin 潘鼎新

Pao Ch'ao 鮑超

pao-chia-ch'u 報價處

Pao-min 保民

Peiyang 北洋

pei-yang ta-ch'en 北洋大臣

P'eng-lai 蓬萊

P'eng Yü-lin 彭玉麟

Pien-ching 汴京

Pien Pao-ti 卞寶第

P'ing-ch'üan 平泉

San-chia-tien	三家店
Seng-ko-lin-ch'in	僧格林沁
Shao Yu-lien	邵友濂
Shan-hai-kuan	山海關
Shen-mu-an	神木廠
Shen Pao-chen	沈葆楨
Shen Pao-ching	沈葆靖
Shih-ching	石井
Shih Ta-k'ai	石達開
Shuang-ch'iao	雙橋
Su-Sung-T'ai	蘇松太
Sun Ch'uan-yüeh	孫傳樾
Sung	宋
Sung Chin	宋晉
Sung Ch'un-ao	宋春鰲
Sungkiang	松江
Taku	大沽

Ta-ling-ho	大凌河
T'ai, Lake	太湖
Taikoktow	大角島
Taiping	太平
Tan-yang	丹陽
T'ang	唐
Ta-pieh Shan	大別山
Tar baga tai	塔爾巴哈台
Te-ch'un	德椿
Te-chou	德州
Teng-chou	登州
t'i-t'iao	提調
t'i-yung	體用
t'ieh-kuan	鐵官
T'ien-chi	恬吉
Ting Jih-ch'ang	丁日昌
Ting Kung-chen	丁拱辰

Ting Pao-chen 丁寶楨

Ting Shou-tsun 丁守存

Ting Ta-i 丁達意

Ts'ai Hsi-yung 蔡錫勇

Ts'ai Kuo-hsiang 蔡國祥

Tsai Shih 蔡石

Tsao-chiang 采江

Ts'ao-chou 曹州

Tse-hai 測海

Tseng Chi-tse 曾紀澤

Tseng Kuo-ch'üan 曾國荃

Tseng Kuo-fan 曾國藩

Ts'eng-pu 曾步

Tso Tsung-t'ang 左宗棠

Tsung-li ko-kuo shih-wu ya-men 總理各國事務衙門

Tsungli Yamen 總理衙門

Tu Wen-lan 杜文瀾

T'ung-chi 濟治

T'ung-chih 恫強

Tung Hsun 咸綏韜均

tzu-ch'iang 韜

Wang En-hsien 王恩

Wang Shih-shou 王世

Wang T'ao 王德文

Wang Te-chün 王德

Wang Wen-shao 王文

Wang Yang-ming 王陽

Wang Yu-ling 王有

Wei-ching 威

Wei-hai-wei 威海

Wei Yüan 魏

Wen-hsiang 文

Wen Ti 文子

Wen Tzu-shao 溫

通同董自恩世王德文陽有威海魏文子

韶明齡靖衛源祥帝紹

Wu-ch'ang 武昌

Wu Chia-lien 吳嘉廉

Wu-lung Shan 烏龍山

Wu-sung 吳淞

Wu Ta-ch'eng 吳大澂

Yakub Beg 阿古柏

yang-wu 洋務

yen-t'ieh lun 鹽鐵論

Ying Kuei 英桂

Ying Pao-shih 應寶時

Yo-chou 岳州

Yü-yüan 馭遠

Yüan 圓

Yung-an 永安

Yung Wing 容閎

Bibliography

CHINESE AND JAPANESE MATERIALS

Chang Chih-tung. <u>Chang Wen-hsiang-kung ch'üan-chi</u> [The complete works of Chang Chih-tung]. Taipei, Wen-hai ch'u-pan-she, 1963.

Chang Po-ch'u. "Shang-hai ping-kung-ch'ang chih shih-mo" [The Shanghai Arsenal from its beginning to the end], <u>Jen wen yüeh-k'an</u> [Men and literature monthly], 5.5:1-14 (1934).

Chao T'ieh-han. <u>Huo-yao te fa-ming</u> [The invention of gunpowder]. Taipei, Kuo-li li-shih po-wu-kuan, 1960.

Ch'en Chen, ed. <u>Chung-kuo chin-tai kung-yeh-shih tzu-liao</u> [Materials on the history of modern Chinese industry]. Vol. III, Peking, San-lien shu-chü, 1957.

Cheng Shih-hsü. "Ming-Ch'ing liang-tai chün-ch'i pien-ke chi ch'i ying-hsiang" [The evolution of military weapons during the Ming and Ch'ing Dynasties and their influence], <u>Hsin Chung-hua</u> [New China], 2nd series, 2.6:59-70 (June 1944).

Chiang Shih-jung, ed. <u>Tseng Kuo-fan wei-k'an hsin-kao</u> [Previously unpublished letters of Tseng Kuo-fan]. Shanghai, Chung-hua shu-chü, 1959.

<u>Chiang-nan chih tsao-chü ch'üan-an</u>. [The complete account of the Kiangnan Arsenal]. Shanghai, Kiangnan Arsenal, no date.

Ch'ing-shih pien-tsuan wei-yüan-hui. [Ch'ing history editorial committee] in cooperation with Chung-kuo wen-hua yen-chiu-so [The Institute of Chinese Culture], ed. <u>Ch'ing-shih</u> [History of the Ch'ing Dynasty]. 8 vols. Taipei, Kuo-fang yen-chiu-yüan.

<u>Ch'ou-pan i-wu shih-mo</u>. [The complete account of the management of barbarian affairs]. Taipei, Kuo-feng ch'u-pan-she, 1963.

Chou Shih-ch'eng. <u>Huai-chün p'ing-nien-chi</u>. [Record of the pacification of the Nien by the Huai Army]. Shanghai, 1877.

Chou Wei. <u>Chung-kuo ping-ch'i shih-kao</u>. [Draft history of Chinese weapons]. Peking, San-lien shu-tien, 1957.

Chu Shou-p'eng, ed. <u>Kuang-hsü-ch'ao tung-hua hsü-lu</u> [Tung-hua records continued for the Kuang-hsü reign].

Ch'üan Han-sheng. "Ch'ing-chi te chiang-nan chih-tsao-chü" [The Kiangnan Arsenal at the end of the Ch'ing dynasty], <u>Li shih yü-yen yen-chiu-so chi-k'an</u> [Bulletin of the Institute of History and Philosophy Academia Sinica], 23;145-59 (1951).

Chung-kuo chin-tai-shih tsung-shu pien-hsieh-tsu [Modern Chinese history compendium editorial committee], ed. <u>Yang-wu yun-tung</u> [Foreign matters movement]. Shanghai, Jen-min ch'u-pan-she, 1973.

Chung-kuo jen-ming ta-tzu-tien. [Chinese biographical dictionary]. Hong kong, T'ai-hsing shu-chü, 1931.

Fang Hao. "Min-mo hsi-yang huo-ch'i liu-ju wo-kuo chich shih-liao" [Materials on the entry of Western firearms to China at the end of the Ming], <u>Tung-fang tsa-chih</u> [Eastern Miscellany], 40: 49-54 (January, 1944).

Feng Chün-kuang. <u>Hsi-hsing jih-chi</u> [Diary of western travel]. 1881.

Hatano Yoshihiro. <u>Chugoku kindai kōgyō shi no kenkyū</u> [Studies on China's modern industrial history]. Kyoto, Toyoshi-kenkyu-kai, 1961.

Hsia Tung-yüan. "Lun Ch'ing-ch'eng-fu so-pan chin-tai chun-yung kung-yeh te hsing-chih" [On the characteristics of the modern industries operated by the Ch'ing government], Hua-tung shih-ta hsüeh-pao [Journal of East China Normal University], 1:50-66 (1958).

Hsieh Yen-keng. "Li Hung-chang yü chia-wu chan-ch'ien te ping-kung-yeh chien-she" [Li Hung-chang and the establishment of military industry prior to the Sino-Japanese War]. Doctoral dissertation, Taipei, Kuo-li Cheng-chih ta-hsüeh, 1968.

Huang Chia-mo. Chia-wu chan-ch'ien chih t'ai-wan mei-wu [Coal in Taiwan prior to the Sino-Japanese War]. Taipei, Chung-yang yen-chiu-yüan chin-tai-shih yen-chiu-so, 1961.

Hu-pei ping-kung-kang-yao-ch'ang t'iao-shuo piao-tse [Itemized discussions and charts on the Hupei arsenal, steel and powder works]. 1910.

Hu-pei ta-hsüeh cheng-chih ching-chi chiao-yen-shih. [Hupeh University political and economic research institute], ed. Chung-kuo chin-tai kuo-min ching-chi shih chiang-i [Lectures on the history of the people's economy of modern China]. Peking, Kao-teng chiao-yu ch'u-pan-she, 1958.

Kan Tso-lin. "Chiang-nan chih-tsao-chü chih chien-shih" [A simplified history of the Kiangnan Arsenal], Tung-fang tsa-chih [Eastern Miscellany] 11.5:46-48, 11.6:21-25 (1914).

Kitayama Yasuo. "Chugoku ni okeru kan'ei gunji no ichi kosatsu" [An investigation of government operated military industry in China], Hisutoria [History], 9:1-8 (August 1954).

Ko Shih-chün, ed. Huang-ch'ao ching-shih wen-hsü-pien [Continuation of the collected documents on statecraft]. Shanghai, 1888.

Kuo Ting-yee. Chin-tai Chung-kuo shih jih-chih [A day-by-day record of recent historical events in China]. 2 vols. Taipei, Chung-yang yen-chiu-yüan chin-tai-shih yen-chiu-so, 1963.

Kuo Ting-yee, et al., eds. Hai-fang Tang [Maritime defense archives]. 5 vols. Taipei, Chung-yang yen-chiu-so, 1957.

Li Chung-chio. Ch'ieh-wan lao-jen ch'i-shih-sui tzu-hsü [The autobiography of Li Chung-chio]. No date. Held by the Institute of Modern History Academia Sinica, Nankang, Taiwan.

Li En-han. "Ch'ing-mo chin-ling chi-ch'i-chü te ch'uang-chien yü kuo-chan" [The establishment and development of the Nanking Arsenal in the late Ch'ing dynasty], Ta-lu tsa-chih [The Continent Magazine], 33.12:7-14 (December 31, 1966).

Li En-han. Tseng Chi-tse te wai-chiao [The diplomacy of Tseng Chi-tse]. Taipei, Chung-yang yen-chiu-yüan chin-tai-shih yen-chiu-so, 1966.

Li Hung-chang. Li Wen-chung kung ch'üan-chi [The complete works of Li Hung-chang]. Taipei, Wen-hai ch'u-pan-she, 1965.

Li Kuo-ch'i. Chang Chih-tung te wai-chiao cheng-tze [Chang Chih-tung's foreign policy]. Taipei, Chung-yang yen-chiu-yüan chin-tai-shih yen-chiu-so, 1970.

Li Kuo-ch'i. Chung-kuo tsao-ch'i te t'ieh-lu ching-ying [Early Chinese railroad enterprise]. Taipei, Chung-yang yen-chiu-yüan chin-tai-shih yen-chiu-so, 1961.

Lien-ch'in ping-kung chi-shu fa-chan chung-hsin [Combined logistical military industry technical development center], ed. Ping-ch'i fa-chan shih [History of weapons development]. Taipei, Lien-ch'in ping-kung chi-shu fa-chan chung-hsin, 1969.

Liu Chin-tsao, ed. Ch'ing-ch'ao-hsü wen-hsien t'ung-kao [The Ch'ing dynasty continuation of the general study of literary remains]. Taipei, Hsin-hsing shu-chü, 1965.

Liu K'un-i. Liu Chung-ch'eng kung (K'un-i) i-chi [Posthumous collection of Liu K'un-i's writings]. Taipei, Wen-hai ch'u-pan-she, 1966.

Lü Shih-ch'iang. Chung-kuo tsao-ch'i te lun-ch'uan ching-ying [Early steamship enterprise in China]. Taipei, Chung-yang yen-chiu-yüan chin-tai-shih yen-chiu-so, 1962.

Lü Shih-ch'iang. "Feng Kuei-fen te cheng-chih ssu-hsiang" [The political thought of Feng Kuei-fen], Chung-hua wen-hua fu-hsing yüeh-k'an [Chinese cultural renaissance monthly] 4.2:1-8.

Lü Shih-ch'iang. Ting-Jih-ch'ang yü tzu-ch'iang yun-tung [Ting Jih-ch'ang and the self-strengthening movement]. Taipei, Chung-yang yen-chiu-yüan chin-tai-li-shih-so, 1972.

Mou An-shih. Yang-wu yun-tung [The foreign matters movement]. Shanghai, Jen-min ch'u-pan-she, 1961.

Onoue Etsuzo. "Chūgoku ni okeru kindai kōgyō no ishoku yōmu undo no ichi sokumen" [The transplanting of modern industry to China--an aspect of the foreign matters movement], Rokkodai ronshu 5.3:67-86 (October 1958).

Pao Tsun-p'eng. Chung-kuo Hai-chün-shih [History of the Chinese navy]. Taipei, Hai-chün ch'u-pan-she, 1951.

Pao Tsun-p'eng, Li Ting-i, and Wu Hsiang-hsiang, eds. Tsu-ch'iang yun-tung [Self-strengthening movement], Chung-kuo chin-tai-shih lun-ts'ung [Compendium on modern Chinese history]. 1st series, vol. 5. Taipei, Chung-cheng shu-chü, 1959.

Saegusa Hirone. Gendai Nihon bunmei shi [Contemporary Japanese cultural history]. Vol. 14. Gijutsushi [History of technology]. Tōyō keizai shimpo sha, 1940.

Shen Pao-chen. Shen Wen-su kung cheng-shu [Public papers of Shen Pao-chen]. 7 chüan. 1880.

Shen Yün-lung, ed. Hsien-tai cheng-chih jen-wu shu-p'ing [Critiques of contemporary political personages]. 2 chüan. Taipei, Wen-hai ch'u-pan-she, 1966.

Shiba Kakichi. Nihon heiki hensen monogatari [The evolution of Japanese weapons]. Tokyo, Aiyoshi Shigekazu, 1942.

Sun Yu-t'ang, ed. Chung-kuo chin-tai kung-yeh-shih tzu-liao [Materials on the history of modern Chinese industry]. Vol. 1, 1840-1895. Peking, K'o-hsüeh ch'u-pan-she, 1957.

Ta-ch'ing hui-tien [Collected Statutes of the Ch'ing dynasty]. No date.

Tien-chin fu-chih [Gazetteer of Tientsin]. 1876.

Ting Jih-ch'ang. Fu-wu kung-tu [Public papers on governing Kiangsu]. 50 chüan. 1877.

Ting Jih-ch'ang. Ting Chung-cheng cheng-shu [Political papers of Ting Jih-ch'ang]. Manuscript, Sterling Library, Yale University.

Tseng Kuo-fan. Tseng Wen-cheng kung ch'üan-chi [The complete works of Tseng Kuo-fan]. Taipei, Shih-chieh shu-chü, 1964.

Tseng Kuo-fan. Tseng Wen-cheng kung shou-shu jih-chi [Handwritten diary of Tseng Kuo-fan]. 1909.

Tso Tsung-t'ang. Tso Wen-hsiang kung ch'üan-chi [The complete works of Tso Tsung-t'ang]. Taipei, Wen-hai ch'u-pan-she, 1964.

Tsugai Yoshio. Nihon sangyō kigyō shi gaisetsu [Outline history of Japanese industry]. Tokyo, Zeimukeiri kyōkikai, 1969.

Wang Erh-min. Ch'ing-chi ping-kung-yeh te hsing-ch'i [The rise of military industry in the late Ch'ing dynasty]. Taipei, Chung-yang yen-chiu-yüan chin-tai-shih yen-chiu-so, 1963.

Wang Erh-min. Huai-chün chih [History of the Huai Army]. Taipei, Chung-kuo hsüeh-shu chu-tso chiang-chu wei-yüan-hui, 1967.

Wang Erh-min. "Lien-chün te ch'i-yüan chi ch'i i-i" [The origin and significance of the Lien Army], Ta-lu tsa-chih [The Continent Magazine] 34.6:10-13 (March 31, 1967); 34.7:22-29 (April 15, 1967).

Wang Erh-min. "Nan-pei-yang ta-chen chih chien-chih chi ch'i ch'üan-li chih k'uo-chang" [The establishment of the commissioners of northern and southern ports and the expansion of their authority]. Ch'ing-chi chi chin-tai-shih yen-chiu lun-chi [Collected research articles on late Ch'ing and recent history], Ta-lu tsa-chih shih-hsüeh tsung-shu [Continent magazine conpendium on history]. Series 1, vol. 7, 192-99. Taipei, Ta-lu tsa-chih-she, 1967.

Wang Erh-min. <u>Wan-ch'ing cheng-chih ssu-hsiang shih-lun</u> [On the history of late Ch'ing political thought]. Taipei, Hsüeh-sheng shu-chü, 1969.

Wang T'ao. <u>T'ao-yüan wen-lu wai-pien</u> [Supplement to the literary record of Wang T'ao]. Hong Kong, 1882.

Wei Yun-kung. <u>Chiang-nan chih-tsao-chü chi</u> [Record of the Kiangnan Arsenal]. 10 chuan. Shanghai, Wen-pao shu-chu, 1905.

Yang Chia-lo, ed. <u>Yang-wu yun-tung wen-hsien hui-pien</u> [Collected documents on the foreign matters movement]. 8 vols. Taipei, Shih-chieh shu-chü, 1963.

Yao Wen-nan, ed. <u>Shang-hai hsien hsü-chih</u> [Gazetteer of the Shanghai district continued]. Shanghai, 1918.

Yü Yüeh, ed. <u>Shang-hai hsien-chih</u> [Gazetteer of the Shanghai district]. Shanghai, 1871.

<u>Yü-che hui-ts'un</u> [Collected edicts and memorials]. Peking, Hsieh-hua shu-chü. 1892-1911.

WESTERN LANGUAGE MATERIALS

"Ammunition." <u>Encyclopedia Britannica</u>. 1910-1911. I.

"Ammunition, Artillery." <u>Encyclopedia Britannica</u>. 1967. I.

"Artillery." <u>Encyclopedia Britannica</u>. 1910-1911. II.

"Artillery." <u>Encyclopedia Britannica</u>. 1967. II.

Banno Masataka. <u>China and the West, 1858-1861: The Origins of the Tsungli Yamen</u>. Cambridge, Mass., Harvard University Press, 1964.

"Battleships." <u>Encyclopedia Britannica</u>. 1963. III.

Bennett, Adrian. <u>John Fryer: The Introduction of Western Science and Technology into Nineteenth-Century China</u>. Cambridge, Mass., East Asian Research Center, Harvard University, 1967.

Beresford, Charles. <u>The Breakup of China</u>. New York and London, Harper and Brothers, 1899.

Biggerstaff, Knight. *The Earliest Modern Government Schools in China*. Ithaca, N.Y., Cornell University Press, 1961.

Boulger, Demetrius. *The Life of Sir Halliday Macartney*. London, John Lane, 1908.

Brunnert, H. S., and Hagelstrom, V. V. *Present Day Political Organization of China*. Taipei, Book World Company, 1963.

Chang Chun-ming. "The Genesis and Meaning of Huan K'uan's 'Discourses on Salt and Iron'," *Chinese Social and Political Science Review* 18.1:1-52 (April 1934).

Chang Chung-li, and Spector, Stanley, eds. *Guide to the Memorials of Seven Leading Officials of Nineteenth Century China*. Seattle, University of Washington Press, 1955.

Chang, Hao. *Liang Ch'i-ch'ao and Intellectual Transition in China, 1890-1907*. Cambridge, Mass., Harvard University Press, 1971.

Chen, Gideon. *Lin Tse-hsu: Pioneer Promoter of the Adoption of Western Means of Maritime Defense in China*. Peiping, Yenching University, 1935.

Chen, Gideon. *Tseng Kuo-fan: Pioneer Promoter of the Steamship in China*. Peiping, Yenching University, 1935.

Chu, Wen-djang. "Tso Tsung-t'ang's Role in the Recovery of Sinkiang," *Tsing Hua Journal of Chinese Studies* 1.3 (September 1958).

Cohen, Paul A. *Between Tradition and Modernity: Wang T'ao and Reform in Late Ch'ing China*. Cambridge, Harvard University Press, 1975.

Dean, Britten. *China and Great Britain: The Diplomacy of Commercial Relations, 1860-1864*. Cambridge, Mass., East Asian Research Center, Harvard University, 1974.

deBary, Wm. Theodore, Chan, Wing-tsit, and Watson, Burton, comps. *Sources of Chinese Tradition*. New York, Columbia University Press, 1960.

"Description of the Shanghai Imperial Arsenal, in 1869," *Shanghai Newsletter*, June 1869.

Deyrup, Felicia Johnson. *Arms Makers of the Connecticut Valley, A Regional Study of the Economic Development of the Small Arms Industry*. Northampton, Mass., Smith College Department of History, 1948.

Duchaxel, Capt. "L'arsenal Chinois de Kiangnan," *Revue Mar et Coloniale* 26:638-44 (February 1873).

Feuerwerker, Albert Murphey, Rhoads and Wright, Mary C., eds. *Approaches to Modern Chinese History*. Berkeley and Los Angeles, University of California Press, 1967.

Feuerwerker, Albert. *China's Early Industrialization: Sheng Hsüan-huai (1844-1916) and Mandarin Enterprises*. Cambridge, Mass., Harvard University Press, 1958.

Feuerwerker, Albert. *The Chinese Economy, ca. 1870-1911*. Ann Arbor, Center for Chinese Studies, University of Michigan, 1969.

Folsom, Kenneth E. *Friends, Guests, and Colleagues: The Mu-Fu System in the late Ch'ing Period*. Berkeley and Los Angeles, University of California Press, 1968.

Fryer, John. *An Account of the Department for the Translation of Foreign Books at the Kiangnan Arsenal with Various Lists of Publications in Chinese Languages*. Shanghai, American Presbyterian Mission Press, 1880.

Fung Yu-lan. *A History of Chinese Philosophy*. 2 vols. Translated by Derk Bodde. Princeton, Princeton University Press, 1952.

Goodrich, L. Carrington. "Note on a Few Early Chinese Bombards," *Isis* 35:211 (1944).

Goodrich, L. Carrington, and Feng Chia-sheng. "The Early Development of Firearms in China," *Isis* 36:114-23 (1945-1946).

Great Britain. Foreign Office. "General Correspondence, China." (Foreign Office series 17 and 233, Admiralty series 1) Manuscript archives filed at the Public Record Office, London.

"Greekfire." *Encyclopedia Britannica*. 1962. Vol. X.

Hsu, Immanuel C. Y. China's Entrance into the Family of Nations: The Diplomatic Phase, 1858-1880. Cambridge, Mass., Harvard University Press, 1960.

Hsu, Immanuel C. Y. "The Great Policy Debate in China, 1874: Maritime Defense vs. Frontier Defense," Harvard Journal of Asiatic Studies, 25:212-28 (1964-1965).

Hummel, Arthur W. Eminent Chinese of the Ch'ing Period. Washington, D.C. 1943-1944; reprint edition, Taipei, Literature House, 1964.

Kennedy, Thomas L. "Chang Chih-tung and the Struggle for Strategic Industrialization: The Establishment of the Hanyang Arsenal, 1884-1895," Harvard Journal of Asiatic Studies 33:154-82 (1973).

Kennedy, Thomas L. "The Establishment of Modern Military Industry in China," Chung-yang yen-chiu-yüan chin-tai-shih yen-chiu-so chi-k'an (Bulletin of the Institute of Modern History Academia Sinica) 4.2:779-823 (December 1974).

Kennedy, Thomas L. "Industrial Metamorphosis in the Self-Strengthening Movement: Li Hung-chang and the Kiangnan Shipbuilding Program," Hsiang-kang chung-wen ta-hsüeh chung-kuo wen-hua yen-chiu-so hsüeh-pao (Journal of the Institute of Chinese Studies of the Chinese University of Hong Kong) 4.1:207-28 (1971).

Kennedy, Thomas L. "The Kiangnan Arsenal 1895-1911: The Decentralized Bureaucracy Responds to Imperialism," Ch'ing-shih wen-t'i 2.1:17-37 (October 1969).

Kennedy, Thomas L. "The Kiangnan Arsenal in the Era of Reform 1895-1911," Chung-yang Yen-chiu-yüan chin-tai-shih yen-chiu-so chi-k'an (Bulletin of the Institute of Modern History Academia Sinica) 3.1:269-346 (July 1972).

Kennedy, Thomas L. "Self-Strengthening: An Analysis Based on Some Recent Writings," Ch'ing-shih wen-t'i 3.1:3-35 (November 1974).

Kim, K. H. Japanese Perspectives on China's Early Modernization: A Bibliographical Survey. Ann Arbor, Center for Chinese Studies, University of Michigan, 1974.

Liang Ch'i-ch'ao. *Intellectual Trends in the Ch'ing Period*, trans. by Immanuel C. Y. Hsu. Cambridge, Mass., Harvard University Press, 1959.

Lissak, Ormond M. *Ordnance and Gunnery*. New York, John Wiley and Sons, 1915.

Liu, Kwang-Ching. *Anglo-American Steamship Rivalry in China, 1862-1874*. Cambridge, Mass., Harvard University Press, 1962.

Liu, Kwang-Ching. "The Confucian as Patriot and Pragmatist: Li Hung-chang's Formative Years, 1823-1866," *Harvard Journal of Asiatic Studies*, 30:5-45 (1970).

Medzini, Meron. *French Policy in Japan during the Closing Years of the Tokugawa Regime*. Cambridge, Mass., East Asian Research Center, Harvard University, 1971.

"Mine, Naval." *Encyclopedia Britannica*. 1967. XV.

Morse, Hosea Ballou. *The International Relations of the Chinese Empire*. 3 vols. London, Hazell, Watson and Viney, Ltd., 1910 and 1918.

Morse, Hosea Ballou. *The Trade and Administration of the Chinese Empire*. Taipei, Cheng-wen Publishing Company, 1966.

Ommundsen, H. and Robinson, E. H. *Rifles and Ammunition*. New York, Cassell and Co., 1915.

"Ordnance." *Encyclopedia Britannica*. 1910-1911. XX.

Pong, David. "Modernization and Politics in China as Seen in the Career of Shen Pao-chen (1820-1879)." Ph.D. dissertation, University of London, 1969.

Powell, Ralph L. *The Rise of Chinese Military Power, 1895-1912*. Princeton: Princeton University Press, 1955.

Rawlinson, John L. *China's Struggle for Naval Development, 1839-1895*. Cambridge, Mass., Harvard University Press, 1967.

Reischauer, Edwin O. and John K. Fairbank. *East Asia: The Great Tradition*. Boston, Houghton Mifflin Company, 1958.

Schwartz, Benjamin. In Search of Wealth and Power: Yen Fu and the West. Cambridge, Mass., 1964; Harper Torchbook ed., New York, Harper & Row, 1969.

Shen, Han-yin Chen. "Tseng Kuo-fan in Peking, 1840-1852: His Ideas on Statecraft and Reform," Journal of Asian Studies 27.1:61-80 (November 1967).

"Ship." Encyclopedia Britannica. 1963. XX.

"Small Arms, Military." Encyclopedia Britannica. 1967. XX.

Smith, Thomas C. Political Change and Industrial Development in Japan: Government Enterprise, 1868-1880. Stanford: Stanford University Press, 1955.

Spector, Stanley. Li Hung-chang and the Huai Army: A Study in Nineteenth-Century Chinese Regionalism. Seattle, University of Washington Press, 1964.

Teng, Ssu-yu, and Fairbank, John K. China's Response to the West: A Documentary Survey, 1839-1923. Cambridge, Mass., 1954; paperback edition, New York, Atheneum, 1963.

Tsiang, T. F. "Sino-Japanese Diplomatic Relations, 1870-1894," The Chinese Social and Political Science Review 17.1:1-106 (April 1933).

Wakeman, Fredrick. "The Huang-ch'ao ching-shih wen-pien," Ch'ing-shih Wen-t'i 1.10:8-22 (February 1969).

Wang Erh-min. "China's Use of Foreign Military Assistance in the Lower Yangtze Valley, 1860-1864," Chung-yang Yen-chiu-yüan chin-tai-shih yen-chiu so chi-k'an (Bulletin of the Institute of Modern History Academia Sinica) 2:535-83 (June 1971).

Wang Ling. "On the Invention and Use of Gunpowder in China," Isis 37:160-78 (1947).

Williamson, Alexander. Journeys in North China, Manchuria, and Eastern Inner Mongolia; with some account of Corea. London, Smith, Edler and Co., 1870.

Wilson, H. W. Ironclads in Action: A Sketch of Naval Warfare from 1855 to 1898. 2 vols. Boston, Little, Brown and Co. 1896.

Wright, Mary C. *The Last Stand of Chinese Conservatism: The T'ung-chih Restoration, 1862-1874.* Stanford, 1957; paperback ed., New York, Atheneum, 1966.

Yung Wing. *My Life in China and America.* New York, Henry Holt, 1909.

Index

air bursting shells, 36
Alcock Convention, 71
Anking Arsenal, 35-36, 42, 175
anti-imperialism, 149
arms and ammunition, modernization of, 153-154
arms monopoly, 3, 4-6, 6-7, 12, 16, 121-122
Armstrong Company, 106, 107, 110-111, 129-130, 199 n. 17
arsenal finance, 154
arsenal locations, 155-156
Artillery and Musketry Division, 42-43, 48, 144

Beresford, Lord, 140, 141
Board of Revenue, 60, 61-62
Board of War, 143
Boxer Uprising, 147
Bracegirdle, Mr., 114
breechloading guns, 199 n. 17
breechloading rifles, 191 n. 28
bronze, early development, 3
Buchheister and Company, 134
built-up ordnance, 106-107, 129-130, 132, 199 n. 17
Butterfield and Swire, 196 n. 15

cartridges, initial production, 64, 191-192 n. 29; center fire, 109, 201 n. 28; rim fire, 201 n. 28
Chang Chao-tung, 91, 177
Chang Chih-tung, 111, 122, 123, 129, 142, 177; on the location of the Kiangnan Arsenal, 136-137
Chang Shih-ch'eng, 10
Chekiang Arsenal, 177
Chekiang Powder Plant, 177
Chen Ting-ching, 45
Ch'en-chia Kang, rocket plant, 63
Cheng Ch'eng-kung (Koxinga), 12
Chia-chia-ku Tao. See East Arsenal
Chiang Chung-yüan, 15
Chiang-nan chih-tsao tsung-chü. See Kiangnan Arsenal
Chiao-pin-lu k'ang-i (Protests from the Study of Chiao-pin), 29-31
Chin-ling chih-tsao-chü. See Nanking Arsenal
Chin-ou, 83, 86, 162
China Educational Mission, 82

China, foreign relations;
with Britain, 26-28, 71,
136; with France, 26-28,
71, 136; with Japan,
79, 88-90, 136; with
Russia, 28-29, 117;
with U.S., 136
China Merchant Steam
Navigation Company, 115-
116, 152, 195-196 n. 15;
establishment, 85
Chu I-hsin, 121
Chu-Yüan-chang, 9
Ch'un, Prince, 122, 177
Chung Yün-ku, 125
Ch'ung-hou, 42, 50-53,
55-56, 71-72, 175
Coal mines, modern, 94,
97, 112, 118, 152
Compound engine, 100,
198 n. 5
Confucianism; attitude
toward monopolies,
5-6; in early Ch'ing
dynasty, 18-23; influ-
ence on ordnance de-
velopment, 9, 16, 149-
150
copper mines, modern,
118
Cornish, Mr., 130, 134
cost of production,
154-155

Davidson, Daniel
McKensie, 73-74
debates on salt and
iron, 5

East Arsenal, Tientsin,
72-76, 143-144, 175-
176; establishment,
50-52.
economic modernization,
152
educational moderniza-
tion, 152-153
electrical equipment,
first produced in
China, 117
Ever Victorious Army,
39,45
explosive shells, 13, 36,
40, 41, 49, 188 n. 21

Feng Chün-kuang, 48, 54,
65, 81, 83-85, 86; pro-
posals for shipbuilding
and industrial develop-
ment, 83-85
Feng Kuei-fen, 36, 43;
reform proposals, 29-33
firearms, early develop-
ment, 2, 8-10
Fo-lan-chi gun, 10
Foochow Arsenal, 175-176
Foochow Dockyard, 78, 80,
87, 88, 102; bombardment
of, 121, 123
foreign technicians, 35,
36, 39, 40, 42-43, 45, 52,
53, 54, 59, 60, 63, 64,
66, 68-70, 72-74, 76-77,
82, 93, 105, 107, 112,
113-114, 115, 117, 123,
127-128, 130, 133, 134,
138, 139, 142, 155, 158-
159
fuses, 40, 41, 50

gatling guns, 68, 114, 115
gingals, 10, 50, 114, 140,
145, 154
Giquel, Prosper, 88, 89,
127
Gordon, George, 45-46
Greek fire, 8, 182 n. 9
Greenwood and Battey, 75
grenades, 8
gun powder, 2-3, 40, 52,
63, 72-75, 114-115, 116,
118; discovery of, 7-8;
introduction to Europe;
prismatic (brown), 130,
142, 192 n. 30, 205 n. 20;
smokeless, 131, 133, 134,
206-207 n. 30

Hai-an, 82, 86, 93, 161
Hai-kuang Szu. See West
Arsenal
Hai-kuo t'u-chih (Illus-

trated gazetteer of the maritime nations), 22
Han Tien-chia, 39, 40, 48, 175, 177
Hanyang Arsenal, 122, 123, 129, 133, 177-178
Hart, Robert, 35, 51
Ho Ch'ang-ling, 21
Ho Ching, 84
Ho Kuei-ch'ing, 26
Hotchkiss Rifle, 131
Hsia Shih, 177
Hsiang Army, 24, 38, 136
Hsien-feng, Emperor, 27
Hsü Chien-yin, 177
Hsü Ching-ch'eng, 129
Hsü Kuang-ch'i (Paul Hsü), 11
Hsü Shou, 36
Hsüeh Fu-chen, 177
Hsüeh Huan, 29
Hsüeh Pei-yung, 177
Hu Lin-i, 15
Hua Heng-fang, 36, 177
Huai Army, 38, 41, 49, 59, 61, 76, 82, 88, 114, 116, 140; relationship with Nanking Arsenal, 67; relationship with Tientsin Mobile Arsenal, 70-71, 113
Huang-ch'ao ching-shih wen-pien (Collected Documents on Statecraft), 21, 125
Huang-ku, 36
Huang Mien, 15
Hunan Arsenal, 177-178
Hung-i-ta-p'ao, 11, 12
Huo-ch'i shuo-lüeh (A Discussion of Firearms) 44-45, 46

I-fu, 140
Ignatiev, Nicholas, 28
imperial leadership, influence on the ordnance industry, 156-157
imperialism, 159-160
industrialization, balanced, 83-84, 122, 152
iron, early development, 3, 4; modern, 97, 112; monopoly, 5-6

Japanese Navy compared to China's, 89
Japanese Ordnance Industry, compared to China's, 89-90, 128, 132, 136
Jui Lin, 177

K'ang-hsi, 12
Kao-ch'ang Miao. See Kiangnan Arsenal
Kawakami, General, 133
Kiangnan Arsenal, 1, 175-176; control, 80-81, 104; costs, 111-112, 138-139; distribution of products, 49, 65, 110-111, 114, 135-136, 165-169, 192 n. 32; establishment, 45-49, 59, 62; expenditures, 170-171; facilities, 62-63, 105; Hunanese influence, 124-125; income, 61-62, 102-103, 124, 163; indebtedness, 138; initial operations, 53-55; personnel, 62, 66, 103, 112, 123, 125-126, 127-128; production: ammunition, 64-65, 105, 108, 109-110, 131, 134, 164; guns, 64, 105-109, 123, 130-131, 164; machinery, 63-64, 105, 135, 164; mines, 110, 164; powder, 164; prismatic powder, 130; small arms, 64, 109, 123, 131-134, 164; smokeless powder, 131, 134; steel, 134-135; torpedoes, 110; purchasing, 103, 128; shipbuilding, 58-62, 79-87, 92-95, 99-102, 129, 161-162; supply, 111-112, 123, 136; strategic vulnerability, 105, 123,

136-137, 139
Kiangnan magazine rifle, 133
Kirin Arsenal, 177-178
Korea, Chinese military assistance group, 117
Koxinga. See Cheng Ch'eng-kung
Krupp, 106, 121, 129-130, 131, 134, 199 n. 16, 199 n. 17, 205 n. 22
Kuang-fang yen-kuan (institute for the study of foreign languages), 39
Kuei-liang, 28
K'un-ming Lake, 144
Kung Chao-yuan, 114, 177
Kung Chen-lin, 14, 15, 36
Kung Chih-t'ang, 15, 36
Kung, Prince, 27, 28, 29, 35, 42-43, 45, 57
Kwangtung Arsenal, 177-178
Kwangtung Cartridge Plant, 177-178
Kwangtung Powder Plant, 177-178
Lai Ch'ang, 175
Lanchow Arsenal, 87, 175-176
Lay-Osborn Flotilla, 40, 46, 52, 72
Lee Rifle, 131, 133
Legalism, 3-6, 20-22
Li Chih-tsao (Leo Li), 11
Li Chung-chio, 124
Li Hsing-jui, 105, 125
Li Hsiu-ch'eng, 25-26, 34
Li Hung-chang, 29, 30, 33, 37, 45, 46, 49, 50, 53, 54, 62, 63, 65, 72, 80, 90, 92, 99, 100, 104, 128, 130, 131, 133, 175; and Huai Army, 38, 70; and Kiangnan Arsenal, 58-59, 78, 81-83, 86, 93, 95, 102, 110-111; leadership in ordnance industry, 76-77; and Nanking Arsenal, 67-70; and Navy Yamen, 122; and Nien Rebellion, 55; and Shanghai-Soochow Arsenals, 40-41; and Taiping Rebellion, 25, 38-41; and Tientsin Arsenal, 55-56, 71-76, 115-119, 142-146; relationship with Tseng Kuo-fan, 25; views on arsenal establishment, 57; views on education, 42-44, 82; views on heavy ordnance production, 106-108; views on machine production, 41-42, 47-48; views on maritime defense, 93; views on shipbuilding, 58-59; views on strategic industry, 96-98; views on western ordnance, 38-39
Li Shan-lan, 36
Li Tsung-hsi, 85, 86
Lien Army, 76, 116, 194 n. 52
Lin Tse-hsü, 13, 15
Liu Ch'ang-yu, 51, 175
Liu Ch'i-hsiang, 141; director of Kiangnan Arsenal, 126-139
Liu Jung, 126
Liu K'un-i, 100-101, 114, 133, 135, 177
Liu Ming-ch'uan, 54, 177
Liu Ping-chang, 41, 177
Liu Tso-yu, 40, 68, 69, 175
Liu Yü-lung, 41
Livadia, Treaty of, 117
Lo Jung-kuang, 41
Lo Ping-chang, 15
Lo Ta-kang, 15
Lo Tun-yen, 61
Lu Ch'uan-lin, 177
Lung-hua. See Kiangnan Arsenal

Ma Hsin-i, 61, 62, 72

Ma-wei, battle of, 110, 121, 122
MacKenzie, John, 107
Macartney, Halliday Dr., 40, 41, 45, 49, 67-70, 127, 175
magazine rifle, 131, 133, 206 n. 26
Maritime Defense Fund, 94, 95, 100-102, 103, 107, 116, 122, 143
Maritime Defense Policy 1875, 92-98, 99, 106, 112
Maritime vs. Frontier Defense Controversy, 90-92
Mannlicher Rifle, 129, 133
Martini-Henry Co., 121
Mauser Rifles, 64, 129, 131, 133
McIlwraith, 73
Meadows, 51, 52, 72, 73, 175
Mei Ch'i-ch'ao, 100, 101
mines, 14, 15, 110, 113, 117, 201-202 n. 32
Moslem Rebellion, 78, 87, 108
Muller, Mr., 65
Murata Rifle, 129, 133

Nanking Arsenal, 55, 102, 106, 175-176; control, 112-113; costs, 141; distribution, 114; establishment, 49-50; expenditure, 173; facilities, 68, 113-114, 139-140; income, 112-113, 140, 173; location, 141-142; management, 68-70, 141; personnel, 114; production, 68, 114, 140; relationship with Huai Army, 67; relationship with Kiangnan Arsenal, 67; shipbuilding, 140; supply, 114
Nanking Powder Plant, 177-178; establishment, 114-115; expenditure, 174; facilities, 114, 140; income, 140-141, 174; production, 114, 141
Nan-yang ta-ch'en. See Southern Commissioner
Nanyang, 94, 100-102, 107, 108, 113, 135-137
Naval Academy, at Tientsin Arsenal, 118
Navy Yamen, 102, 103, 122, 128, 129, 130, 140, 142, 144
Nerchinsk, Treaty of, 13
New Southgate Engineering Company, 143
Nieh Ch'i-kuei, 125-128, 129
Nien Rebellion, 48, 49, 50, 54, 55, 58, 60, 192 n. 32
Ning-yüan, battle of, 11
non-military production, 151-152
North China Herald, 142, 143
Northern Commissioner, 28, 32, 42, 58, 65, 67, 72, 81, 93, 94, 96, 98, 99, 100-102, 104, 112-113, 119, 122; leadership in the ordnance industry, 157-158
Nurhachi, 11

ordnance industry, status during Sino-Japanese War, 146-147

paddle wheel propulsion, 190, n. 11
P'an Ching-ju, 125
P'an Chun-te, 177
P'an Lu, 177
P'an Shih-ch'eng, 14
P'an Ting-hsin, 41, 50
Pao Ch'ao, 117
Pao-min, 101, 103
Pei-yang ta-ch'en. See Northern Commissioner
Peiyang, 94, 100, 102, 107, 110-111, 113, 117, 135-

240

136, 137, 144-146
Peking Field Forces Arsenal, 116, 177-178
P'eng Yu-lin, 100, 101
percussion caps, 14, 17, 36, 41, 50, 183-184 n. 23
personnel and administrative costs, 155
Pien-ching, battle of, 8
Pien Pao-ti, 121-122
Pong, David, on proposals to halt shipbuilding, 195 n. 8
propeller drive, 60, 190 n. 11
provincial arsenals, 78, 97-98, 99, 121, 175-178
Putnam Machine Company, 36

Quick firing guns, 130-131, 205 n. 22

raw material, costs, 154-155
Remington Rifles, 64, 74, 109-110, 117, 131, 133
rifling, 199 n. 16
rockets, 8, 49-50, 63
Rodriquez, Johannes, 11
Russel Steamship Line, 116, 139, 195-196 n. 15

self-strengthening, 31-33, 35, 57, 58, 77, 149-151
semi-colonialism, 150-151
Seng-ko-lin-ch'in, Prince, 42, 48, 49
Shanghai Arsenals, 38-45, 175-176
Shansi Arsenal, 177-178
Shantung Arsenal, 177-178
Shao Yu-lien, 111
Shen Pao-chen, 88, 89, 90, 107; views on shipbuilding, 100; views on strategic industry, 93-95, 97
Shen Pao-ching, 48, 53, 73, 144
Shensi Arsenal, 177-178
Shih Ta-k'ai, 15
Sian Arsenal, 87, 175-176
Sino-French War, logistics, 111, 114-115, 117, 125; stimulates reform in ordnance industry, 121-123
Sino-Japanese Treaty of Friendship and Commerce 1871, 88
Sino-Japanese War, logistics, 136-137, 140, 141, 144-146
Soochow Arsenal, 40, 49, 175-176
Southern Commissioner, 28, 32, 58, 59, 62, 65, 68, 80-81, 93, 94, 96, 98, 99, 100-102, 103, 104, 107, 110, 112, 113, 119, 122; leadership in ordnance industry, 157
Spector, Stanley, on control of the Nanking Arsenal, 203 n. 42
standardization of arms, ammunition, and equipment, 119-120, 128-129
Statecraft, School of, 20-22, 23-24, 29-33, 150
steel industry, 112, 123, 134-135, 143, 199 n. 16
Stewart, Mr., 53, 56, 72, 142, 175
Sun Ch'uan-yueh, 177
Sung Chin, 80
Sung Ch'un-ao, 177
Sungkiang Arsenal, 40, 175-176
Sungkiang Magazine, 105
Szechwan Arsenal, 177-178

Ta-ling-ho, battle of, 12
Taiwan Arsenal, 177-178
Taiwan Crisis 1874, 88-90
Taku Forts, 14, 27, 68-70

106, 107, 109
Te-ch'un, 52
technological modernization, 152
telegraphy school, at Tientsin Arsenal, 118
t'i-yung, theory of reform, 32
Tientsin Arsenal, 71; control, 72-73, 104, 115; costs, 117; distribution, 114, 116, 117-118, 144-146; expenditure, 172; facilities, 73, 74-75, 116, 117; income, 55-56, 117, 142-143, 145-146, 172; management, 146; mint, 144; palace grounds improvements, 144; production, 75-76, 110, 116, 117, 130, 142, 144-146; shipbuilding, 118, 143; steel, 143; supply, 118. See also East Arsenal, West Arsenal
Tientsin Massacre, 67, 71
Tientsin Mobile Arsenal, 70-71, 175-176
Ting Army, 117
Ting Jih-ch'ang, 39, 40, 44, 45-48, 50, 54, 55, 56, 57, 62, 80, 88, 91, 175; views on machine production, 48; views on shipbuilding, 59
Ting Kung-chen, 14
Ting Pao-chen, 177
Ting Shou-tsun, 14
Ting Ta-i, 177
traditional civilization, changes in, 1-2
traditional ordnance and ammunition, production in Chihli, 51
Tsai Shih Rock, battle of, 8
Ts'ai Hsi-yung, 177
Ts'ai Kuo-hsiang, 36
Tseng Chi-tse, 126

Tseng Kuo-ch'üan, 35, 38, 111, 121, 125, 127, 129, 131, 139
Tseng Kuo-fan, 15, 29, 34, 45, 48, 49, 54, 55, 57, 60, 61, 62, 65, 67, 72, 78, 91, 103, 125, 175; and Anking Arsenal, 35-36; views on reform, 24-25; views on machine production, 37; views on shipbuilding at Kiangnan Arsenal, 58-60, 80; and Yung Wing, 37-38
Tso Tsung-t'ang, 38, 87, 91, 92, 101, 103, 107, 125, 126, 175
Tsung-li ko-Kuo shih-wu ya-men. See Tsungli Yamen
Tsungli Yamen, 29, 35, 41, 42, 43, 50, 51, 53, 59, 79, 84-85, 90, 91, 104; establishment, 28
Tu Wen-lan, 61
Tung Hsun, 62
tzu-ch'iang. See self-strengthening

Verbiest, Ferdinand, 12-13

Wade, Sir Thomas, 73-74, 90
Wang En-hsien, 177
Wang Shih-shou, 134
Wang T'ao, views on ordnance production, 44-45, 46
Wang Te-chün, 48, 71, 118
Wang Wen-shao, 177
Wang Yang-ming, 10
Wang Yu-ling, 29
Ward, Fredrick Townsend, 39; brother of, 46
Wei-ching, 83, 161
Wei Yüan, 13, 22, 31
Wen-hsiang, 28
Wen Tzu-shao, 177
West Arsenal, Tientsin, 56-57, 71, 72, 74, 143, 148, 175-176; establish-

ment, 52-53
Western ordnance, introduction to China, 10-12; employment and production during: 17th and 18th centuries, 12-13; Opium War, 13-14; Taiping Rebellion through 1865, 14-15, 24, 25, 29, 36, 38-45
Woolwich Company, 131
Wu-lung Shan Arsenal, 68, 113
Wu Chia-lien, 36
Wu Ta-ch'eng, 177

Yakub Beg, 87
<u>Yen-t'ieh lun</u>. See debates on salt and iron
Ying Kuei, 175
Ying Pao-shih, 60
<u>Yü-yüan</u>, 86, 93, 110, 162
<u>yüan</u> (Chinese dollar), 187 n. 15
Yung Wing, 37-38, 46, 48, 54, 59
Yunnan Arsenal, 177-178

Studies of the East Asian Institute

THE LADDER OF SUCCESS IN IMPERIAL CHINA, by Ping-ti Ho. Columbia University Press, 1962.

THE CHINESE INFLATION, 1937-1949, by Shun-hsin Chou. Columbia University Press, 1963.

REFORMER IN MODERN CHINA: CHANG CHIEN, 1853-1926, by Samuel Chu. Columbia University Press, 1965.

RESEARCH IN JAPANESE SOURCES: A GUIDE, by Herschel Webb with the assistance of Marleigh Ryan. Columbia University Press, 1965.

SOCIETY AND EDUCATION IN JAPAN, by Herbert Passin. Teachers College Press, Columbia University, 1965.

AGRICULTURAL PRODUCTION AND ECONOMIC DEVELOPMENT IN JAPAN, 1873-1922, by James I. Nakamura. Princeton University Press, 1966.

JAPAN'S FIRST MODERN NOVEL: UKIGUMO OF FUTABATEI SHIMEI, by Marleigh Ryan. Columbia University Press, 1967.

THE KOREAN COMMUNIST MOVEMENT, 1918-1948, by Dae-Sook Suh. Princeton University Press, 1967.

THE FIRST VIETNAM CRISIS, by Melvin Gurtov. Columbia University Press, 1967.

CADRES, BUREAUCRACY, AND POLITICAL POWER IN COMMUNIST CHINA, by A. Doak Barnett. Columbia University Press, 1967.

THE JAPANESE IMPERIAL INSTITUTION IN THE TOKUGAWA PERIOD, by Herschel Webb. Columbia University Press, 1968.

HIGHER EDUCATION AND BUSINESS RECRUITMENT IN JAPAN, by Koya Azumi. Teachers College Press, Columbia University, 1969.

THE COMMUNISTS AND CHINESE PEASANT REBELLIONS: A STUDY IN THE REWRITING OF CHINESE HISTORY, by James P. Harrison, Jr. Atheneum, 1969.

HOW THE CONSERVATIVES RULE JAPAN, by Nathaniel B. Thayer. Princeton University Press, 1969.

ASPECTS OF CHINESE EDUCATION, edited by C. T. Hu. Teachers College Press, Columbia University, 1969.

DOCUMENTS OF KOREAN COMMUNISM, 1918-1948, by Dae-Sook Suh. Princeton University Press, 1970.

JAPANESE EDUCATION: A BIBLIOGRAPHY OF MATERIALS IN THE ENGLISH LANGUAGE, by Herbert Passin. Teachers College Press, Columbia University, 1970.

ECONOMIC DEVELOPMENT AND THE LABOR MARKET IN JAPAN, by Koji Taira. Columbia University Press, 1970.

THE JAPANESE OLIGARCHY AND THE RUSSO-JAPANESE WAR, by Shumpei Okamoto. Columbia University Press, 1970.

IMPERIAL RESTORATION IN MEDIEVAL JAPAN, by H. Paul Varley. Columbia University Press, 1971.

JAPAN'S POSTWAR DEFENSE POLICY, 1947-1968, by Martin E. Weinstein. Columbia University Press, 1971.

ELECTION CAMPAIGNING JAPANESE STYLE, by Gerald L. Curtis. Columbia University Press, 1971.

CHINA AND RUSSIA: THE "GREAT GAME," by O. Edmund Clubb. Columbia University Press, 1971.

MONEY AND MONETARY POLICY IN COMMUNIST CHINA, by Katherine Huang Hsiao. Columbia University Press, 1971.

THE DISTRICT MAGISTRATE IN LATE IMPERIAL CHINA, by John R. Watt. Columbia University Press, 1972.

LAW AND POLICY IN CHINA'S FOREIGN RELATIONS: A STUDY OF ATTITUDES AND PRACTICE, by James C. Hsiung. Columbia University Press, 1972.

PEARL HARBOR AS HISTORY: JAPANESE-AMERICAN RELATIONS, 1931-1941, edited by Dorothy Borg and Shumpei Okamoto, with the assistance of Dale K. A. Finlayson. Columbia University Press, 1973.

JAPANESE CULTURE: A SHORT HISTORY, by H. Paul Varley. Praeger, 1973.

DOCTORS IN POLITICS: THE POLITICAL LIFE OF THE JAPAN MEDICAL ASSOCIATION, by William E. Steslicke. Praeger, 1973.

JAPAN'S FOREIGN POLICY, 1868-1941: A RESEARCH GUIDE, edited by James William Morley. Columbia University Press, 1973.

THE JAPAN TEACHERS UNION: A RADICAL INTEREST GROUP IN JAPANESE POLITICS, by Donald Ray Thurston. Princeton University Press, 1973.

PALACE AND POLITICS IN PREWAR JAPAN, by David Anson Titus. Columbia University Press, 1974.

THE IDEA OF CHINA: ESSAYS IN GEOGRAPHIC MYTH AND THEORY, by Andrew March. David and Charles, 1974.

ORIGINS OF THE CULTURAL REVOLUTION, by Roderick MacFarquhar. Columbia University Press, 1974.

SHIBA KŌKAN: ARTIST, INNOVATOR, AND PIONEER IN THE WESTERNIZATION OF JAPAN, by Calvin L. French. Weatherhill, 1974.

EMBASSY AT WAR, by Harold Joyce Noble, edited with an introduction by Frank Baldwin, Jr. University of Washington Press, 1975.

REBELS AND BUREAUCRATS: CHINA'S DECEMBER 9ERS, by John Israel and Donald W. Klein. University of California Press, 1975.

HOUSE UNITED, HOUSE DIVIDED: THE CHINESE FAMILY IN TAIWAN, by Myron L. Cohen. Columbia University Press, 1976.

INSEI: ABDICATED SOVEREIGNS IN THE POLITICS OF LATE HEIAN JAPAN, by G. Cameron Hurst. Columbia University Press, 1976.

DETERRENT DIPLOMACY, edited by James William Morley. Columbia University Press, 1976.

CADRES, COMMANDERS AND COMMISSARS: THE TRAINING OF THE CHINESE COMMUNIST LEADERSHIP, 1920-45, by Jane L. Price. Westview Press, 1976.

SUN YAT-SEN: FRUSTRATED PATRIOT, by C. Martin Wilbur. Columbia University Press, 1976.

JAPANESE INTERNATIONAL NEGOTIATING STYLE, by Michael Blaker. Columbia University Press, 1977.

CONTEMPORARY JAPANESE BUDGET POLITICS, by John Creighton Campbell. University of California Press, 1977.

THE MEDIEVAL CHINESE OLIGARCHY, by David Johnson. Westview Press, 1977.

ESCAPE FROM PREDICAMENT: NEO-CONFUCIANISM AND CHINA'S EVOLVING POLITICAL CULTURE, by Thomas A. Metzger. Columbia University Press, 1977.

THE CHINESE CONNECTION, by Warren Cohen. Columbia University Press, 1978.

PATTERNS OF JAPANESE POLICYMAKING: EXPERIENCES FROM HIGHER EDUCATION, by T. J. Pempel. Westview Press, 1978.